Reading Roman Declamation – Calpurnius Fla

Beiträge zur Altertumskunde

———

Herausgegeben von Susanne Daub, Michael Erler, Dorothee Gall, Ludwig Koenen und Clemens Zintzen

Band 348

Reading Roman Declamation – Calpurnius Flaccus

Edited by
Martin T. Dinter, Charles Guérin, Marcos Martinho

DE GRUYTER

ISBN 978-3-11-068513-8
e-ISBN (PDF) 978-3-11-040155-4
e-ISBN (EPUB) 978-3-11-040163-9
ISSN 1616-0452

Library of Congress Cataloging-in-Publication Data
A CIP catalog record for this book has been applied for at the Library of Congress.

Bibliographic information published by the Deutsche Nationalbibliothek
The Deutsche Nationalbibliothek lists this publication in the Deutsche Nationalbibliografie;
detailed bibliographic data are available on the Internet at http://dnb.dnb.de.

© 2019 Walter de Gruyter GmbH, Berlin/Boston
This volume is text- and page-identical with the hardback published in 2017.
Printing and binding: Hubert & Co. GmbH & Co. KG, Göttingen
♾ Printed on acid-free paper
Printed in Germany

www.degruyter.com

Acknowledgements

The papers in this volume stem from a conference held at the Maison de la Recherche, Université Paris-Sorbonne in February 2014, which has been generously supported by the Institut Universitaire de France.

Special thanks in the name of the co-organisers and all participants are due to Charles Guérin (UPEC), whose travails and organisational skills made this event possible – *gratias tibi agimus*.

The present book is the second in a series of three edited volumes that showcase current research in Roman Declamation under the heading 'Reading Roman Declamation'. A volume on Ps-Quintilian has appeared with De Gruyter in 2016, one on Seneca the Elder (OUP) will be published in 2018.

We would also like to thank the editors of this series as well as the editorial team at De Gruyter, Katharina Legutke and Mirko Vonderstein, for their swift, kind and professional co-operation. Antonia Ruppel's and Astrid Khoo's astute copy-editing has made life easier for all of us, many thanks to them. Astrid Khoo has also kindly compiled the *index locorum* and the *index rerum* for this volume.

Last but not least, we acknowledge with gratitude a significant contribution towards the production costs of this volume by the Institut Universitaire de France.

Martin T. Dinter (King's College London)
Charles Guérin (Université Paris Est-Créteil)
Marcos Martinho (University of São Paulo)

https://doi.org/10.1515/9783110401554-001

Table of Contents

Martin T. Dinter and Charles Guérin

Introduction:
Calpurnius – a postmodern author?

Every generation of students has their particular frame of cultural reference of which those teaching make frequent use. We will find that in a similar way Roman declamation can rely on its audience's awareness of its generic conventions: pirates, ghosts, evil stepmothers, blind sons and violent tyrants people a world as weird as it is wonderful and provide ample fodder for teachers of rhetoric and their students. They discuss (in all seriousness) fictional court cases so as to provide training to future lawyers and display a firework of rhetorical skill. When read sociologically, rhetorical education fosters social reproduction and helps to shape a young man's attitudes and behavior; it teaches him how to be a Roman citizen. For he will train to navigate the Roman concept of *patria potestas* that gives a father overbearing legal power over the members of his family; he will argue with fictional tyrants rather than question the authority of actual emperors and thus find his place in imperial hierarchy; he will learn to sort out the social mess that transgressions such as rape cause and absorb the moral precepts and approved values of his peers. In addition, he will imbibe how to reinforce the poor-rich and the slave-free divide through the examples Roman declamation provides.[1] When read from this socio-political perspective we observe how Roman declamation turns Roman boys into Roman men.[2]

What is more, scholars have recently lavished their attention on Roman declamation's *controversiae* (mock legal speeches) and *suasoriae* (mock speeches of advice, usually to some great man) and have allowed these genres to leave their neglected corners. Important studies by Gunderson (2003), Schröder (2003), Berti (2007), Frazel (2009) and Bernstein (2013) have placed *declamatio* centre-stage and illuminate social concepts such as authority, educational practices, cultural context or Roman jurisdiction.[3] A number of recent edited volumes have enriched the field further: Amato, Citti and Huelsenbeck (2015) places its focus on ethics and law in Greek and Roman declamation. Lentano (2015), Poignault and Schneider (2016) as well as Casamento, van Mal-Maeder and Pa-

---

1 Corbeill (2007) 77–81 and Bloomer (2007) 298 analyze declamations' most common themes.
2 Cf. Bloomer (2011) 170–92.
3 The journal *Rhetorica* has dedicated two issues (spring and summer 1995) to Quintilian's oeuvre.

Martin T. Dinter, King's College London and **Charles Guérin**, Université Paris Est-Créteil

https://doi.org/10.1515/9783110401554-002

setti (2016) which concentrates on Quintilian's minor declamations and Dinter, Guérin, Martinho (2016) showcase declamation as self-conscious literary genre, similarly to the volume in hand. Previously Gleason (1996) had smoothed the way for a recognition of rhetoric as the fashioning of the self, as a cultural process that facilitates not merely gender definition – how to be a real man – but also reinforces claims of *paideia*, *Graecitas*, *Romanitas*, and status. In addition, Beard (1993) ingeniously saw declamation as playing the role of myth in earlier Greek culture, in that it provides the source of storytelling Roman culture, and a space for the exercise of this culture's imagination.

Naturally, when placed into its socio-historical context the body of declamations that has come down to us (Seneca the Elder, Ps.-Quintilian and Calpurnius Flaccus) echoes its cultural, social and literary background. These texts are not independent and have to be read within their contexts, but at the same time they also constitute a genre on their own, the rhetorical and literary framework of which remains not yet fully explored. It remains to be asked: what are the poetics of *declamatio?*

As a genre situated at the crossroad of rhetoric and fiction, *declamatio* offers the freedom and ability to experiment new forms of discourse, and calls for both a technical and literary analysis. If one places the literariness of *declamatio* into the spotlight (van Mal-Maeder 2007) – *declamatio* has been hailed by Bloomer as 'the first literary movement of the Roman empire' (2007: 297) – it becomes possible to study it as a realm of genuine literary creation with its own theoretical underpinning, rather than simply reading it as a gratuitous exercise mimicking the practice of real orators.

Of the three Roman authors whose declamations have survived, the corpus of Quintilian has attracted the highest degree of scholarly attention. The Cassino series of commentaries coordinated by Antonio Stramaglia has almost completed its task to provide a commentary on each of Quintilian's *Major Declamations*. In addition Santorelli has made accessible to us Håkanson's previously unpublished research on the *Major Declamations* and Santorelli, Stramaglia and Winterbottom are at present preparing a new Loeb edition of that very *corpus*.[4] What is more, Lentano is currently preparing a research report (Forschungsbericht) for Lustrum that will provide a detailed overview of existing secondary literature. He has also just published a 'profile' of Roman declamation which makes the field ever the more accessible to the interested public.[5] Seneca the Elder is equally enjoying a revival of interest with recent publications including the monographs of

---

4 Håkanson (2014).
5 Lentano (2017).

Berti (2007) and Migliario (2007) as well as Huelsenbeck's Duke Dissertation (2009) and his substantial article (2011). In addition, we now also have Feddern's commentary on Seneca's *Suasoriae* (2013), Huerta Cabrera's UNAM Dissertation (2015) and most recently Lennart Håkanson's posthumously published commentary on *Controversiae* book I edited by Citti, Santorelli and Stramaglia (2016). Finally, an edited volume with papers on Seneca the Elder stemming from our own Reading Roman Declamation project will appear in due course.

Calpurnius text is well served by an excellent Teubner edition.[6] Apart from Sussman's commentary (1994), however, literary scholarship that focuses on Calpurnius Flaccus, as the present volume does, is almost entirely absent. Accordingly, the volume in hand certainly fills a lacuna in that it offers a point of entry to the relatively compact corpus of *excerpta* attributed to Calpurnius Flaccus. Consisting of just fifty-three short excerpts of declamations, Calpurnius' oeuvre in many respects epitomizes Roman Declamation: it exemplifies all its traits and due to its relative brevity also provides a potted version of the genre. Therefore we hope that readers will accept our invitation to read Roman declamation as literature and not just as offering a convenient footnote when on the hunt for a reference on racial prejudice in antiquity (cf. Calp. 2).

The volume we are presenting here stems from the third of a series of three events, each dedicated to one of the three Roman writers under whose names collections of often-fragmentary declamations have survived: Seneca the Elder, Ps.-Quintilian and Calpurnius Flaccus. The volume features contributions by both junior and senior scholars from the USA, France, Italy, the Netherlands and the UK and has brought together some of the most productive scholars currently working in the field of Roman declamation. Readers will notice the varying length of the contributions. We are grateful to De Gruyter that we are able to accommodate not only the key-note speeches at full length (Balbo and Schneider) but also a number of contributions that have been expanded considerably from the versions presented in Paris.

In what follows we shall provide a brief overview over the content of this volume so as to facilitate easier access.

In a substantial piece, **Mannering** subjects Calpurnius to a masterly literary analysis, which yields important fresh insights. He highlights how declamations in this collection tend to be connected into sequenced clusters according to certain themes, by turns ostensible and discreet; and, conversely, seemingly *un*connected declamations tend to respond to each other in discursively explicit ways. Those

---

6 Håkanson (1978).

clusters of declamations which are grouped by thematic connections demonstrate to the reader how rhetorical variety and innovation can be mined from numerous situations which closely resemble each other. By taking this authorial approach, Calpurnius shows us how creative stagnation can be obviated by constantly turning out new insights from and about the declamatory world's limited troupe of stock characters. The converse lesson in Calpurnius also applies: those declamations which follow each other without any obvious thematic or situational resemblance are written and positioned in such a way as to demonstrate the possibility for making discursive connections between otherwise unrelated scenarios.

Spielberg concentrates on several of Calpurnius' declamations that have parallel treatments in Seneca. Calpurnius 30 is almost identical to Seneca 2.4, and every scrap of Calpurnius' declamation corresponds to something that Seneca ascribes to some rhetor, most frequently Latro, in that declamation. Although it is impossible to prove influence, the number of correspondences is striking and may suggest direct engagement with Seneca's corpus as Calpurnius tries to outdo the Senecan declaimers in key epigrams. This suggests that *aemulatio* and continual re-adaptation of models was an integral part of declamation, as a standard set of scenarios proliferated and compilations like Seneca's own collected the cleverest conceits and *sententiae*. A *sententia* from Calpurnius 3, meanwhile, which also appears under the same theme in the *Major Declamations* (3.6), appears to be borrowed from another declamation by Latro (2.7.5). Even without assuming direct dependence, comparing the form and technique of these *sententiae*, as well as the arguments they outline, helps clarify Calpurnius' particular style, and this in turn lets us consider declamation as a dynamic genre whose artistry, even at the level of the epigram, changes in accordance with changing literary taste.

Balbo's chapter addresses general problems about the definition of proverbial material in declamation and investigates some examples of proverbial material in the corpus of Calpurnius Flaccus. He outlines the problematic relationship between *proverbs* and *sententiae*: scholars do not fully agree on how to distinguish between these two categories. As *sententiae* in Roman declamation express general concepts, sometimes pseudo-philosophical ones, and are usually brimming with ethical content, mostly without any authorial identification, they are often reusable (and reused) which blurs the lines of distinction even further. Accordingly, Balbo uses a wider-than-usual definition of the term 'proverb' to test what can be included, and to examine how proverbs differ from *sententiae*.

Within the framework of declamatory studies, the *vir fortis* (*brave man*) character plays a pivotal role and can be found in every collection of Roman declamations. One aspect of the themes involving a *vir fortis* that deserves further analysis concerns family relations during wartime, with a particular focus on family conflicts between father and son, or among brothers. **Casamento's** chapter takes a closer look at the declamatory theme of family strife by analyzing closely Calp. 32 and 36 together with 21, in which the figures of war heroes and military contexts are used to stage family conflicts. By showcasing in detail how Calpurnius' *argumenta* are construed Casamento also highlights the originality of Calpurnius' work and showcases how the themes of desertion and cowardice are employed in a novel way.

Schneider's contribution examines the nine excerpts from the *Miles Marianus* declamation (Calp. 3) in Calpurnius Flaccus' corpus, a topic prominent as well in Cicero, Quintilian, Valerius Maximus and Pseudo-Quintilian. Inspired by an authentic incident that occurred during the invasion of the Cimbri and Teutons in 104 BC, *Miles Marianus* is one of the most famous and controversial subjects of antiquity. Schneider's chapter focuses on the themes of sexual morality and transgression. By pinpointing parallels and variations in Calpurnius' and Ps.-Quintilian's versions of the theme, she attempts to distil the sexual norms underlying this discourse.

The identity of the author to whom the manuscript tradition ascribes this collection unanimously remains shrouded in mystery. **Santorelli's** detailed analysis of Calpurnius' metrical and accentual *clausulae* in this volume, however, suggests that he should be dated to the second half of the second century CE and implies that Calpurnius has been influenced by the teaching practices in use in the schools of rhetoric of the African provinces.[7]

Calpurnius Flaccus was first edited by Pierre Pithou in 1580. The text was improved by distinguished scholars of the seventeenth and eighteenth centuries: Johann Friedrich Gronov (1665), Ulrich Obrecht (1698), and Pieter Burman, (1720), the latter drawing on the conjectures of other fine emenders (especially Johannes Schultingh). The first editor to apply modern editorial methods was Georg Lehnert (Teubner, 1903), but his work was far surpassed by the Swedish scholar Lennart Håkanson (1978). **Winterbottom** comments on the development of editorial technique as seen over this four-hundred-year period, and assesses

---

7 For an overview of previous attempts to date Calpurnius see Sussman (1994) 6–9.

the qualities that these very different scholars brought to their task. Last but not least, on the small scale of Calp. *Decl.* 13 he then exemplifies how classical philology has been evolving and maturing by discussing the conjecture suggested for this passage.

In the final section of this introduction we wish to highlight just a few themes and concepts that are 'good to think with' (to borrow a phrase from Lévi-Strauss) and which occur throughout the corpus of Calpurnius.

Calpurnius certainly is an author aware of his burden of the past, his coming after. He playfully accepts this challenge by providing us some of the most layered – not to say convoluted – cases which have come down to us, outdoing his predecessors. This is declamation not for beginners. He truly provides food for thought or at least amuse-gueules for connoisseurs initiated to the genre of declamation. By combining well-known declamatory laws and re-arranging or complicating stock situations, Calpurnius achieves remarkable innovation whilst not straying far from the recognizable boundaries of his genre, a process Mannering in this volume has dubbed 'Declamation 2.0'.[8] One needs but cite one example to showcase the level of sophistication Calpurnius' cases demand from those attempting to declaim them.

46. THE RAPIST'S SON, CONDEMNED WITHOUT A TRIAL

The Laws: 1. The law concerning raped women. 2. One may execute one's children without a trial.

The Situation: A certain man committed rape and then ran away. From the rape the girl conceived a child and gave birth. Then the rapist returned, the girl demanded his death. The man wants to execute his son without a trial. The rape victim opposes this. (trl. adapted from Sussman).[9]

As in several other examples dealing with rape, Calpurnius' case creates an entire social fabric involved in or even resulting from one particular crime. Indeed, throughout his corpus rape's ramifications provide near endless material for variation and combination to create multi-layered situations which will tease a declaimer's brains: *The Girl Who Was Abducted, Then Violated By a Youth* (Calp. 41 *Rapta ab Ephebo Stuprata*) as well as *The Blinded Rapist* (Calp.

---

8 Some *excerpta* such as Calp. 26 (*Tria Praemia Sacerdotis* – The Priest's Three Rewards) even combine three laws and a calamitous situation.
9 *Indemnatus raptoris filius. Lex raptarum. Indemnatos liberos liceat occidere.*
Quidam rapuit et fugit. De raptu puella concepit et peperit. Reverso raptore puella mortem raptoris optavit. Filium ille indemnatum vult occidere. Rapta contradicit.

43 *Raptor Excaecatus*) both fall within this very category.[10] The latter example in itself combines the rape subject with one of declamation's favorite afflictions, which complicates many a case: blindness. By placing blindness centre-stage the pair Calp. 9 and 10 offer up a discourse on blindness and regained sight that showcases this declamatory obsession. What is more, the entire corpus features a web of *fama/infamia*, a hallowed rhetorical technique common also in all other declamatory collections, spanning the full scale of permutations this versatile motif allows.[11] May it be the twin brother intent on committing suicide because – so he laments – his brother was led to ruin his own reputation by working as a male prostitute[12] and who thereby makes a good reputation a matter of life and death; or the elderly priest of Mars who seeks to protect his third son through self-sacrifice by turning the same argument the other way round: the renown of an old man does not count, but the potential of a youngster does.[13] Reputation also is central to the argument of Calp. 32. Here the orator son argues that the father should not be acquitted as reward for the soldier son, in order to protect their father's reputation; the acquittal would raise doubts about their father's innocence.[14]

To conclude, allow us to address the question in the title of this introduction which provocatively dubs Calpurnius a postmodern author. The French philosopher Lyotard discusses two key grand narratives of modernity in his work *The Postmodern Condition* (1979): a speculative narrative and a narrative of emancipation.[15] Under these grand narratives, all social institutions such as law, education and technology combine to strive for a common goal for all humanity: absolute knowledge or universal emancipation. Knowledge thus acquires a vocation and

---

10 And there are further declamations dealing with rape across the corpus: cf. Calp. 16; 34; 51.

11 For the use of *Fama* in Ps.-Quintilian's corpus cf. Dinter (2016).

12 *ipsa famae suae naufragia delatus* (Calp. 20; 19.14: 'he was brought to the very shipwreck of his own personal reputation').

13 *Melior quidem **fama** seniorum, spes tamen minoribus maior est.* ('Old men have a better reputation, but there is greater hope for the young.') (Calp. 26; 25.10)

14 *Publicae utilitatis est omnium reorum iudicari causas, ne aut nocens evadat poenam aut innocens patiatur **infamiam.*** ('It is for the public good that all cases should be judged, lest a guilty man evade his punishment or an innocent man suffer infamy.') (Calp. 32; 29.2)

*Innocentiam patris dum liberare quaeris, **infamas.** Homini verecundo in eiusmodi crimine longe gravior est **fama** quam poena.* (Calp. 32; 29.5) ('While you seek to prove the innocence of your father, you slander him. In a charge of this sort, the loss of reputation weighs far more heavily on an honourable man than punishment.')

15 French title: *La condition postmoderne: rapport sur le savoir.* All quotes are from the 1984 translation by Bennington and Massumi.

a role for the greater good.[16] This concept also fits well with the socio-political reading of Roman Declamation: it teaches Roman boys to be Roman men and Roman citizen by instilling them with a set of values and a sense of justice. Calpurnius' corpus, however, complicates this reading by providing scenarios whose intricacies makes us question common values and laws. According to Lyotard the two grand narratives of modernity have been liquidated by the rise of technology and the spread of capitalism, and a universal consensus is thus no longer possible. He therefore suggests: 'We must thus arrive at an idea and practice of justice that is not linked to that of consensus' (1984: 66). He also proposes a focus on individual 'little narratives', their differences from each other, and the fact that they should not all be judged by the same criteria. 'Once the grand narratives have fallen away, we are left only with the diverse range of language games [to use Wittgenstein's terminology], and the aim of postmodern criticism should be to do justice to them by allowing them to be heard in their own terms.'[17] When applied to Calpurnius this postmodern point of view would encourage us to read his oeuvre as questioning the grand narrative of Roman Declamation by introducing little narratives, each of which so individual that it demands to be heard on its own terms. For Calpurnius' cases there are no easy answers. In our literary tradition Calpurnius constitutes the endpoint of Roman Declamation. While his small corpus features all the characteristics of the genre, Calpurnius' overwrought cases also signpost his status as declamatory successor.

Reading Roman Declamation has been the motto of our project. While we are aware that declamation is often regarded as an outlier and left aside by literary scholars, the contributions to this volume exemplify what happens when the same theoretical skills and sophistication we are applying to much of Latin literature nowadays are brought to declamation: a genre with its own set of generic rules and characteristics is starting to emerge. The present volume (and the two related ones) shall contribute to the ongoing re-evaluation of Roman Declamation.

---

16 Malpas (2003) 27.
17 Malpas (2003) 30.

Jonathan E. Mannering*

Declamation 2.0 –
Reading Calpurnius 'Whole'

How different our understanding of Roman declamation would be if Calpurnius were its only surviving spokesperson. He constructs no authorial persona like Seneca's genial father figure to preface his collection or provide running commentary to frame reader response to a parade of contestants.[1] And without even the aid of theoretical advice in the form of *sermones* from a Quintilianic Master, the brevity of his declamations leaves little textual ground to find one's bearings.[2] Calpurnius' declamations, all fifty-three, are supplemented by nothing more than the laws and scenarios, and only the first nine present speeches for both sides of the case.[3] These formal differences from the writings of Seneca the Elder and ps.-Quintilian indicate, I would suggest, that Calpurnius presumes familiarity with declamation on the reader's part, and even personal experience both in and of extemporaneous oratory. If Seneca's ten-volume highlight reel is suitable for the casual aficionado, and if the author of the *Major* and *Minor Declamations* crafts robust speeches for rhetorical edification, then Calpurnius' collection can be read as offering *advanced* lessons in how to declaim insofar as he deprives the reader of commentative signage and of the reassuring guidance of a masterly author. Calpurnius lays down a new set of challenges in virtue of the distinctive way he himself recedes almost entirely out of sight.

This chapter considers what Calpurnius' textual schoolroom teaches us about how to declaim, and why we might, by endeavouring to read Calpurnius'

---

* I offer deep thanks to John Henderson and the editors for their patience and scrupulous attention to this chapter.

1 Janson (1964) 116–24 charts Seneca's contributions to prefatorial convention. Exploring the relationship between paternal authority and memory, Gunderson (2003) 57 observes how Seneca labours to "use his memories to ensure the reproduction of [a] particular economy of desire [for rhetorical performance] for his sons' and subsequent generations".

2 Gunderson (2003) 62–69 explains how the Master of the *Minores* constructs himself as surrogate father figure. For the unity and purpose of ps.-Quinitilian's *Maiores*, see Hömke (2009) 240–255; (2007) 116–27. Stramaglia (2016) 25–48, however, questions the distinction between 'school pieces' and 'show pieces', and endeavours to discern the rhetorician who shapes the fictive declaimer in the *Maiores*.

3 The MSS history and theories for the purpose of the text's publication are described by Sussman (1994) 16–21.

Jonathan E. Mannering, Loyola University Chicago

https://doi.org/10.1515/9783110401554-003

unique 'book' sequentially and as if it were complete. Calpurnius' mission is broadly like that of the other authors of Roman declamation – to develop rhetorical versatility and sharpen skills of *inventio* – but it is undertaken, I propose, according to two particular methods of pedagogy made possible by the unique format of his book: declamations in his collection *tend* to be connected into sequenced clusters according to certain themes, by turns ostensible and discreet; and, conversely, seemingly *un*connected declamations *tend* to respond to each other in discursively explicit ways. Those clusters of declamations which are grouped by thematic connections will demonstrate to the reader how rhetorical variety and innovation can be mined from numerous situations which closely resemble each other. By taking this authorial approach, Calpurnius shows us how creative stagnation can be obviated by constantly turning out new insights from and about the declamatory world's limited troupe of stock characters.[4] The converse lesson in Calpurnius also obtains: those declamations which follow each other without any obvious thematic or situational resemblance are written *and* positioned in such a way as to demonstrate the possibility for making discursive connections between otherwise unrelated scenarios. Differentiating similitudes, connecting the unconnected, Calpurnian pedagogy operates *interstitially*, his lessons on rhetorical and intellectual innovation rendered manifest through the way his declamations are juxtaposed and respond to each other in virtue of their proximity. Calpurnius challenges his reader to maintain optimal creative flexibility across his sequencing of declamations in order for us to appreciate how innovative departures and also, complementarily, credible connections may be devised.

This chapter comprises five sections: the first three *controversiae* of Calpurnius' book will be read as introducing rhetorical techniques which inform the rest of the collection; four *controversiae* (Calp. 14, 15, 16, 17) will then be read as a sequenced group organised around crises of personal identity and character; four other *controversiae* (Calp. 18, 19, 20, 21) will be read for their shared rhetorical technique of comparative figurations and mimetic substitutions; another four *controversiae* (Calp. 23, 24, 25, 26) will be read together for the ways in which speakers deploy and interpret the language of law; and a selection of nine *controversiae* (Calp. 9, 10, 11; 33, 34; 36, 37; 52, 53) will demonstrate how Calpurnius juxtaposes particular declamations to elicit surprising discursive connections between otherwise unrelated topics. Taken together, these declamations corroborate Calpurnius' testimony to the salutary benefits of declamatory exercise, and to the rhetorical and intellectual skills declamation can develop.

---

4 On role playing in Roman declamation, see Mal-Maeder (2007) 3–9, 41–46.

1 Calpurnian Cornerstones: Calp. 1 (Deciphering Intention) ~ 2 (Legal Language) ~ 3 (Figuration)

In one killer of an opening, the first *controversia* demonstrates a rhetorical tactic central to forensic argumentation and practiced throughout much of Calpurnius, namely, manipulating the meaning of an opponent's oral testimony to one's advantage.[5] A mother has killed her tyrant-husband as well as her son for staging a coup, and as her reward asks that her remaining son be spared, promising to kill him herself if he ever shows the same despotic inclinations (1.1–6).[6] The prosecution does not trust she will act on her oath: '*occidam,*' *inquit. quanta nobis ante patienda sunt, dum occidere tyrannum femina possit et mater velit?* (1.7–8).[7] Across the first four words of Calpurnius' book, the singular, willful determination of the individual is brought under the evaluative scrutiny of the societal collective. From the incipient moment that *occidam* flashes as the thrilling opener of the speech, the word's singular volitional certainty, the avowed commitment to act on the part of the speaking *ego*, is called immediately into question as *first*-person is cordoned and isolated from the community by pithy *third*-person *inquit*, which effectively differentiates, and distances, the (heretofore) unidentified speaker of *occidam* from the declaimer now speaking; first-person *plural* (*nobis*) promptly dominates the criticism thereafter, and the concerns for the commonwealth assume urgent priority over the desires of the individual. Despite her proven track record, this tyrant-slayer is labelled dually as woman (*femina*) and mother (*mater*); as capability (*possit*) and volition (*velit*) are associated with each of these characteristics respectively, the woman's original promise to take care of the killing and her overall trustworthiness are undermined along gendered lines.[8] It is the womanly 'will' latent in *occidam* that the prosecution

---

5 According to Quintilian, the task of dealing with the oral evidence of witnesses in law courts is an exceptional challenge (*ingens dimicatio*, 5.7.3), which can be accomplished either by a set speech (*actio*, 5.7.3–8) or, more usually, by cross-examination (*interrogatio*, 5.7.9–32). Declamation thus presents a further challenge to the orator who cannot cross-examine a live witness but must craft extemporaneous responses to imaginary oral testimony.

6 Excerpts of Calpurnius Flaccus are cited according to page and line numbering of Håkanson (1978). Translations, with my own changes, are drawn from Sussman (1994), and are provided wherever paraphrase does not suffice.

7 '"I shall kill him," she tells us. But how much must we first endure until a woman is able, and a mother is willing, to kill a tyrant?'

8 The fictional world of declamation permits male speakers to craft arguments against and on behalf of women and other socially marginalised groups as opportunities to experiment with unconventional social views, and not necessarily to redefine *mores* in the world outside the classroom; cf. Mal-Maeder (2007) 95–107.

calls into question with his conclusive emphasis on *velit*, the verb which occupies the centre of his four-sentence prosecutorial speech and which prepares us for the final rhetorical climax. The second quotation from the woman's testimony serves to corroborate the doubt already perceived from her womanly capabilities – '*non possum mortem filii mei videre*' (1.8 – 9)[9] – and ultimately justifies the prosecution's final stance: *hoc est ergo quare illum velimus occidere* (1.9 – 10).[10] Together, *velimus* and *occidere* coalesce into the prosecution's message, as volition and capital punishment are construed as the sole responsibility of the community (*velimus*), not the individual (*occidam*). The speech is constructed in ring composition, as the prosecution rhetorically divests the desire and duty to guard against tyrants away from the original promise of the lone female individual (*occidam*; *velit*), and invests this responsibility in the hands of society writ-large (*velimus occidere*). Selecting only two sentences from the testimony of the opposing side, the prosecuting orator subsumes an individual's will under collective and (unmistakably) masculine agency. Indeed, the one-line counterargument of the first *controversia* in defence of the mother recognises how judiciously the prosecutorial speech has exploited the subjunctival uncertainty of *occidam*, and reminds the jury that the woman has earned her reward from what she has done in fact, not what she may or may not do in future: *petit praemium, non quod accipiat, sed quod accepit* (1.12).[11] The concluding indicative communicates greater assurance, relieving the anxiety a jury might experience from the uncertainty inherent to the subjunctive.

The book's second *controversia* also takes issue with the testimony of a mother, one who has given birth to a dark-skinned son (1.14), and both argument and counterargument are considerably longer than those of the first.[12] Here, the prosecution appeals to the law of natural heredity, adducing examples from numerous ethnic groups known throughout the Roman territories (2.7 – 12), to prove the child's father is an Ethiopian slave; the defence offers a variety of possible natural causes for the child's skin colour, such as a blood disorder or prenatal trauma (2.23 – 3.4).[13] In considering the laws of nature, the second *controversia*

---

9 "I am incapable of looking upon the death of my son."

10 'That is precisely why we want to kill this man!'

11 'She seeks the reward, not the one that she may receive, but the one that she has received.'

12 Respectively, 4 and 1 MSS lines for the argument and counterargument in first *controversia*, 21 and 19 for those in the second.

13 The same scenario is the subject of a lost speech ascribed to Quintilian, conjectured by Winterbottom (1984) 290 to be a major declamation. Plutarch (*De Sera Numinis Vindicta* 563a) tells of a Greek woman who gives birth to a black child and successfully exculpates herself in court by claiming descent from an Ethiopian great-grandparent. Aristotle, in his theory of phenotype in-is also an opportunity for Calpurnian declamation to consider the nature of law, a topic that will unite a cluster of subsequent speeches.[14] The prosecution stakes its argument on observable phenomena, that hereditary features are as predictable as the unchanging laws of nature, and appeals to the jury's shared general knowledge of natural phenomena to strain the mother's credibility: *miramur hanc legem esse naturae...?* (2.4–5).[15] Using a rhetorical technique similar to that of the first *controversia*, the prosecution calls the language of the woman's testimony into question, only in this instance by taking a discursively *preemptive* approach to discrediting her: the first word of the prosecution's ethical *sententia*, *nonnumquam incredibiliter peccare ratio peccandi est* (2.1–2),[16] anticipates the first words of her excuse, '*non semper*,' inquit, '*similes parentibus nascuntur*' (2.2–3).[17] As *nonnumquam* outsmarts *non semper*, the prosecution casts doubt over the woman's claim about possible irregularities in inherited parental traits while re-casting the child's aberrant skin colour in view of psychoanalytic considerations of the *rationale* behind criminal behaviour committed for its own sake (viz. *peccare ratio peccandi est*). The prosecution may then marshal empirical evidence from nature in order to elucidate his thesis that bearing a child by a slave can only be an act of perversity which defies belief (viz. *incredibiliter*).

On the other hand, the defence for the woman is the first speech in Calpurnius to consider the role of fortune and accident in human experience, a declamatory *locus communis*.[18] The speech underscores the limits of human understanding of nature's mysteries and the internal workings of the human body; he suggests that the infant may have suffered a prenatal injury (*multum fortunae etiam intra uterum licet*, 2.24–25),[19] and reminds us that skin colour can change

---

heritance (*De Generatione Animalium* IV 3, 768a14–21), suggests that atavistic relapse (λύσις) can occur through the paternal as well as the maternal line, with the result that offspring resemble their grandparents. He does not indicate whether it is possible that features can be unexpectedly inherited over more than two generations, as is the case in this declamation; cf. Connell (2016) 292–324; Henry (2006) 258–263, 276–278.

14 Calp. 22, 23, 24, 25, discussed below.

15 'Are we surprised for this to be a law of nature...?' For the way in which Roman declamation connects natural law to *pietas* and patriarchal authority, and how Cicero had developed the concept of natural law as immutable principle in accordance with Stoic thought, see Citti (2015) 95–112.

16 'On occasion the reason for committing a heinous act is the opportunity to do so in a manner that invites disbelief.'

17 '"On occasion," she tells us, "children don't take after their parents."'

18 Cf. Fairweather (1981) 184 with n. 7; Bonner (1949) 61–63.

19 'Much of its misfortune may even be inside her womb.'

with prolonged exposure to or shelter from the sun.[20] With a clincher redolent of Heraclitus, the defence reminds the jury that nature's immutable law is its eternal mutability: *tantum tempori licet quantum putas licere naturae* (3.4–5).[21] As the prosecution had worked to unite the jury against the woman by ascertaining 'our' shared understanding (viz. *miramur*) of nature's laws, the pointedly singular address to the lone jury member (*putas*; also *vides*, 2.23, 2.25) by the defence complicates collective wisdom, inviting each juror as an individual to question his own understanding of nature and consider alternative possibilities to explain the child's skin colour. Whereas the prosecution had undermined the woman's intellectual grasp of the laws of nature, the defence targets *each* of our own intellects, introducing a degree of reasonable doubt warranting careful reflection. Throughout the rest of his book, Calpurnius' declaimers will pose provocative questions that can challenge the reader's preconceptions about justice and equity as much as the fictive jurors', effectively conflating the reader with the jury in order to put our own consciences under scrutiny.[22]

The third *controversia* is Calpurnius' only one set during a specific period of Roman history, and also features the only speech to corroborate an argument with examples drawn from history. The third *controversia* nonetheless does influence the rest of the book rhetorically, as it introduces a technique which will feature elsewhere in the book, namely that of Calpurnian "figuration", or conceptual substitution. In this rhetorical strategy, certain elements of the scenario are implicitly analogised to other elements or even broader thematic preoccupations.[23] In addition, the sequence of the speeches in the third *controversia* itself tests the reader's preparedness for the forensic joust, for unlike the first two *controversiae*, the first speech here is given in defence, not in prosecution. Any pattern of argumentation that may have been established by the first two *controversiae* – i.e. prosecution first, then defence – is suddenly altered, and the aspirant declaimer is thus compelled to manoeuvre by starting with a defence speech before considering the prosecution and, thus, adapting his expectations and hon-

---

20 Cf. Sussman (1994) 98–99, *ad loc*. Pliny (*NH* 7.50–51) recounts extraordinary variations in the transmission of characteristics from parents to children. Although there are no pertinent similarities between the explanations offered by this defence speech and the 'Andromeda Effect' of Chariclea's conception in the *Aethiopica*, the speaker's effort to propose possible explanations could be guided by the same spirit as Heliodorus' plot-generating innovativeness to test the limits of credibility and challenge norms of acceptability; cf. Olsen (2012) 310–320; Reeve (1989) 82–84.
21 'Grant as much time as you think nature allows for this process.'
22 Cf. Calp. 52, discussed below.
23 Cf. Calp. 18, 19, 20, 21, discussed below.

ing intellectual agility in the process of reading. In the scenario, set during the Cimbrian War of 113 – 101 BCE, a soldier from Marius' army has killed a relative of Marius, a tribune, who tried to assault him sexually (3.7– 8).[24] The concluding sentences for the defence denigrate the character of the would-be rapist in strikingly nationalistic terms: *stuprum minatus est militi suo? minus est quod nobis Cimbri minantur* (3.17– 18).[25] The soldier's bodily integrity is figured here as Roman territory, and the slain officer is cast as a greater 'threat' to Roman statehood and morality than the notoriously savage enemy at her borders. In this instance, the Calpurnian method of figuration has fused two distinct conceptual elements, a soldier's body and Roman territory, into a formidable rhetorical challenge to the opposing party. Insinuating that attempted male *stuprum* is a more dangerous form of invasiveness than any alien force could pose is sufficiently damning to the prosecution's case that the speaker for the other side endeavours to minimise the 'threat' of the ex-tribune's actions as those of someone who did not have to be killed but merely warned off (viz. *quem satis fuit* _minari_, 3.22).[26]

For the next six *controversiae*, speeches for both sides of the case are delivered, and the rest of the cast of declamation's troupe of characters are introduced to populate the remaining scenarios, including stock villains such as stepmother (Calp. 4), brothel keeper (Calp. 5), rich man and tyrant (Calp. 6, 7), as well as virtuous war hero (Calp. 8) and patriarch (Calp. 9). From Calp. 10 to 53, only one side of the argument is provided. Whether this reduction in content is the result of authorial choice or the condition of the manuscripts cannot be ascertained. However, the juncture at which counterarguments cease will be the focus of subsequent analysis in Section 5 to *see* – the impairment of sight and vision governs the scenarios for Calp. 9, 10 and 11 – if there may be latent pedagogical purpose behind this noticeable turn. The following sections will consider the groups of *controversiae* outlined in my introduction.

---

24 Based on a real case, this scenario is also the topic of ps.-Quint. *DM* 3, the temporal dislocation of which affords the declaimer of the second century CE (or later) safe opportunity to discuss sodomy for purposes of defining Roman morality; cf. Schneider in this volume; (2004) 35; Gunderson (2003) 24, 153 – 90; Walters (1997a) 40.

25 'He threatened your soldier with sodomy? What the Cimbri are threatening us with is far less serious!' The charge of *stuprum* would apply to unlawful sexual acts between citizens and primarily affect the passive partner; cf. Williams (2010) 103 – 136, 191– 196; Fantham (1991) 270. In Roman declamation, the more typical topic for debate in cases of sexual assault is the responsibility women bear in maintaining their chastity; cf. Brescia (2015) 75 – 93.

26 'It would have sufficed just to threaten him off.'

2 Identity Crises: Calp. 14 ~ 15 ~ 16 ~ 17

It is tempting to read one feature of the scenario of Calp. 13 as though it were preparing the reader for the forensic challenge presented by Calp. 14. Just as the dispute in Calp. 13 is waged between opponents who were socially and professionally equivalent, i.e. two medical doctors, so does the argument of Calp. 14 take place between symmetrical opponents, i.e. two sons of the same father. Calp. 14 confronts a new rhetorical challenge, though, of differentiating between equivalents, a challenge not explicitly required of the previous *controversia* since both doctors claimed credit for the same deed (poisoning a tyrant). To this end, Calp. 14 adopts a rhetorical strategy which will be used in this and the following three *controversiae*: subversive re-fashioning of personal identity through *para-doxical* juxtaposition and, even, conflation of otherwise antithetically determined social roles and ethical standards in a bid for claiming moral *orthodoxy*. In this series of four, the identity of characters central to each case is compromised by behaviour, whether actual or imputed, which runs counter to the moral values which uphold and are bespoken by their social roles. A disinherited son must convince a jury of his filial piety (Calp. 14); a soldier known for his bravery must come to grips with an act of cowardice (Calp. 15); a civil magistrate is accused of acting like a tyrant (Calp. 16); and a man contends with the loss of his citizenship, his freedom and, potentially, his bodily integrity (Calp. 17). All four speeches work to reconcile crises of personal identity, whether for purposes of exculpation or incrimination.

In Calp. 14, a disinherited son, or *abdicatus*, has deigned to settle the account of his bankrupt father, secure his release from a moneylender, and even grant him freedom from servitude to himself (14.7–12). The father dies, and the disinherited son disputes the family estate with the other son.[27] In a two-pronged attack on his brother, the *abdicatus* crafts a daring argument on the grounds that he is owed a portion of the estate in his role as his father's former owner (*utor patroni actione, non filii*, 14.22).[28] However, he uses his professed legal status and his actions as one-time *patronus*, or slave owner, to redound upon his innate filial *pietas*.[29] This declamation works to restore the rightful dy-

---

27 For how declamation distorts the historical realities of Roman *abdicatio*, see Fantham (2004) 65–82. For the theme of disowning in declamation from late antiquity, and also its connection to the law of nature, see the discussion of Libanius by Johansson (2015) 269–286.
28 'I am entering the plea of a former master, not a son.'
29 The son must persuade the jury that he was effectively his father's *patronus* and, thus, legally owed a portion of the estate even though his father was technically under the temporary ser-

namic of authority and devotion which should obtain between fathers and sons and which has been disturbed by the extraordinary circumstance of a son temporarily acquiring his own father as a slave. Once a father had become his own son's personal property, patriarchal authority was both erased and grotesquely subverted; in turn, the speaker's selfhood had undergone an extraordinary crisis by assuming a dual role of son and slave owner in relation to his father *qua* slave. The speaker endeavours to resolve his untenably complex dual identity and ultimately prove himself a more dutiful son than the brother who was never disowned. First, the *abdicatus* deftly raises the issue of filial duty by conspicuously refraining to lay claim to *pietas* in explicit terms, characterising himself by modest litotes in the opening line (*me fuisse nec impium docui*, 14.13),[30] and recalling his father's chronic lamentation over the negligence of his other son (*quotiens de huius impietate conquestus*, 15.7).[31] Through his actions as slave owner, the *abdicatus* has proven himself, paradoxically, a more dutiful son than his brother, thereby resolving his impossibly hybridised identity of *patronus-filius*. As he concludes with a request for only a portion of the estate to cover funeral expenses (15.12–14), the *abdicatus* redeems his own character *qua* son, subordinating his role of *patronus* to that of *filius*, while also underscoring the failures of his brother to care for their father in life and death.[32]

The speaker of Calp. 15 also grapples with compromised selfhood, but here the defendant fails to reconcile his dual identity as decorated veteran and cowardly deserter. Although he was exempt from military service for prior acts of heroism, the courageous man, or *vir fortis*, in question disobeyed a general's command to go to war and deserted; rather than accept the general's offer of exemption from capital punishment – an offer, the speech portrays, made *not* out of clemency – the war hero sues for his own execution (15.16–19).[33] He encapsulates his present condition thusly: *miserum me, cuius nec infamia potest latere*

---

vitude of an *addictus*, or free man assigned to serve as slave to his creditor for unpaid debt, and not exactly the same status of slave; cf. Sussman (1994) 136.

30 'I have demonstrated that I have not been lacking in filial devotion.'

31 'How many times did our father complain about his son's lack of filial devotion!'

32 The affordability of burials for Romans of modest means is an elusive subject. According to the *Lex Libitinae Puteolana* people who abandon corpses would incur fines if caught; families living in this region during the Augustan era were otherwise responsible for paying the local contractor what might have been the minimal fee of HS 30; cf. Dumont (2003) 72.

33 Deserters were traditionally executed, sometimes in spectacular ways, although there is little historical evidence for extreme harshness in the imperial period; cf. Phang (2008) 120–123, 137–138; Sussman (1994) 139.

nec gloria (15.23 – 24).[34] The veteran's present condition, defined simultaneously by infamy and glory, is untenable, and renders his life unlivable. Pardoning him now would be an unusual brand of punishment (*novum genus damnationis ignoscere*, 16.5 – 6) inasmuch as his worthless life would be prolonged indefinitely.[35] As he becomes conscious once again of the importance of social standing, the soldier commits himself to execution with a renewed sense of *libido moriendi*, if not to confirm his former heroic status fully, then at least to undo his shame in the eyes of his community.[36] The final question encapsulates his comprehensive awareness of his betrayal of the soldier's honour code: *cur enim dubitem per infamiam senex emori qui etiam iuvenis optavi saepe per gloriam?* (16.6 – 7).[37] Taking stock of his life, the man ruefully observes that he has lived to approach death from two diametrically different conditions and perspectives, both in his current state of senescence and disgrace and formerly while fulfilling his youthful aspirations to glory. Too late does he appreciate the inevitability of death and – with *emori* placed at the fulcrum of the chiastic antithesis – its disregard for one's age or preparedness; what was formerly under his power to master, namely his personal conduct and deportment, has been squandered by him later in life. His concluding question is hardly rhetorical.

In Calp. 15, a war hero recriminates himself for acting the coward. A similar situation informs Calp. 16, in which one of the central characters is accused of behaving like his negative counterpart. In this case, a civil magistrate is said to have acted like a depraved autocrat, but, unlike the previous *vir fortis*, this *magistratus* is portrayed as showing no regret for his actions. The magistrate is on trial for putting a young man to death for raping a woman who said nothing to condemn the accused other than weep in silence (16.9 – 11). It is possible the magistrate had presumed her tears were the result of shame and embarrassment at her violation by the accused, but the prosecution takes the approach of casting the girl's tearful silence as a display of compassion for the accused, and of branding the magistrate's interpretation of her tears as callous insensitivity to

---

34 'I am in agony, I, neither whose disgrace nor glory can be concealed!' Though not unique to Calpurnius, the striking inversion of the usual '*me miserum*' could be symptomatic of the soldier's tormented condition; cf. Sussman (1994) 140 n. ad loc.

35 Shaming punishments for soldiers otherwise came in a variety of forms; cf. Phang (2008) 140 – 142.

36 Should the judgment be cast in favour of the commanding officer, the soldier's express desire for suicide would be thwarted as he could not exercise his own *liberum mortis arbitrium*; cf. Hill (2004) 183 – 212.

37 'For why should I hesitate to die as an old man during the period of my disgrace, I, who even as a young man often desired to die during my period of glory?'

compassion.[38] The prosecution dares the magistrate to commit to his original line of legal justification, and casts his testimony, however paraphrased, as evidence of megalomania: *dicat nunc: 'libuit et licuit'. civis haec, an regis oratio est?* (16.19 – 20).[39] The magistrate's testimony is portrayed as the conflation of individual desire with execution of law. The snappish, heart-beat fluidity of one letter replacing another (*libuit-licuit*) reflects the subconscious ease with which a civil functionary (viz. *civis*) can suddenly fail to differentiate his personal inclination from state *licence*. Such a failure to distinguish one's own preferences from one's official responsibilities is one of the early symptoms of decline into tyrannical hubris (viz. *regis oratio*).[40] The prosecution also calls attention to the way in which the magistrate exercised the judgment of the girl by perversely interpreting her silence as incrimination: *'tacuit,' inquit. o mira et muta sententia!* (16.20 – 21).[41] The oxymoronic rejoinder casts the magistrate's claim that the girl was silent as 'unspeaking sentiment', illustrating how tyrants exploit the inscrutability of their own silences which can arbitrarily be trans*mut*ed into death-dealing.[42] Unlike the *patronus-filius* and *desertor-vir fortis*, the *civis-rex* here is not conscious of his dual identity, and it is the prosecution's task to make the case. And where the disinherited son acts as a model of filial *pietas* and the disgraced veteran accepts his only honourable exit, the silent defendant in Calp. 16 poses a threat to the commonwealth which must be eliminated by vigorous prosecution.

The last speaker in this series of compromised personalities is beset by multiple crises of identity, and, potentially, of body. The '*Paedagogus Cruciarius*' of Calp. 17 is a poor man charged with residing as a non-citizen, sold into slavery, and condemned to crucifixion by his rich owner for not rescuing his wastrel son from being killed in an act of adultery (17.6 – 10). Twice has the poor man experienced dramatic inversions of selfhood, first being transformed from Roman citizen to foreigner (*audio me subito peregrinum*, 17.12 – 13),[43] and second from free agent to slave (*unum non est in servitutem nasci et libertate multari?*,

---

38 Sussman (1994) 142 – 143 traces possible legal antecedents which may have influenced the magistrate's decision for capital punishment in a situation involving rape.
39 'Now let him say, "It was my will, and it was legal!" Is this the language of a fellow citizen or of a king?'
40 The jingly phrase itself may derive from everyday discourse; cf. Sussman (1994) 144 n. ad loc.
41 '"She was silent," he said. Oh, what a marvelous and mute statement!'
42 For the stock tyrant in declamation, see Berti (2007) 99 – 110; Sussman (1994) 145 n. ad loc.; Tabacco (1985) 18 n. 46, 66 – 67. Dunkle (1971) 12 – 20 considers the influence of declamation's tyrants on Roman historiography.
43 'I hear that I have suddenly become a foreigner.'

17.17–18).[44] The poor man faces yet a third, fatally compromising 'split' to his selfhood, specifically with regard to his body, now subject to the crucifix.[45] In order to spare his body from being splayed into asphyxiated dissolution, the poor man ironically uses his track record of misfortune as the *crux* of his plea, blaming the rich man for entrusting his son to someone historically crisscrossed by bad luck: *non esse felicem iam tum scire potuisti* (17.19).[46] A man prone to such personal misery could hardly have influenced the rich man's son to behave without restraint, and ultimately the father should be held accountable for indulging his son at every turn (*multa largiebaris, indulgebas omnia, nihil umquam negabas*, 17.22–23).[47] As to whether a lifetime of bad luck can save this man from hanging and preserve his bodily integrity, the reader is ultimately left, appropriately, in suspense, even as this line of declamations featuring characters who struggle with maintaining the integrity of their selfhoods comes to a close.

3 Mimetic replications: Calp. 18 ~ 19 ~ 20 ~ 21

The premises of Calp. 17 and 18 serve as productive foils to each other. If a life of indulgence can turn a young man to behave self-destructively in Calp. 17, the converse holds true in Calp. 18, where a number of disinherited sons petition their fathers, assembled in a *curia*, to reinstate them on the grounds that their characters have been reformed by poverty (18.2–4; *egestate correcti*, 18.9).[48] In spite (or, in virtue) of its resemblance to the preceding declamation, Calp. 18 marks a departure from the forensic preoccupations of the previous quartet, which had endeavoured to reconcile impossibly compromised selfhoods. For Calp. 18 introduces a new rhetorical strategy to feature in the next sequence of *controversiae*, that is, the total replacement, or substitution, of one form of personal identity by another. Such mimetic replication of selfhood is effected in this and the next three declamations by various means, specifically epigraph-

---

44 'Is it not one and the same thing to be born into slavery and to be punished with the loss of your freedom?' This punishment is according to a declamatory law which appears to reflect Athenian legislation; cf. Sussman (1994) 147–148.

45 The diametric crisis posed to the pedagogue's body could be visualized powerfully if we care to imagine an X-shape for this particular cross, but these suspension structures could take many forms; cf. Samuelsson (2013) 90–142.

46 'You could have known even then that I was not lucky.'

47 'You kept lavishing him with many possessions, you kept indulging his every whim, you never denied him a thing.'

48 Even for declamation, the senate house is an unusual setting for this case, which would normally take place before a court; cf. Sussman (1994) 150–151.

ical inscription (Calp. 18), ritual self-sacrifice (Calp. 19), genetic twinhood (Calp. 20), and, finally, the plastic arts (Calp. 21).

With regard to Calp. 18, a father speaks in favour of admitting the disowned sons to their former status in light of their manifestly changed character (*tamquam alia natura*, 18.13–14), ever since his own son committed suicide after his initial refusal. The father concludes his speech by addressing his son in an explicit effort to recall him to the family name even though he is dead (*te... vel in morte revocabo*, 18.17). To this end, not only will he inter the body in the family tomb, he will inscribe his family name next to his son's on the epitaph (*inferam maiorum sepulcris et elogio, quod optasti, nomen inscribam*, 18.17–18). Through a form of *revocatio post mortem*, the son's wish is fulfilled (viz. *quod optasti*) as he is re-admitted to his family by means of the inscription of his name alongside that of his ancestors.[49] The inscription functions as a legal and material substitute for the son himself, its very form symptomatic of his father's loss and regret.

The limits and consequences of disinheritance are tested again in Calp. 19, where yet another young *abdicatus* is at the centre of attention, only this time volunteering himself to be sacrificed to end a plague (18.20–22).[50] His father contests the action, but the son makes a pithy three-line objection on grounds he is no longer bound by his father's authority. Where the son in question in the previous declamation had already died, the suspense of this case is heightened further as this son begins his speech on the verge of actually embracing death (*amplexus sum mortem*, 19.1).[51] But where the father in the previous case had the power to replace his son only by nominal inscription, here it is the father who is ironically supplanted by something else. First, the son makes clear he owes his life's breath to his father*land* (*spiritum... patriae profundam*, 19.2–3), and, second, he affirms he no longer has a *father* to obey (*me scio patrem non habere*, 19.4). Within two sentences, the young man's *pater* has been fully replaced by his *patria*. It is even possible to view the nature of this substitutive wordplay as having been influenced by the previous declamation. In Calp. 18, a deceased young man was re-admitted to his family by means of the addi-

---

49 The father's name, presumably denied to the son after *abdicatio*, would revert to the son if successfully reinstated; cf. Sussman (1994) 153 n. ad loc. In imperial Latin funerary epigraphy, the nuclear family was the primary focus of certain forms of familial obligation; cf. Saller (1994) 95–101; Saller and Shaw (1984) 132, 134–139. For Latin epigraphic habits as indicators of the value of Romanisation throughout the imperial provinces, see Meyer (1990) 78–81.

50 Hardly any cases of human sacrifice are attested in the ancient world, and only three in all of declamation; cf. Sussman (1994) 154.

51 A figure without parallel in declamation; cf. Sussman (1994) 154 n. ad loc.

tion of his *name* to the family tomb, but in Calp. 19 it is the etymological connection between *pater* and *patria* that makes a different kind of onomastic substitution possible. In the latter case, all ties between father and son are severed, and filial commitment is redirected towards self-sacrificing devotion to country.

The onomastic transferences of Calp. 19 pave the way for more creative turns of language in Calp. 20, which concerns the radical, total replacement of one man's identity by a morally corrupt doppelganger. Here the speaker makes an appeal for suicide because his twin brother has hired out himself as a prostitute, thereby destroying his own reputation (19.6–7).[52] By virtue of their identity as twins, he reasons, the brothers have been known throughout their community all their lives; such unavoidable notoriety constitutes the essence of the speaker's dilemma: *nostis nos... etenim pluribus noti sumus quam et aetas et verecundia postulat* (19.10–11).[53] The speaker's point is communicated through strikingly thick discourse, which draws attention to the connection between his shared identity with his brother and their public notoriety in linguistic terms: for the community to *know* anything (*nostis*) is to *know* them (*nos*), since their shared lives to date have always been subject to public *knowledge* (*noti sumus*).[54] As a twin, it is impossible for the speaker to avoid public scrutiny, or ever to separate his own identity from his brother's.[55] Now that his brother has turned himself into a male prostitute, the speaker's identity and reputation have also been irrevocably co-opted by that of a prostitute. The untenable situation for the man is then posed as an ethical crisis for the wider Roman community; to refuse the man's appeal to kill himself would be to permit two conflicted standards of morality to co-exist: *qua in civitate prostitui licet, mori non licet? an utrumque congruere aestimatis huic ordini et vitam turpem permittere et ab honesta morte pro-*

---

52 On the legal basis for an appeal for voluntary suicide in declamation, see Sussman (1994) 155. On free male prostitution and *infamia*, see Williams (2010) 40–50.
53 'You all know us; and indeed the fact is that we are personally known to more people than both our age and modesty require.'
54 For the sexual meaning of *nosco*, see Sussman (1994) 155–156 n. ad loc.
55 The angst of this declamation's speaker – and the scenario of *DMin.* 270, where a twin secures the death of the man who raped and caused the suicide of her sister – might help corroborate the reading of Plautus' *Menaechmi* offered by Mencacci (2007) 47–68, who assumes twins in ancient Rome were perceived as sharing inseparably similar identities. On the other hand, we might read this declamation's scenario not as reflecting common perceptions of twins in Roman culture but as inheriting (duplicating?) generic conventions from Plautine New Comedy. For the relationship between declamation and comedy, see Mal-Maeder (2007) 1–39. Figurations of pairs and doublings do become a dominant topos in post-Vergilian epic, most vividly as the organising structure of twinhood in Statius' *Thebaid*; cf. McAuley (2016) 321–344; Korneeva (2011) 71–143; O'Gorman (2005) 29–45.

hibere? (19.15 – 17).[56] The *congruence* of antithetical moral standards, both as located in his own selfhood and in society (*civitas*), is precisely what the jury, figured as social order (*ordo*), must not tolerate; only his own honourable death can redeem (what is effectively) his own disgraceful life.

Another kind of doppelganger, one born not from the womb but created from the painterly arts, is at the centre of Calp. 20. A soldier has killed his brother in combat, and requests as his reward for past feats of heroism that this particular exploit not be commemorated in a mural;[57] the father of the two sons opposes the request (19.21 – 20.1). The father's speech arises from his shattering revelation that intrafamilial violence can be committed without violating the law (*didici salvis legibus parricidium posse committi*, 20.7),[58] and explores the limitations of language to express grief and outrage. Where words fail to communicate the significance of his son's death, the visual arts can be employed to portray the moment and its meaning for all to see: *cetera iam non sunt narranda, pingenda sunt* (20.7 – 8).[59] The father insists that narration should yield to visual representation, and, with an irony at once restrained and unrelenting, confronts the son's evident misgivings about the public commemoration of his fratricide by discoursing on the relationship between the human body and the visual arts. First, the father distils the fratricide and its commemoration into respective 'liquid' essences, i.e. blood and paint, in order to expose the inconsistency of the position of his son who did not refrain from shedding his brother's blood but who is now afraid that his deed would be painted for public viewing: *vana et inepta formido est... colorem timere peius quam sanguinem* (20.8 – 10).[60] Second, the father requests that his son's death be commemorated by other plastic art forms as well: *simuletur hoc factum non tantum colore, sed aere, si possit, et lapide, et quacumque nostrorum corporum materia vel ars aemula est* (20.10 – 12).[61] As each choice of material – paint, bronze, stone – strengthens in durability, so does the father's stance harden, and the crime is further corporealised from two-dimensional to full-relief 'body art' available for public consumption. Additionally, the proposed

---

56 'Is one not allowed to die in a city where one is allowed to be a prostitute? Do you really think this body acts consistently in each case when it permits one person to live a disgraceful life and prohibits another from dying an honorable death?'

57 The only example in declamation of the painting of a war hero's deed as a reward; cf. Casamento in this volume; Sussman (1994) 158.

58 'I have learned that fratricide can be committed while leaving the laws intact.'

59 'Now the rest of the story ought to be painted, not stated formally as the facts in this case.'

60 'Groundless and foolish is... your fearing paint worse than real blood.'

61 'Let this deed be represented not just in paint, but in bronze, if possible, also in stone, and in whatever medium artistic skill also rivals our actual flesh.'

monumentalisation of the moment of fratricide through various artistic media that will endure over time and occupy public space in two and three dimensions stands in complex tension with the evanescence of his son's death;[62] the function of public art to glorify military victory and, thus, social cohesion is confounded by the dissolution of the family unit as it is to be represented in various artistic media. Finally, the speaker refigures the son's action of stabbing as a perverse kind of creative technique, implying the soldier is something of an artist in his own right: *in omnibus pectoribus incisa sunt, in oculis, in animis, in ipsis denique tuis manibus* (20.13 – 15).[63] The son has already engraved (viz. *incisa sunt*), as it were, his crime indelibly on the minds of the community, and even on his own hands.[64] As an artificer of death, the son, using a sword as his artistic instrument, cannot escape his father's *incisive* insight that his engraving tool dug his brother's grave, and the deed has been memorialised throughout the social consciousness irreversibly.

Across these four *controversiae*, personal identities are subject to co-option by unexpected means and media. Epigraphical inscription, patriotic duty, a genetic twin, and artistic representation serve various ways to figure dramatic alteregos, welcome or otherwise. By creative turns Calpurnius demonstrates how a declaimer may tap into conceptual re-figuration for the purpose of invigorating rhetorical inventiveness.

4 The Letter of the Law: Calp. 23 ~ 24 ~ 25 ~ 26 (by way of Calp. 22)

If thematic and conceptual connections are to be discerned across declamations for the Calpurnian brand of pedagogy to be effective, then more explicit *verbal* connections between declamations warrant attention for what these may have to teach. Explicit discursive responses between particular declamations – which are otherwise entirely unrelated – function as a special kind of intertextuality, as sites where semantic meaning and, thus, authority are contested.[65] Several instances of these discursive cross-stitchings between Calpurnius' decla-

---

62 As a 'momentary factual event' military victory must be rendered into monumental format if it is to be successfully translated into political power and to bind the empire together; cf. Hölscher (2006) 27– 29.

63 'Those events have been engraved on all our hearts, on our eyes, on our minds, and, in point of fact, on those very hands of yours.'

64 Cf. Sussman (1994) 160 – 161 n. ad loc.

65 See also the chapter by Spielberg in this volume.

mations will be considered in Section 5. One signal example of Calpurnian intertextuality, however, will be examined here in virtue of its position between one
thematic cluster and another. Calp. 22 shares an intriguing intertextual connection with its predecessor, Calp. 21, but *also* signals a point of departure from the
unifying theme of the preceding cluster – i.e., the topic of mimetic substitutions
of Calp. 18, 19, 20 and 21 – to that of the next – namely, the use of laws in Calpurnian rhetoric and the inherent indeterminacy of legal semantics as explored
by Calp. 23, 24, 25 and 26 – to be discussed in this section.

Both Calp. 21 and 22 make potent use of the verb *cedere*, and interpret the
verb in strikingly different ways. The emphasis on the verb *cedere* calls attention
to the act of yielding, and signals to the reader the beginning of a new lesson in
Calpurnius' study of rhetoric. Mastery of one's argument, the key to rhetorical
success, depends on mastery of the semantic meaning of the discourse employed, which is never inherently stable in meaning and is always subject to slippage in significance. Conversely, control of one's argument also depends on *not*
yielding semantic ground to one's opponent. It is the constant shifting of language's meaning which the emphasis on *cedere* here signals to the reader,
and which introduces the new pedagogical topic in the subsequent cluster of invoking the language of law to one's rhetorical advantage. The language of law,
that edifice of social cohesiveness, is shown to be subject to the same slippage
between its letter and its intention as all language is, and Calpurnius' pointed
use of *cedere* between Calp. 21 and 22 brings to our awareness this quality
and challenge inherent to rhetoric.[66]

In Calp. 21 and 22, fathers speak out against their sons and against what they
perceive as acts of disobedience and betrayal. The arguments of both speeches
are centred on two divergent understandings of the word *cedere*. In Calp. 21,
the father recalls advice he gave to his younger son before he fought his brother
in battle: *cede fratri, cede vel patri; victor eris, mihi crede, si cesseris* (20.6).[67] The
son's refusal to yield to his father's request has brought violence and disarray to
the family; yielding to a father's request is not merely a matter of rigid obedience
to patriarchal authority, but also, as the almost incantatory phonetics of his plea
emphasises, a matter of *trust* in a father's judgment: *cede-cede-crede-cesseris*.[68]
In stark contrast to this act of defiant stubbornness, the son in the following dec-

---

66 The full range of possible controversies between the *scriptum* and *voluntas* of the law which
can determine the outcome of legal disputes are taxonomised by Quint. *Inst.* 7.6.1 ff.; further, Cic.
Inv. 2.121 ff.
67 'Yield to your brother, yield at any rate to your father; a victor you will be, if you yield – believe me.'
68 Cf. Sussman (1994) 159 n. ad loc.

lamation is brought to trial because he *did* yield to someone. In Calp. 22, a young man has killed a tyrant and, exercising his legal right, offered his prize to his stepmother (*cessit novercae praemio*, 20.18), who now wants to marry him; son and father dispute the right to oppose the stepmother's request (20.17–20).[69] Here the father excoriates the son, and in three separate instances frames the ceding of his prize as an act of betrayal. First, in dishonouring his father, the son also dishonours the hierarchy of the traditional household, in which the patriarch should take priority of consideration over a stepmother, and even a natural mother: *novercae praemio cessit, cum haberet in domo patrem cui nemo praeferret in tali honore vel matrem* (21.3–5).[70] Second, the father discredits his son's testimony, undermining the sincerity of his refusal to marry and, thus, the integrity of his character: '*Ego,*' *inquit,* '*praemio* cessi.' *tu ergo non potes revocare quod dederis eamque reprehendere quam paulo ante laudaveris* (21.11–13).[71] The son's efforts to refuse marriage to a woman he deferred to only recently and whom he now wants to impugn expose his motives as inconsistent, contradictory and untrustworthy. Finally, the father issues a warning: *cavendum tibi est ne, si victus... discesseris, dicaris iudicio quoque sic cessisse quasi praemio* (21.13–15).[72] By renouncing his prize in the first instance, the son has set a vexing precedent for his reputation and placed on himself a significant burden of proof. Should he win the *divinatio* only to lose the case against his stepmother, he may be reputed (*dicaris*) as intentionally yielding the trial as he has done his reward, throwing the match, as it were, in her favour, and confirming his innately slippery character. To lose the trial (*victus... discesseris*) is not an option, since failure would incriminate him once again as a deliberate conceder (*cessisse*). The inconsistencies between his professed motives to accuse his stepmother and the original act of conceding his prize define his character as morally *recessive*, predictable only in his unreliable, ever-shifting affiliations. Whereas the son in Calp. 21 betrayed a lack of trust in his father by *not* acquiescing to his request, the son in Calp. 22 is himself untrustworthy *because of* acquiescing to someone else.

---

69 On *divinatio*, in which two or more parties contest the right to act as accuser, see Sussman (1994) 162.
70 'He renounced the reward in his stepmother's favour when he had in his house a father, someone over whom nobody should give preference in such an honour – even a natural mother.' For declamation's *saeva noverca* and her influence on Roman literature, see Pingoud and Rolle (2016) 148–157; Casamento (2002) 101–124; Watson (1995) 92–134; Sussman (1994) 162 n. ad loc.
71 'He tells us, "I renounced the reward." You in that case cannot take back what you have given away and censure a woman whom you honored just a little while ago.'
72 'You have to be on your guard, because if you end up losing the case... people may say you also yielded in the trial just as you had in the reward.'

Semantic ground shifts and yields beneath the surface meanings of *cedere* between Calp. 21 and 22, indirectly preparing the reader for the following group of declamations which explore myriad ways that laws can be interpreted, referenced and adduced to the orator's advantage; centring on the language of law, linguistic signifiers and semiotic significance are negotiated throughout these four declamations. In Calp. 23, a son killed his mother in the act of adultery, and was executed by his maternal grandfather according to his mother's dying claim that he was not actually her son and, thus, not a Roman citizen (viz. *'non es meus'*, 21.22); upon his return, the father appeals to the tribunes (21.18 – 25). Calp. 23 is strongly reminiscent of Lysias' classic set-speech (Lysias 1, *'On the Murder of Eratosthenes'*), in which the defendant casts himself as the human embodiment of Athenian law to justify killing his wife's seducer.[73] Calpurnius' defendant here makes a similar rhetorical manoeuvre – arguing he invested the authority of (Roman declamatory) law in the hands of his son to protect the sanctity of his marriage bed while he was away from home – but also must refute the charge that his son was ever a foreigner. To these ends, the speaker constructs his identity with three explicit references to laws which have defined him as a husband and a father. The appeals to the laws serve the added purpose of casting the credibility of the speaker and his opponents in distinctly *psychological* terms. The argument implicit to this speech is as follows: just as his ex-wife and ex-father-in-law were subject to excessive emotions, like lust and vindictiveness, and, thus, were mentally unfit when adjudicating his son's execution, so too is the speaker a man of rational composure and sound mind *in virtue of* his abiding awareness of the laws throughout his life. Recognition of and adherence to laws is imbricated with cognizant acknowledgment of one's kin; so too, failure to acknowledge one's kin is symptomatic of mental disarray and disregard for the law.

First, with respect to the laws, he reminds the jury that he married this man's daughter and waited out her pregnancy in accordance with the laws of the land and in the presence of witnesses: *huius ego legibus filiam duxi eamque praegnantem simul vidimus* (22.7 – 8). His marriage and fatherhood are determined by their legal status and the fact that both he and his father-in-law have borne witness (*vidimus*) to the due course of events.[74] Years later, the father appointed his son interim *paterfamilias* before he departed on business, impressing on him the law concerning adultery: *ut plus illi necessitatis imponerem, sententiam ves-*

---

73 The law permitting husbands and the male kin they appoint to kill wives caught in adultery had enduring precedent in Greece and possibly in Republican Rome; cf. Sussman (1994) 165.
74 Cf. Sussman (1994) 166 n. ad loc.

trae legis ingessi. denuntiavi postremo futurum ipsius crimen, si non patri paruisset et legi (22.11–14).[75] The son is invested with the law's authority and his father's *patria potestas*, which are co-identified with each other; to disobey one is to disobey the other, and would render the son criminally negligent were he not to act as needed.[76] From the time he was married, the speaker has always conducted his life as a husband and father in active compliance with the laws. In addition, by pointedly referring to the law and its intent as the prerogative of the tribunal hearing his case (viz. *sententiam* <u>*vestrae*</u> *legis*), he implicates the tribunal in the maintenance of social order, and in confirming the justice of his and his son's actions.

As the speaker draws attention to his lifelong cognizance of the law, he simultaneously characterises his former father-in-law and wife as susceptible to overpowering emotions and psychological disturbances which impair cognitive functioning and, in turn, observance of the law. The father-in-law was so consumed by anger at his daughter's death that he was no longer willing to recognize his son-in-law or his own grandson (*quatenus socer saevit ut nec generum velit agnoscere nec nepotem*, 22.3–4). In a similar state of emotional turmoil, the wife was driven to insanity, so consumed by unrestrained lust for her paramour and by terror at the sudden sight of the armed young man that she, too, was incapable of recognising her own family members (*per insanam libidinem stimulis tanti furoris exarserat ut nec suos agnosceret*, 22.14–15; *mater armatum timuit*, 22.20–21). Like father like daughter, these two are prone to succumbing to emotions which prevent them from recognising their own blood relations, a consequence of emotional excess.[77] The father concludes his speech by contrasting himself both with his father-in-law and with his wife: *illa dixit, 'meus non est,' at ego dico, 'meus est.' mater armatum timuit, sed pater servientem, quod est maius, agnoscit* (22.20–21).[78] Whereas the father-in-law and wife were unwilling or incapable of acknowledging the young man due to upheavals of passion, the father, having defined himself as obedient to the law, *does* recognise his own

---

75 'To impose upon him a more powerful sense of his required duties, I forced repeatedly to his attention the decree of your law. Last of all, I duly warned him that he would be subject to censure if he had failed to obey his father and the law.'

76 Perhaps the statute (*sententia*) is from the Twelve Tables; cf. Sussman (1994) 166–167 n. ad loc.

77 As represented through tragic characters such as Ajax, Agave and Herakles/Hercules, psychotic fits typically impair cognitive faculties of recognition and comprehension; cf. Papadopoulou (2004) 257–281; Dobrov (2001) 57–85.

78 'That woman said, "He's not my legal son," but I for my part say, "He is my legal son." The mother feared an armed man, but a father acknowledges as his own a man serving as a slave, and this is something which carries more weight.'

son and, consequently, should be perceived by the tribunal as endowed with rational composure. The sort of person who maintains his rational faculties, free from surfeit of detrimental emotions such as anger, fear or lust, is the sort of person who always recognises his own family members, and also the sort of person who understands and lives according to the law, the commonwealth's foundation. The law is established to defend all who are *compos mentis.*

Whereas the speaker in Calp. 23 vindicates himself by appealing to the laws he has followed throughout his life, the speaker in Calp. 24 seeks to apply the law to the fullest extent, using the language of the law to force – literally – his prosecutor's hand. At the behest of his father, a son is to be executed in accordance with the law concerning those condemned without trial; he wants to be killed by his father's hand, but his father admits he is unable to finish what he had begun (22.24 – 23.2).[79] The speech is guided by a strategy of reverse psychology designed to compound the father's hesitation, to arouse pity for the son's situation, and, ultimately, exculpate the son. First the son cites a legal clause to prove that the duty for execution cannot be performed by a state executioner in cases where the condemned has not faced a judge (*quia nec iuris ratio permittit ut adhibeatur adversum eum carnifex, in quem non fuit iudex*, 23.9 – 11).[80] Then the son compels his father to commit to his legally binding decision, first by availing himself of the law which defends him (*ius quod tibi vindicas, experire*, 23.13 – 14), and second by reminding him of the paternal obligations placed on him by the law (*non potes, pater, legis eiusdem et inrogare supplicium et denegare solacium*, 23.17 – 19).[81] Crisp, rhythmic phonetics evocatively encapsulate the father's powerlessness (*nōn-pó-tes-pá-ter*), an ironic reversal for someone who had originally sought surety and protection from the very same law (viz. *vindicas*; *legis eiusdem*).[82] The more the condemned son speaks, the more the father is disempowered. Although the meaning of the law is clear, its consequences have proven to be paradoxical and impracticable, demanding both capital punishment (*supplicium*) and consolation (*solacium*) for the guilty in question.[83] Insisting on his father to act in accordance with the law is to constrain the father by an untenable predicament. No solution is specified, only, perhaps, the tacit hope that the father will revoke his original condemnation.

---

79 The *lex indemnatorum* conferred on a father the right of life and death over his children; cf. Sussman (1994) 168.

80 Cf. Sussman (1994) 169 n. ad loc.

81 'Father, you cannot propose the same law's execution and deny me its consolation.'

82 Calpurnius' rhythm and prosodic complications are analyzed by Håkanson (2014) 120 – 130 (cf. 134 – 135).

83 Cf. Quint. *Inst.* 7.6.5.

In Calp. 25, a law is invited to speak for itself in its own voice. A rapist who was sentenced to death by his victim has been freed by his war hero brother, who uses his other reward to sue for the death of the raped woman in reprisal; the rapist now pleads for the girl to be spared so he can marry her (23.24–24.4). Surprisingly, the speaker decides to embrace his identity as a rapist so he can use the particulars of the law against rapists to his full advantage.[84] In the opening sentence he refers to the woman in question explicitly as the woman who was raped (*rapta*, 24.5); he openly admits he is unable to prove his sexual violation was committed out of love (*ego... [nec] rebus ipsis ostendo quod amavi*, 24.9); and he freely accepts the judgment that he committed sexual assault (*iniuriam... quod rapui*, 24.10). The penultimate sentence is reserved for the law itself, by which he was formerly condemned, to speak *in propria persona* in his defence, a device used occasionally elsewhere in declamation: *lex dicit: 'raptor aut pereat aut ducat'* (24.10–11).[85] However inaccurately, the voice of law reduces, in virtue of its paraphrased form, the choices available to the rapist to a strictly binary option between death and marriage. Invoking the voice of the law is also a deft manoeuvre to take agency *away* from the rape victim and invest it in the law itself to decide the fate of the rapist. The rapist concludes (viz. *ergo*) that since he was released from the death penalty, he and the raped woman are owed to each other necessarily (*raptori si poena dimittitur, rapta[e] debetur*, 24.11–12)[86] – a provision nowhere explicit in the law itself, but nonetheless made possible by the way it is paraphrased here. The citation of the law adds a veneer of objectivity and authority to a carefully gauged line of reasoning. But even when a law is seemingly allowed to 'speak', its voice can be subject to scrupulous application by a declaimer's guiding ventriloquism.

And just as the law was allowed to speak, in so many words, in Calp. 25, it is the legislator who makes a cameo appearance, of sorts, in the subsequent and final declamation of this series. In Calp. 26, the speaker ventures onto the terrain of collective socio-historical memory, as he divines the intentions of a legislator on whose law he is now making his appeal.[87] Here, a war hero offers to substitute himself for his condemned son who deserted the field of battle (24.14–17).[88] Although a law permits substitutions for punishment, by objecting to the condem-

---

84 For the unique variations of the laws used in this case, see Sussman (1994) 172.

85 'The law says, "A rapist may either die or marry."' For the phrase *lex dicit* in declamation, see Sussman (1994) 174 n. ad loc.

86 'Therefore, if a rapist is released from the punishment, the raped woman is his due.'

87 Proving the intention of the *legumlator* requires that the speaker either impugn the letter of the law or, as here, defend it; cf. Quint. *Inst.* 7.6.8–12.

88 An option based on what is apparently a fictional law; cf. Sussman (1994) 175.

nation of his son the war hero risks setting his personal, domestic preferences in opposition to the will of the state, which demands full accountability from its soldiers in times of war. To resolve any apparent conflict of personal and civic interests, the veteran mounts an interpretation of this law as having been originally drafted with blood ties in mind for the purpose of ensuring the vitality of the state. With a rhetorical question (of which eight dominate the speech as a whole), the father articulates the ideology of his approach to the issue: *resisto orbitati non iure vel sanguine?* (24.22).[89] His request to intervene against the loss of his child is legitimised not only on legal grounds (*non iure*) but, both literally and metaphorically, by the pledge of his own life's blood (*vel sanguine*) for the sake of his blood kin. The association of blood ties with the law, if primarily by means of syntactical parallelism, cues the central rhetorical strategy of the speech, one which is an effort to humanise the process of drafting legislation. The father posits that this law permitting substitutions for punishment was designed by its legislator specifically with *fathers* in mind: *mihi videtur et ille qui primus hanc condidit legem nihil aliud cogitasse quam patrem* (25.1–2).[90] The ring composition of the sentence effects an elevation, even transcendence, of the individual (*mihi*) into the archetypal (*patrem*); the speaker identifies himself as that Everyfather which the legislator – who remains anonymous but is presumed to be known to all (*ille*) and, for that, is sanctified – had in mind exclusively (*nihil aliud*) when passing the law; the historical time frame of the legislator's deliberations in the past (*cogitasse*) is notably underdetermined, locating the drafting of the law at *some* point in Roman history which no sceptic in the jury can verify *or* dispute. The persuasiveness of this hypothetical scenario of a legislator who is unidentifiable yet who *certainly* existed (again, *ille*) drafting his law with fathers in mind gains strength by virtue of its vagueness; each member of the jury can be amenable to the mental time frame of collective historical consciousness, not determined by specific years but by social affiliation. Finally, an agricultural connotation latent in *condidit* cues a developed metaphor, as the father compares himself to an old tree about to be uprooted for new life: *agricolae antiquas arbores exstirpant ut novas inserant; horum virtus spectabitur, nostra delabitur* (25.8–10).[91] The legislator, in virtue of having *implanted* (viz. *inserant*) this law into society's *foundation* (again, *condidit*), is something of a farmer, removing the dead wood from society's orchards (*antiquas arbores*), ensuring that

---

[89] 'Have I not the right to intervene against the loss of my children, even with my own blood?'
[90] 'It seems to me that the particular man who first framed this law also intended no other eventuality than a father [as a substitute].'
[91] 'Farmers uproot old trees in order to plan new ones; my sons' valour is to be looked forward to, but mine is slipping away.' Cf. Sussman (1994) 177 n. ad loc.

the younger generation's excellence and valour (*virtus*), in this case guaranteed by the father's past feats of heroism, will flourish for all to see.[92] The inner workings of the legislator's mind and intent are constructed from agricultural discourse, rooting the importance of the legal tradition in the Roman household as the guarantor of the future burgeoning of the state.

Permutations of the words *lex* and/or *ius* occur in all four of these declamations to signal a unifying conceptual thread, as they demonstrate four distinct ways that laws can be invoked and deployed in forensic argumentation. First, the laws of the land structure the speaker's autobiography and character, redounding to his credibility; next, the full implications of the laws of capital punishment are used to call one's accuser to account, potentially forcing a reversal of charges; the language of the law can *appear* to be quoted authoritatively verbatim, all while undergoing scrupulous paraphrase and calibrated explication; and the irrecoverable intentions of the lawgiver are momentarily conjured from collective memory to foster mindfulness of legal traditions and patriarchal *mores.* Together, these four declamations reflect on myriad ways that legal theory and practice are embedded in the social fabric.

5 'Seeing Things' (like it or not): Calp. 9 ~ 10 ~ 11; 33 ~ 34; 36 ~ 37; 52 ~ 53

Thematic cohesion may in fact obtain across certain groups of declamations in Calpurnius Flaccus, but there are many other declamations which bear no obvious conceptual resemblance to those which immediately precede or follow them. However, when a declamation appears to make a departure into a topic ostensibly *un*related to what has preceded it, Calpurnius, I will argue here, tends to insert unmistakable verbal responses between those *controversiae*, making ostensible *discursive* connections that prompt critical reflection on unlikely pairs of declamations. As the previous analysis of the use of the verb *cedere* between Calp. 22 and 23 indicates, such instances of explicit discursive response serve another goal of Calpurnian pedagogy, namely to challenge the aspirant declaimer to appreciate the versatility and applicability of language and rhetorical techniques by witnessing how the *same* words may be used to dramatically different effect in otherwise unrelated speeches. The following case studies consider four clusters of declamations, the unity of which is defined primarily by explicit verbal connections, and only secondarily (if at all) by thematic connections.

---

92 A rare but not unattested use of *specto*; cf. Sussman (1994) 177 n. ad loc.

The role of sight and vision is prominent in Calp. 9 and 10, but these two declamations, together with Calp. 11, will be considered here with regard to the particular pedagogical function they may have to serve in Calpurnius' book as a whole. Calp. 9 and 10 make a fitting pair not only because of their oddly similar situations – one father loses his sight, another miraculously regains his – but also because these two declamations occur at a pivotal juncture in the book itself: Calp. 9 is the last of Calpurnius' fifty-three declamations to provide a counterargument. We cannot know if this cut-off is an intentional change in approach by the author or the result of an unfortunate loss in the manuscripts – the counterargument of Calp. 9 is itself a lacunose sentence and a half – but Calp. 9's and 10's shared topical interests in sight and seeing *in conjunction with* the cessation of counterarguments *seem*, I will suggest, to demand a new level of rhetorical skill from the student of Calpurnius' lessons on declamation, and all the more so when these two declamations are read with Calp. 11 in mind. 'Seeming' is the essence of this metatextual, metapedagogic message, for all three declamations discourse upon the fissures between appearances and reality, seeing and understanding, semantic surfaces and multiform connotations, overt actions and hidden intentions. Over the course of these three declamations, the safety net of Calpurnius' prefabricated model counterarguments is taken away. Because model counterarguments are no longer provided by the author to edify students on the possibilities for arguing from the opposing side, the student is expected, I propose, to provide *his own* counterarguments from this point of the book onward. Now you see the counterarguments, now you –

The student-reader is enjoined, that is, to graduate to a more demanding level of rhetorical and argumentative proficiency by sharpening his awareness of the essential role that discursive indeterminacy plays in forensic argument: the meaning behind any action or word can never be presumed stable, *just as* one's *perceptions* are always subject to manipulation and reappraisal. Why this challenge is levelled at the student at this point in the book may be gleaned better from analysing some of the prominent issues raised by these three declamations.

The circumstances behind the case of Calp. 9 are peculiar in their obscurity. After 'putting away' (viz. *abdita*) his wife and dissolute son, a father retires into seclusion (*secessit in secretum*) only to emerge blinded under mysterious circumstances (8.21–22); despite his wife's claim that she caused his blindness, the father blames his son and seeks retribution in kind (i.e. *talio*).[93] The speech's tone is unusually acerbic for Calpurnius, as the father openly admits he hates his son

---

[93] For the circumstances and phenomenon of blindness through weeping and other afflictions in declamation, see Sussman (1994) 120.

more than whoever actually blinded him *(quam sceleratus es! plus te pater odit quam eum a quo excaecatus est*, 9.9 – 10).[94] This blast of emotional candour may be symptomatic of the speech's broader dilations on transparency and deception, how not only eyes may be blinded but also one's intellectual and emotional faculties. This topic is cued in the introductory sentences by an explication of the double meaning inherent in the forceful verb *excaecare*, meaning to blind utterly. The son is said to have discovered a way to blind both parents in different ways, his father in private (*secreto*, 9.2) in respect of his eyesight, and his mother in public (*in foro*, 9.3) in respect of her mind and maternal instincts. That is, the son's means of defence against blinding his father physically is to dupe his mother emotionally blind into taking the fall for him: *cuius crimen est excaecasse patrem, patrocinium excaecare matrem* (9.14 – 15).[95] The double use of *excaecare* by the father here serves to identify two distinct layers of discursive meaning; this exercise in critical distinction is done not merely for the sake of clever wordplay but to evince the father's own evaluative faculties, which are put into practical use when the father assesses the truthfulness of the son's and mother's confessions. His interpretations of their confessions, therefore, redound to his credit as someone keenly perceptive of character despite his ocular blindness. For example, as the sort of young man who wanted to blind his father (*talis es, adulescens, ut excaecare volueris patrem*, 9.8 – 9), the son's own testimony can never be trusted even when confessed in a court of law: '*non feci*,' *inquit. non crederem, si confitereris* (9.7 – 8).[96] The mother's confession also must not be trusted, not because of criminal intent but because of her misguided maternal instinct to protect her son: '*ego feci.*' *non sceleris, sed matris ista confessio est* (9.16 – 17).[97] This father, a Calpurnian Oedipus, has gained powers of psychoanalytic insight into the intentions lurking behind actions *and* words of those who have wronged him. Indeed, the way the opening sentence of the counterargument begs the jury to believe the son's confession (*credite confitenti*, 9.19 – 20), shows the father's line of attack on the credibility of the son's and mother's confessions to be the most incriminating charge the defence must address.

At the juncture between Calp. 9 and 10, the student-reader is compelled to heighten his awareness of the ever-present slippage between verbal signifiers and signifieds if he hopes – with an *eye* towards eventual rhetorical mastery –

---

94 'What a scoundrel you are! Your father hates you more than the person by whom he was blinded.'

95 'Blinding his mother is the defence in court of one whose crime it is to have blinded his father.'

96 '"I didn't do it," he says. I wouldn't believe it even if you were to confess.'

97 '"I did it," she says. That is the confession of a mother, not a crime.'

to make progress in his declamatory education. To this end, Calp. 10 denies the reader the seeing-eye guidance Calpurnius has offered in the form of pre-fashioned counterarguments, and re-teaches the forensic lessons of Calp. 9 in virtue of its eye-opening topical complementarity: 'Oedipus-in-reverse' is the speaker of Calp. 10, a father who, having lost his eyesight from weeping over two dead sons, miraculously regains his vision in fulfilment of a prophetic dream – but at the cost of his third son's life (10.2–5). According to the circumstances of the case, the father had confided his dream only to his wife that he would see again if his third son died, and has divorced her for telling and, so he infers, vindictively motivating their dutiful son to commit suicide; she now countersues him for unjustified divorce.[98] As it was to the previous speech, the dual meaning of blindness (*caecitas*, passim) is central. But whereas the father of Calp. 9 knew he could *not* trust the confessions of his wife and son, the father of Calp. 10 positively asserts he knows her true intentions. First, to counter his wife's claim that she acted out of love for her husband, the father makes the distinction between originally confiding his dream to her out of a sense of marital *amor* and a father's overriding moral imperative to preserve his household (*numquid discutiunt recti necessitate qui aliquid amore fecerunt?*, 10.11–12).[99] The speaker thus makes his own fatherly priorities manifest to the jury and dissociates himself from blame for his son's death.[100] Having simultaneously rebutted his wife's claim and established himself as a patriarch of moral rectitude, he proceeds to characterise her actions as criminal in terms of the acuteness of his own ocular perception: *decet esse oculos duriores qui scelere reverterunt* (10.13–14).[101] The logic is, to a degree, circular: the fact his eyesight was restored by her vindictive action is proof positive that his eyes are steadier and keener, less likely to be deceived, more skilled at discerning criminal intent. To elucidate his point, the father diagnoses blindness as a condition not affecting ocular health but psychoanalytic acuity. Speaking as someone who could see again by means of a criminal act (*qui, ut scelerate viderem*, 10.24), the father defines blindness as the inability to perceive the character of others, specifically his wife: *non recepi oculos, sed perdidi caecitatem* (10.24–25).[102] The restoration of the father's ocular sight is of no value to him; it is his blindness to his wife's character and criminal intentions that had truly afflicted him before, and that he has now overcome. Even

---

98 On *iniustum repudium* and *divortium* in declamation, see Sussman (1994) 124.

99 'Can it be said that those who have done something out of love attenuate the demands of what is morally right?'

100 Further Sussman (1994) 125 n. ad loc.

101 'Eyes are quite properly tougher which have been restored through a crime.'

102 'I have not recovered my eyesight but lost my blindness.'

without the aid of his eyes, he can now see her true intentions. The concluding lament suggests that the father may weep his eyes into a condition of blindness once again (*iam tempus est fletuum, immo iam tempus est caecitatis*, 11.4–5), but ocular blindness would offer no solace this time around, for even if this father should lose his ability to see the physical world again, he will always see how his ex-wife betrayed him.

The third lesson in this series of discursive explorations of vision and blindness is a treatment of the *converse* implications of the previous two declamations. If sight does not necessarily confer knowledge – indeed, if seeing actually impairs knowing – according to Calp. 9 and 10, then according to Calp. 11 seeming should not induce believing either. This speech is framed by instances of *videre* in the passive, which signal intriguing thematic responsion with the previous two declamations. A poor man has given his three sons in adoption to a rich man with whom he has reconciled; two sons have been killed while committing violent acts; the poor father seeks the restoration of his third son before he can be corrupted by wealth (11.6–11).[103] The first sentence captures the paradoxical nature of the poor man's turn of fortune: *nihil tamen praeter luctus meos gravius quam quod, ubi odia nihil fecere, videatur amicitia plus nocere* (11.12–13).[104] Compounding the poor man's grief is the cruel irony that the period of open hostility (*odia*) between himself and the rich man proved inconsequential (*nihil fecere*), whereas their reconciliation (*amicitia*) gives the appearance (*videatur*) of having caused greater harm (*plus nocere*). The fathers of the previous two declamations could confidently ascertain the intentions of their wrongdoers through powers of insight honed by the loss/restoration of their eyes, but this father is less confident in his ability to comprehend his situation; the passive *videatur* signals a tone of cautiousness in his rhetorical approach, its modest subjectivity calling into question the reliability of his own faculties of perception. The humility of this rhetorical stance, though, redounds to his credit *qua pauper*, the tentativeness of his observation reflective of a modest, sympathetic character. Where the previous two fathers were aggressively perspicacious, this father errs on

---

103 As a particular form of aristocratic exchange, open adoption in Roman society typically occurred between families of the same class in the hopes of creating enduring affective relationships; cf. Lindsay (2009) 62–70, 74–75; Kunst (2005) 35–80; Gardner (1998) 114–208; Sussman (1994) 128. Declamation, however, invents scenarios of adoption conflicts between unrelated families of unequal social classes to explore the social and moral effects of the luxury ethic; cf. Bernstein (2009) 335–343. See further below on Calp. 53.

104 'In spite of what has been said, nothing, with the exception of my own grief, weighs on me more than this: in a situation where our mutual hatred has brought about no consequences, our friendship would appear to be a greater source of harm.'

the side of speculation, expressing a degree of doubt in his perceptual grasp of his situation while coming to terms with his grief. The speech's first sentence also echoes a sentiment of the previous declamation, that the *ostensible* cure to their feud only resulted in greater calamity (cf. *nec remedia quaerenda sunt ubi maior<is> supplicii sanatio*, 10.16–17).[105] The speech's final sentence recalls – deliberately (cf. *recordare*, *infra*) – its opening sentence but with a shift of emphasis: *recordare quantis meis redemerim malis ne adhuc videremur inimici* (12.2–3).[106] The poor man has suffered so many afflictions only for the sake of keeping up appearances, only for a simulation of friendship (*ne... videremur inimici*). Ever since his apparent reconciliation with the rich man has resulted in the loss of two sons, this father has been disillusioned, his outlook clouded. In a world where *seeming* has produced the opposite of what he had best intended, the poor man *sees* to it that his remaining son be rescued before too late.

So we see – at least, we seem to see – what we are supposed to. Calp. 9, 10 and 11 work in coordination to alert the reader to a new stage in Calpurnius' declamatory education; these declamations call attention to the fact that words may always encode their opposite meanings. Once a reader has seen the light of this lesson on semantics, he is empowered to craft his own counterarguments from this point forward, and our author need not supply us with his own prefabricated examples.

If these three declamations serve a broader purpose for the project of the book as a whole, other pairs of adjacent declamations in Calpurnius Flaccus work in conjunction with each other in more localised ways. For example, both Calp. 33 and 34 find an unlikely connection through shared use of a rhetorical device – the explicit appeal to a god (*deus*), a rarity in this book.[107] Calp. 33 finds its inspiration from Catullus 85, but this victim of love, a slave who dared fall for his mistress, a courtesan, is not only 'crucified' emotionally by unrequited desire but actually faces death by the cross (29.10–11).[108] Devoted to the end, the slave cannot believe (*miror*, 29.12) that his mistress could ever think of crucifying someone by any means other than love, inflecting his description of her, *quae nullum umquam nisi amore cruciaverit* (29.12–13), with lyric erudition.[109] Even though the rules of

---

105 'We must not seek remedies where the cure is a source of still greater suffering.'

106 'Recall how great a price I paid in my own misfortunes so that we would not still appear to be enemies!'

107 Calp. 20 (19.14–15) is the only other to invoke *deus*; the language is identical to the invocation at 30.1, discussed below. The hero-priest of Calp. 26, discussed above, mentions the role of the gods in his life (24.19–20), but does not invoke their aid.

108 Free Roman women consorting with slaves was taboo; cf. Sussman (1994) 193.

109 'A woman who never crucified anyone before – except in love.' Cf. Cat. 76.10; 85.2; 99.4, 12.

Roman law do not have to obtain strictly in the distorted realm of declamation, the premise of this speech strains credibility, in that a slave is permitted to avail himself of a fair hearing by a panel of tribunes and plead for his life before enfranchised citizens.[110] In order to legitimise his right to speak, I would suggest, the slave endeavours to overcome the social difference between himself and his jury by making productive use of multivalent connotations inherent in his language. Like the crucifix itself, which, *qua* passion, transfixes the speaker's mind and which, *qua* instrument of execution, will soon wreck his body, the speaker's own identity is defined according to two levels of discursive meaning, insofar as he is both a slave in legal status and also enslaved to *amor*. By defining himself in two distinct yet analogous ways, the slave makes it possible, if not inevitable, for the jury to identify with him: what gives a slave authority to plead for his life, if only in the realm of declamation, is the fact that we have all been enslaved to *amor* at one time or another. Furthermore, the slave makes an appeal to Love as a patron deity so that the jury may identify with him on emotional as well as theistic terms. Since he is beholden to a power more than human, to accuse him is to accuse the emotion, properly understood to be a god, which masters him and, thus, is to court impiety: *accusatur a nobis amor, et homo qui deum nostrum patitur?* (29.14–15).[111] Social differences between a slave and jury of enfranchised citizens are erased when social strata are measured according to *ontological* differences between human (*homo*) and god (*deum*); the slave can thus refer to himself and the jury as members of a community of nominal equals (viz. *a nobis*) without offending social sensibility. By appealing to a god, the slave bridges the legal and social divisions between himself and his jury, who come to view their relationship to the slave not in terms of social hierarchy but broadly as a shared species of human beings. The members of the jury are encouraged to identify themselves with the slave along emotional, theistic and, possibly, religious lines.

If a slave can appeal to a god to exculpate himself in the unpredictable world of declamation, then a rapist can just as easily swear by a god in order to incriminate himself in the very next speech. In Calp. 34, a father keeps his raped daughter under lock and key; the rapist pleads she come before a magistrate to pass judgment on him, presumably because he is confident she will opt to marry him (29.18–19).[112] First the speaker appeals to the laws concerning rape, noting that only the victim, not her father, can act as judge over the perpetrator; he freely admits his guilt and demands his female judge be released (*sum reus, sed ex-*

110 On *latio auxilii*, see Sussman (1994) 147–48.
111 'Are we charging Love with a crime, and also a man who submits to this god of ours?'
112 Cf. Sussman (1994) 194.

hibe iudicem meum, 29.21– 30.1).[113] In the final sentence, the rapist sheds light on the untenability of the current situation, where the rapist is the one who walks free and the victim is imprisoned: *pro deum atque hominum fidem! in qua civitate raptor solutus est? in ea rapta vincitur* (30.1–2).[114] The exclamatory invocation of a god (if, like *fidem*, *deum* is accusative) and of the social contract (*hominum fidem*) generates colonic rhythm, revving propulsive momentum for the conclud-ing rhetorical question-and-answer. The invocation also foregrounds an ethical implication that the health of the state (*civitas*) is predicated on the integrity of the contract between gods and men (if, like *hominum*, *deum* is genitive). The tight parallel structure of the final two clauses makes provocative use of the passive voice: both *raptor* and *rapta* are not free agents but subject (*solutus est/vincitur*) to powers beyond their control. In order to honour the heavenly and social contracts, therefore, it is urgently incumbent upon the jury to act and set the *civitas* to order. In contrast to the slave of the previous speech, who invoked a god to bring an end to his trial, the self-confessed culprit here appeals to a god – and even expands on the slave's exclamation from *pro deum* to *pro deum atque hominum fidem* – to bring his *iudex-rapta* before him. And where the slave aligned himself with the jury in order to free himself as an individual, the appeal of the rapist centres on the divine sanctity of social order.

Permutations of *velle*, *nolle* and *malle* coordinate Calp. 36 with 37, which act as foils to each other while examining the nature and psychological processes of desire and personal preference in the context of troubled relationships between fathers and sons. In one, a father seeks to have his son, a deserter, executed so he will not be enslaved to the perverted clutches of his new master, a wealthy general (*dives-imperator*, 30.21–31.2); in the latter, a son disputes his disinheri-tance over alleged misappropriation of estate funds (31.10 – 12).[115] In the first, the father clarifies his intentions towards his son for the benefit of the jury: *cre-ditis, iudices, quod filio meo bene inimicus velit, pater nolit? profiteor mortem me filii mei non quidem velle, sed malle* (31.4–5).[116] The sequence of verbs in the con-trafactual rhetorical question refines the jury's appreciation of the father's inten-tions: by designating the wealthy general as inimical and, thus, incapable of

---

113 'I am the guilty one; now produce my judge!'
114 'By God and all that men consider sacred! In what kind of state is a rapist set free? In one where the rape victim is kept imprisoned!'
115 For the laws, peculiar to declamation, governing these scenarios, see Sussman (1994) 198, 200.
116 'Gentlemen of the jury, do you not believe that my enemy wishes my son well, but that his father doesn't? I hereby declare that I certainly do not desire my son's death, but I do prefer it to the alternative.'

good will towards his son, the father is, by asyndetic contrast, not inimical and, it can be inferred, of good intention. Furthermore, the father's intentions cannot be characterised as an active death-wish (*non velle*) for his son, but as a preference (*malle*) for an honourable death over a disgraceful life (cf. *o fili, morere constanter!*, 31.7).[117] With assiduous care, the father avoids associating *velle* and its connotations of active desire, which would be unseemly in regard to a son's death, with himself explicitly. The contrafactual rhetorical question allows him to pirouette around *velle* (cf. *pater nolit*), and his positive claim to his true intentions (*profiteor*) is framed in terms of a preference between the lesser of two evils (*non quidem velle, sed malle*). The way in which ideas of desire and choice are delicately categorised and sequenced here bespeaks the thoughtfulness of the father's rationale, eliciting empathy for his predicament and sympathy for his judgment.

In what almost could be heard as a direct rejoinder to the earnest reasoning of Calp. 36, the son of Calp. 37 turns the same discourse of desire and preference *against* his father. This son used his father's money to buy the freedom of a mistress he loved, not the mistress the father loved, and is disinherited; he explains how incredulous he was that his father, an old man, was ever serious in his instructions to buy the freedom of a mistress, interpreting his father's expressions of love as teasing mockery of his own amorous attachment (*rideri me... opinabar a patre*, 31.12).[118] If these two adjoining declamations can be construed together along discursive coordinates of *velle-nolle-malle*, then a certain quasi-chiastic arrangement emerges: where the father of the previous declamation works his way rhetorically through stages of desire (*velit*), antipathy (*nolit*) and ultimately towards reluctant preference (*malle*), this son declares his personal preferences (*mallem*, 31.16) *before* discussing matters of personal volition (*velis nolis*, 31.17). First, the son claims that his preferences had long been known to his father (*sciebas utique quid mallem*, 31.16), and he concludes by criticising his father for behaving in a manner inappropriate and altogether imbalanced for his age: *<im>-paria sunt nobis in amore tormenta: primum quod amor, velis nolis, in senectute frigidior est* (31.16–18).[119] The vigour of *amor* blooms and fades, grows hot and

---

117 'My son, die with steadfastness!' The asyndeton and marked contrast is striking even for declamation; cf. Sussman (1994) 199 n. ad loc.
118 'I thought that my father was having a laugh at me.' This scenario is heavily influenced by New Comedy; cf. Mal-Maeder (2007) 1–39; Sussman (1994) 200.
119 'We have unequal torments in love: in the first place because, whether you like it or not, your sexual passion has grown colder in old age.' For the striking asyndeton, disjunctive coordination and literary parallels of *velis nolis*, see Sussman (1994) 201 n. ad loc.; *tormenta* is a strong but not unprecedented word for amatory contexts: cf. Sussman ibid.

cold, in accordance with a man's age and *irrespective of* personal desire. 'Like it or not', the father refuses to accept that he is past his sexual prime, that *amor* is not subject to his personal volition or patriarchal authority. The father of the previous declamation, in contrast, can exercise his full volitional agency over his particular case, as he considers what he wants, does not want, and ultimately prefers. Juxtaposed as such, these two declamations emerge as productive foils to each other as they explore the psychic routes fathers and sons may take to arrive at a fuller understanding of their will, their desires and their preferences.

Finally – and whether Calpurnius himself 'liked it or not' – Calp. 52 and 53 amount to the conclusion to his book. Both speeches end with signal uses of *redimere*; together, they take into thoughtful *account* the *value* of human life, both for society and for the Roman household, in the discourse of commercial and legal exchange. In Calp. 52, a war hero falls into the hands of pirates, only for a slave owner to purchase (viz. *redemit*) him as a gladiator before the state paid his ransom; after winning his freedom in the arena, he is summoned to military service, despite the fact disgraced individuals (*infames*) are technically barred (39.4–8).[120] The speech is remarkable not only for how the man grapples with his own worth and reputation as a soldier, lately disgraced by his time spent as a gladiator, but for how he holds the state accountable for abandoning him to the slave owner. Paronomastic (and anagrammatic) word play – *gladiatorem me fecit non pir-a-ta, sed pat-ri-a* (39.15) – even suggests the citizen-soldier has been treated worse by his *patria* than his captor *pirata*.[121] The speech is framed by references to *fortuna* and the influence blind luck has exerted over his multiple role reversals in life.[122] Luck may have turned him from a free man into a slave, a war hero into a gladiator (39.8–9), but by speech's end the soldier refrains from assigning all responsibility to misfortune alone: *'fortunae,' inquit, 'fuit.' quousque fortunam facimus humanorum negotiorum ream? esto; fortuna fecit ut caperer.*

---

120 Cf. Sussman (1994) 238. Edwards (1997) 71–72 observes that gladiators could not become soldiers during the Republic, and Knapp (2011) 265–289 observes that *infamia* would have been an elite phenomenon stigmatising those who might harbour political and, as in this case, military aspirations.

121 'It wasn't a pirate who made me a gladiator – it was my fatherland.' Cf. Sussman (1994) 240 n. ad loc.

122 *Could* this topical fixation on *fortuna* in our book's penultimate declamation be cued by the concluding sentiment of the collection's *ante*penultimate declamation, Calp. 51, with its ironic twist on the Vergilian view of the proper delineation between *fortuna* and *virtus*? The language and spirit of the sentiment expressed in *disce, infelix puer, natalium tuorum, disce fortunam* (Calp. 38.23–39.2) recall Aeneas' parting words to his own son, *disce, puer, virtutem ex me verumque laborem, / fortunam ex aliis* (*Aen.* 12.435–436).

quis fecit ut nemo redimeret? (39.22–24).[123] As Calpurnius' book draws to its end, the role of human agency assumes a renewed centrality to declamatory argumentation. The renouncement of chance, of all mitigating circumstances, is courted through the resonant first-person rhetorical question (*facimus*), implicating the jury *and* readership in resolving his predicament. Ruling out *fortuna*, the speaker confronts his community with its inaction on his behalf, asking why he was not rated of sufficient value for his military service to be bought back (*redimeret*) from his captors before he was commoditised as human traffic for the commercial benefit of a manager of gladiators (*lanista*, 39.5).[124] Now, because his social value was debated while in captivity, his present status has been so compromised by his life as a gladiator that the soldier poses something of a legal conundrum for his community: *et, si victoria solita provenerit, post rudem triumphabo?* (39.24–25).[125] If the soldier fights with his customary heroism and earns a triumph, it is not clear whether an ex-gladiator can be paraded as the paragon of civic and military virtue.[126] The state may desire to conscript him once again, but its penurious self-interests have manufactured a potential crisis for the state insofar as its communal identity would then be embodied by the compromised identity of the soldier-gladiator as promulgated on the public platform of the triumph.

If the open question of the penultimate speech forestalls the reconciliation between individual and state, and leaves the reader with a sense of self-reflective mindfulness of the mutual obligations shared between individual and state, the final speech of the book gestures towards a healing of rifts, if only within the domestic sphere, and does so along strikingly similar lines of economic discourse. A rich man and poor man adopted each other's sons in a display of reconciliation; the rich man condemns his new son without trial, and the poor man's son presents his case for suicide, presumably in fear of his adoptive father's immi-

---

123 'The opposition says, 'This was your bad luck.' How long shall we make luck answerable for human affairs? So be it; luck was responsible for my capture. Whose responsibility was it that nobody bought my freedom?' For observations on the striking sound effects and polyptoton of *fortuna* here, and also possible parallels to Juvenal's attack on *fortuna*, see Sussman (1994) 241 n. ad loc.

124 The language of mercantile acquisition is ill-suited to codes of traditional heroism in light of Euryalus' inauspicious use of *emere* while vowing to 'buy honour with his life' during his night raid (*Aen.* 9.205–6); cf. Coffee (2009) 83–84.

125 'And after all that, if the usual victory occurs, shall I take part in the triumphal parade after my discharge as a gladiator?'

126 Beard (2007) 187–218 documents the qualifications for the Roman triumph.

nent reprisal (40.2–5).[127] In three sentences, the poor man pleads for his adopted son's life, arguing it would not be merited (*indignum*, 40.7) to lose both his natural son and the son which friendship has substituted for him (*quod nunc substituit amicitia*, 40.8–9). Although his current son is the result not of nature but of the legal process of adoption, to demonstrate his profound fatherly attachment the poor man derives the etymological essence of (filial) love (*amo*) from the amicable relationship (*amicitia*) on which his present state of fatherhood was established: *amo enim iuvenem quem non genui meo sanguine, sed redemi* (40.9–10).[128] The final word of Calpurnius' book (*redemi*) is otherwise a term of economic exchange, but one which, according to this argument, has produced an enduring bond of affection beyond calculable value.[129] Similar to the way in which the soldier's ransom was not deemed worthy of payment by his state (cf. *ut nemo redimeret*), the father's use of *redimere* here reveals how layers of value and worth which undergird the ostensibly objective discourse of economic and social exchange are always subjectively determined. Where the soldier was left suspended in captivity, unpaid for by his community – and so decides to leave his jury in suspense with his unanswerable rhetorical questions – the poor father uses similar language of exchange to bid for a *redemptive* conclusion to his predicament, and to the book itself.

6 Calpurnius Altogether

Calpurnius Flaccus' book designs new methods for appraising and approaching declamation in practice, and demonstrates how the stagnation to which declamation, constrained by its stock characters and guiding premium on paradoxical *sententiae*, is prone can be mitigated. By connecting pairs and strings of declamations with thematic and discursive ligatures, Calpurnius challenges aspirant orators to appreciate how similar declamatory situations can be differentiated and enlivened, and, conversely, how unrelated situations can be crafted to resonate with each other. Other clusters which I have seen, or seem to have seen, and not discussed here could be grouped along the following themes or primary

---

127 Cf. Sussman (1994) 242. Like the exposed infant, the figure of the adoptee is a polyvalent character in Roman declamation, and can be portrayed as an active, aggressive agent or, more commonly, the object of potential violence; cf. Bernstein (2009) 343–351.
128 'I do indeed love the young man whom I did not father of my own seed, whom I acquired in the contract.'
129 The verb 'indicates that the exchange of sons was a formal guarantee of friendship and reconciliation' (Sussman (1994) 243 n. ad loc.).

characters: heroic men, or *viri fortes* (Calp. 26 ~ 27 ~ 28 ~ 29); ruminations on the differences between correlation and causation (Calp. 35 ~ 36 ~ 37 ~ 38 ~ 39 ~ 40); the express desire for suicide (Calp. 41 ~ 42 ~ 43 ~ 44 ~ 45).

The organisation of the book in its present state obviates comfortable or symmetrical configurations of the author's declamations. Instead, as I have argued, Calpurnius' lessons on declamation are communicated most effectively when the unlikely collection is read 'straight through' to experience the rhetorical twists and conceptual turns taken from one topic to the next. Calpurnius' book, therefore, becomes something of an obstacle course, but one in which the author shows how particular challenges can be overcome. Unlike Seneca's anthology, which invites the reader to dip into a single topic in no particular order to witness the proliferation of multiple forensic perspectives, and unlike ps.-Quintilian's collections, which invite analysis of the rhetorical contours of lengthy, robust set-pieces on each its own terms, Calpurnius challenges the reader to assess how a stock declamatory character or situation can be used differently and re-invented from one declamation to the next and to discover similitudes between unrelated scenarios. Calpurnius' method of teasing out connections and patterns between declamations tests the aspirant declaimer's rhetorical faculties to find daring new ways to innovate and persuade.

Lydia Spielberg*

Non contenti exemplis saeculi vestri: Intertextuality and the Declamatory Tradition in Calpurnius Flaccus

As a text, the excerpted *sententiae* of Calpurnius Flaccus are in good company. They were apparently transmitted at an early stage as part of a corpus of '*excerpta x rhetorum minorum*', and are found in extant manuscripts along with the pseudo-Quintilianic *Minor Declamations* and the excerpted tradition of Seneca the Elder.[1] Putting Calpurnius himself in context, however, is more difficult. He cannot be dated with certainty, much less set into an identifiable literary and scholastic milieu such as the community of speakers who populate Seneca the Elder's selection of the greatest hits of Augustan and Tiberian declamation.[2] But Calpurnius does fall into the same tradition as our other sources of Latin (and often Greek) declamation, using the same stock characters, declamatory laws and rhetorical *loci* in themes that sometimes have exact parallels elsewhere in the corpus. There are places, moreover, where one of Calpurnius' excerpts replicates the shape or thought of a passage found in another, prior source of declamation, most often in the compilation of Seneca the Elder.

Seneca's depiction of a lively society of teachers, students, amateurs and audiences is one of the most striking and valuable aspects of his work, a reminder that declamation was always an oral, performative practice.[3] By presenting ex-

* I am very grateful to Cynthia Damon and James Ker for their helpful comments on early drafts of this chapter.

1 On the transmission and ms history of Calpurnius, see Håkanson (1978) iii-v; Sussman (1994) 19 – 20; little can be said about the other '*decem rhetores minores*', but they may have included Gellius' friend Antonius Julianus (Lehnert (1908) 479 – 80; Schanz-Hosius (1922) 153). Sussman (1994) 20 observes that Calpurnius, by contrast to the other declamatory corpora, does not seem to have exerted much influence in the Middle Ages.

2 Scholars have traditionally dated Calpurnius to the second century CE on linguistic and stylistic grounds. See Weber (1898) 17 – 20, Sussman (1994) 7 – 9, but also the critique of Tabacco (1994) 188. An association with the M. Calpurnius who was suffect consul in 96 and the Calpurnius Flaccus who is the addressee of Pliny 5.2 is often assumed (Brzoska (1897) 1371 – 72; Syme (1968) 146 – 47; Sussman (1994) 6 – 7). For the most recent discussion, proposing a later date than has generally been assumed, see Santorelli in this volume.

3 On orality in declamation, see Imber (2001) 203 – 04.

Lydia Spielberg, Radboud University

https://doi.org/10.1515/9783110401554-004

cerpts from multiple declaimers on the same theme, Seneca shows how one speaker's *color* or particularly famous epigram could spawn imitation, contentious discussion, and even parody, as speakers strove to innovate and outdo their predecessors and colleagues.[4] Famous anecdotes about plagiarists, misattribution and faulty imitation similarly make clear that a serious student of declamation had to be broadly familiar with the range of previous treatments of a theme in order to evaluate the effectiveness of a novel expansion in the *divisio* or a daring new twist on an old *color*.[5] Seneca represents his work as just such a textual link, by which new generations of speakers can continue to interact with the past greats of the genre: his sons are admirable, he says, in their desire to know their predecessors as well as the *exempla* of their contemporaries:

> *Contr.* 1.*praef*.6: *Facitis autem, iuvenes mei, rem necessariam et utilem quod non contenti exemplis saeculi vestri prioris quoque vultis cognoscere. Primum quia, quo plura exempla inspecta sunt, plus in eloquentiam proficitur... Deinde ut possitis aestimare in quantum cotidie ingenia decrescant et nescio qua iniquitate naturae eloquentia se retro tulerit.*[6]

Many aspects of Seneca's claims about imitation and the decline of eloquence have been well explored.[7] Here, I consider a more pragmatic question: how did later declaimers use texts of earlier declamation, and how do such identifi-

---

4 Cf. Connolly (2007) 243: 'The spotty quality of the *Controversiae* 'narrative' evokes the droll repartee of what Seneca suggests is a typical day spent in declamation.' On a competitive 'society of declaimers' in Seneca, see Sussman (1978) 15–16, Bloomer (1997) 129–37; on some of the problems involved in trying to reconstruct 'live' declamation based on Seneca's miscellany of excerpts from declamations performed possibly decades apart, see Berti (2007) 28–31, Feddern (2013) 60. For the critical evaluation of individual declaimers and their styles, see Sussman (1978) 118–31, Fairweather (1981) 190–247, Berti (2007) 183–218.

5 On the importance of comparison in Seneca's declamatory world: Connolly (2007) 237–54, Peirano (2013) 96–97.

6 'Moreover, o young men of mine, you are doing something both necessary and useful in that, not being satisfied with the models of your era, you wish to become familiar with those of a prior one, too. First, because the more models that are examined, the more progress is made in eloquence... Secondly so that you can judge how greatly talent is shrinking daily and by some natural inequity eloquence is regressing.' (For Calpurnius, Seneca the Elder (*Contr., Suas.*) and the *Major Declamations* (*Decl. Mai.*), I use the text of Håkanson's Teubners; for the *Minor Declamations* (*Decl. Min.*) that of Shackleton Bailey's Teubner. For ease of reference, the Teubner page and line numbers are given in parentheses after the declamation and section numbers in references to Calpurnius and the *Major Declamations*. Thus: Calpurnius 3, 3.15 = Calpurnius 3, page 3 line 15 in Håkanson's edition. All translations are my own.)

7 See. e.g. Sussman (1972), Gunderson (2003) 34–35, Berti (2007) 22–24; Fantham (1978) deals with the (paradoxical) relationship between imitation of good models and the decline of oratory in first-century CE rhetorical theory more broadly.

able 'intertexts' relate to the practices and expectations of subsequent communities of declaimers, students and audiences? The object of this paper is to fill in such a community for Calpurnius. While his excerpts cannot be compared directly to those of competitors and students, they can be set against textual predecessors and even successors where a Calpurnian *controversia* or sententious conceit duplicates one in Seneca the Elder or pseudo-Quintilian. Close correspondences between excerpts of Calpurnius Flaccus and those in the *Controversiae* of Seneca the Elder give an idea of the technical adaptations that the later declaimer made to his models, but also point to a looser form of 'intertextual' engagement with declamatory *loci* that underlay all performances of declamation.[8] In order to make sense of Calpurnius' adaptations, however, it will first be necessary to look at intertextuality more broadly, and to ask what it means for two declamations to be intertextually related.

1 Declamation and Intertextuality

The idea of intertextuality provides a neutral term for referring to the fact that every text is made up of verbal links to other texts.[9] Nevertheless, it is only relatively recently that scholars have tried to move beyond intertextuality as the evaluation of one-to-one relationships between individual (usually poetic) texts to consider 'intertextual' relationships within genres, oral traditions, and cultural as well as literary traditions.[10] Declamation is especially well suited to this more complex intertextual analysis, because declaimers both worked within a tradition of common themes and tropes and overtly emulated specific *lumina* of successful speakers.[11] Both of these forms of 'intertextuality' or even 'allusion' need to be taken into account when considering an individual speaker like Calpurnius.

Because declamation is a fundamentally transient and oral practice, in which the same ideas and even phrases were constantly reused and varied, it is more difficult to identify certain intertextual links between the corpora that

---

8 Cf. van Mal-Maeder (2007) 36.
9 Conte (1986) 29. Cf. Hinds (1998) 22–34.
10 See in general Baraz and van den Berg (2013) and the articles in the special issue of *AJP* that their essay introduces.
11 Cf. Conte (1986) 37–38.

we have than it is to identify the presence of a 'literary' text in a declamation.[12] Even when individual epigrams and their attributions are cited by multiple subsequent authors, this is not clear evidence of textual dependence, since such anecdotes were also transmitted through popular tradition.[13] The extent to which Quintilian knew of Seneca's compilation is still debated, and the situation is still more difficult for the authors of the declamations transmitted under his name. In his discussion of the *Minor Declamations*, Dingel rightly distinguishes between topoi present in the 'tradition' and the author's dependence, much more difficult to demonstrate, on a particular prior declaimer, let alone a written source.[14] One scholar has recently gone so far as to state that even among Seneca's declaimers, one should not assume direct influence unless Seneca or one of his speakers makes it explicit.[15]

To a certain extent, this must be true. Declamation was on the whole conservative, in the sense that the same *controversiae* and the same argumentative strategies persisted over time, appearing in both Latin and Greek corpora and rhetorical handbooks of all periods.[16] From an educational perspective, the cause and utility are clear: the teacher reused his notes, training his pupils on the same strategies in the same curriculum from which he had learned.[17] For skilled speakers like the *scholastici* of Seneca, the writers of the pseudo-Quintilianic *Major Declamations* (*Decl. Mai.*), or, as I will show, Calpurnius, the fairly fixed cast of 'Sophistopolitans' and their conflicts meant that there was a premi-

---

12 Cf. Sussman (1978) 154 on the difficulties of detecting the use of Seneca the Elder in later authors (declamatory and not); cf. Pasetti (2009) and Pingoud and Rolle (2016) 147–48 on literary allusions in later declamations.

13 For some specific examples of anecdote transmission, see Dingel (1988) 23–24.

14 For Quintilian and Seneca, see Sussman (1978) 161–63 and Fairweather (1984) 535; for the *Minor Declamations* Dingel (1988) 25–31, who concludes that Seneca was not used, although material from individual Senecan declaimers may have been.

15 Feddern (2013) 61.

16 Simmonds (1899) 81–83 gives lists of 'identical' and 'more or less cognate' subjects in the Latin declamatory corpora, and Bornecque (1902) 75–76 lists themes in Seneca with parallels in the Greek corpora; Russell (1983) 21–39 sketches the typical scenarios of 'Sophistopolis;' the commentaries of Winterbottom (1984) on the *Declamationes minores*, Innes and Winterbottom (1988) on Sopatros, and Sussman (1994) on Calpurnius Flaccus give parallel themes at each *controversia*. Greek and Latin declamation do not overlap completely. For example, while a few themes from Greek and Roman history appear in the Latin corpora, there is nothing like the concentration of (fictitious) scenarios involving historical figures (usually orators) found in Libanius or Sopatros, on which see Kohl (1915).

17 On the pedagogical advantages of standard *controversiae*: Winterbottom (1982) 64–66; on repetition, Bornecque (1902) 76–77; for the monotony of schoolroom declamation, cf. Juvenal 7.154.

um for being cleverer, more subtle, or simply novel in one's treatment of topoi and even individual epigrams that the audience had heard many performers treat before.[18]

This is intertextual emulation whose point of reference is often an active oral tradition rather than any particular individual.[19] Thus Seneca praises Vincius for treating a well-worn idea 'with elegance and novelty, although it was treated well by everyone' (*Contr.* 1.4.11: *et pulchre dixit et nove sensum etsi ab omnibus bene dictum*). Ingenuity could also be displayed by producing *aliquid novi*, and Seneca sometimes notes where a speaker contributed a novel idea, often in a dramatic moment in the 'plot' of the declamation.[20]

The presence of a topos, however, does not obviate the possibility of direct emulation of predecessors.[21] Declaimers competed in each speech to outdo not (only) an anonymous tradition, but specific, known, antecedents. Seneca's declaimers imitate, improve upon and mock each other; they argue about the treatment of themes, the phrasing of epigrams and the standards for good and bad declamation. In some respects, the Augustan and Tiberian sub-culture that Seneca records may be anomalous, a temporally particular flowering of declamation that seems distinct from the educational context in which much of our later declamatory corpus, at least in the textual form that is preserved, can be set.[22] But in other respects, much the same conventions of competition and display seem to obtain in other works, too, especially in the 'show declamations' of the *Major Declamations* and the *lumina orationis* preserved in Calpurnius.[23] Orators might

---

18 On imitation and emulation in declamation, see Berti (2007) 172–78; 251–64.

19 Welch (2013) 72–73; Nicholson (2013) 10–13 and LeVen (2013) 32 have useful general remarks on intertextuality between textual and oral traditions, what LeVen terms 'textual collectives'.

20 For example, the moment when the handless hero surprises the adulterers (*Contr.* 1.4.10), the moment in the *controversia* about the murder of Cicero where Popilius arrives (*Contr.* 7.2.14), and the moment when the stepmother names her natural daughter as an accomplice to the poisoning of her stepson (*Contr.* 9.6.16).

21 Hinds (1998) 40 and 38–47.

22 On Seneca the Elder in his Tiberian context, see Bloomer (1997) 110–25, Connolly (2007) 237–54; Winterbottom (1982) 64 is a reminder that some of the declamation in Seneca may have taken place in a school setting.

23 For the traditional distinction between exercises for students of rhetoric under the instruction of a teacher (school declamation), and 'adult' or 'show' declamation, see Seneca *Contr.* 9.*praef.*1 and Quintilian *Inst.* 2.10.10–12; for modern discussions see Sussman (1994) 3–5, Hömke (2002) 21–29 and (2007), Berti (2007) 149–54. The Latin *Declamationes minores*, and Greek collections such as Sopater are generally put in the former category (cf. Winterbottom (1984) xi–xii), Seneca the Elder and the *Major Declamations* in the latter (Hömke (2002) 41–43 and *passim*). Calpurnius' excerpts are difficult to place in this schema. Common stylistic

use declamation to keep in practice as well as to entertain themselves, and professional teachers gave flashy 'show' declamations to attract patrons and advertise the merits of their schools. The reputation for turning out a good *sententia* was valuable social currency for professionals, students and amateurs alike.[24]

Seneca the Elder is the source for many of the anecdotes that give evidence for the ancient reading of intertextual relationships as intentional allusions whether by poets or declaimers. Among the best known is Ovid's declaration that he openly borrowed a line from Vergil with the intention of its being recognised as such (*Suas.* 3.3.7).[25] Arellius Fuscus' response to an accusation that he plagiarised a *sententia* from the Greek rhetor Adaeus shows a similar awareness of emulation as engagement with an individual predecessor's words:

> *Contr.* 9.1.13: *aiebat non commendationis id se aut furti, sed exercitationis causa facere. Do, inquit, operam ut cum optimis sententiis certem, nec illas surripere conor sed vincere. Multa oratores, historici, poetae Romani a Graecis dicta non subripuerunt sed provocaverunt.*[26]

Plagiarism, the 'dark side' of intertextuality, is a charge that is frequently levelled in Seneca's pages. Its currency complicates easy claims about the appreciation of

---

features suggest that they are excerpts from a single rhetor's declamations (and not a commonplace book drawn from the performances of multiple speakers); it also seems probable that excerption was made for scholastic purposes; the excerpted *sententiae*, however, have more in common with those embedded in the *Major Declamations* or found in Seneca's corpus than with the generally more prosaic *Minor Declamations* (Sussman (1994) 17–18). A clear distinction between scholastic and public-entertainment contexts for imperial rhetoric is unlikely: Stramaglia (2010) 136–43, Korenjak (2000) 24–26.

24 What Seneca terms a *sententia* is much broader than the technical sense of *gnome:* an epigrammatic, well-turned phrase, whether expressing a universal truth or capping an argument or narrative portion. Cf. Quintilian's distinction between *sententiae* in their strict sense and *sententiae* as 'brilliant sparks, particularly those used to cap a sentence' (*Inst.* 8.5.2: *lumina autem praecipueque in clausulis posita*). Cf. Feddern (2013) 36–38 and Breij (2006) for Quintilian's typology of *sententiae* (in the broad sense) with examples from surviving declamations. On sententious skill as a way of achieving social distinction, see Sinclair (1995) 122–32; cf. McGill (2013) 149–53 on plagiarism charges as a strategy for dismissing competitors' *sententiae*. On 'metarhetoric', see Winterbottom (1983) 67–74 on Gorgias, Cicero, and late Greek declaimers and Stramaglia (2016) on the *Major Declamations*; Sussman (1994) 18 n.58 discusses a metarhetorical moment in Calpurnius 42.

25 For discussion, see Hinds (1998) 22–23, Peirano (2013).

26 'He said that he did it not to gain credit for the *sententia* or to steal it, but rather as practice. 'I make an effort to compete with the best phrases; I don't try to steal them but to beat them.' This text has some difficulties: *surripere* is Kiessling's emendation, adopted by Håkanson, for the transmitted *corrumpere*, and the last line is found only in the excerpted tradition but is generally assigned here by editors.

emulative allusion in imperial literary culture, but also shows how attentive audiences might be to the original source of a clever idea or an ingenious *sententia*.[27] Epigrams, in the pages of Seneca, belong to their authors, and overly close imitation or outright borrowing can be cast as an attempt to gain credit for the wit of another.[28] But Fuscus' claim goes beyond a defence of plagiarism to become a declaration of Roman *aemulatio* and competitive allusion. The adaptation of specific *sententiae* is imagined to serve an educational purpose (*exercitationis causa*), a recognised function for 'competitive' translation and paraphrase.[29] Under the 'Fuscan' model, there is direct and conscious adaptation of a prior declaimer's idea or wording, which is intended to be recognised as an innovation that both serves the adapting speaker's technique and improves on the original.[30]

Seneca complains about the modern plagiarists who 'easily speak the *sententiae* put out by superb speakers as if they were their own', but makes this a failure of audiences whose ignorance allows *sententiae* to be wrongfully attributed:

> Contr. 1.praef.10: *Sententias a disertissimis viris iactas facile in tanta hominum desidia pro suis dicunt, et sic sacerrimam eloquentiam, quam praestare non possunt, violare non desinunt. Eo libentius quod exigitis faciam, et quaecumque a celeberrimis viris facunde dicta teneo, ne ad quemquam privatim pertineant, populo dedicabo.*[31]

In this programmatic statement, Seneca sets out the ideal conditions for a successful declamatory community: when famous *sententiae* are in the 'public domain', then plagiarism or emulation can be decided on aesthetic and intentional criteria. In reality, of course, the dissemination of any such compendia could provide a later speaker with *sententiae* to pass off as his own with minimal mod-

---

27 McGill (2013) 146–77 and *passim*.

28 Plagiarism accusations in Seneca have now been treated comprehensively by McGill (2013), 145–76, especially 147–52; cf. Peirano (2013) 95–96.

29 Cf. Cicero *De. Or.* 1.155, Quintilian *Inst.* 10.5.2–10. Beall (1997) 215–16 summarises the evidence for translation as an education practice.

30 Cf. Berti (2007) 254 and Russell (1979) on imitation and emulation in ancient literary theory.

31 'Amid people's widespread laziness, they easily speak the *sententiae* put out by superb speakers as if they were their own. Thus they never cease assaulting that most sacred eloquence, that they are not capable of attaining. So I shall do what you demand all the more willingly, and I will dedicate to the public whatever I possess skilfully said by famed speakers, so that they cannot be the private property of anyone.' Cf. *Suas.* 2.19. For an in-depth discussion of this passage, see McGill (2013) 61–69 and Peirano (2013) 96.

ification. Yet there is relatively little of this in subsequent declamations; common ideas, and even unusual ones, are found varied rather than simply repeated.

Here, too, it is important to remember that Seneca was not the only textual source for declamation: individual *rhetores* left treatises, *commentarii*, and even published speeches.[32] Seneca notes as well where individual *sententiae* were *laudatae* or *circumlatae*, a sign that they had achieved firm fame in and even beyond declamatory circles.[33] Both Tacitus and Quintilian describe young men keeping and disseminating notebooks of especially good *sententiae*, while the excerpted tradition of Seneca the Elder and the excerpts of Calpurnius Flaccus show that Seneca was not describing the taste of his own era alone when he conceded that his sons were chiefly interested in models for *sententiae*.[34] Whether Calpurnius was a teacher, a show-declaimer, or an amateur, he had both specific examples and a broad background of the tradition for competing with and reusing the material of the declaimers of the past as well as those in his own scholastic environment.[35]

In order to see how a Calpurnian reworking of a traditional *locus* or a specific *sententia* might have been effective, however, a model of intertexuality is needed that has elements both of the precise borrowings that Seneca points out among his declaimers and the free play within an anonymous tradition where 'what needs to be established is that such an utterance is a real possibility at a given moment'.[36] A useful concept is what Lowell Edmunds terms 'synchronic intertextuality' or what contemporary media studies would term the 'meme': a phrase or topos that has an identifiable origin but gains compounding levels of allusive meaning as it is repurposed and reused.[37] Bart Huelsenbeck, similarly, has usefully introduced the idea that literary traditions are 'built collaboratively

---

32 This has been shown most clearly for sources of Seneca the Elder: Sussman (1978) 79–83; Huelsenbeck (2009) 22–25.

33 Berti (2007) 181–82.

34 Taste for epigrams: Seneca *Contr.* 1.*praef.*22, Quintilian *Inst.* 8.4.29; cf. Berti (2007) 159–60. Notebooks: Quintilian *Inst.* 2.11.7, Tacitus *Dial.* 20.4. Fairweather (1981) 40–41 suggests that Seneca the Elder's work might be have originated as such a personal commonplace book. Hagendahl (1936) 299–313 discusses the excerpted tradition, which may have begun as early as the fourth century (300 n.1).

35 To avoid repeated circumlocutions, I will generally refer to Calpurnius' adaptation of 'Senecan material' with the understanding that we cannot be certain that there was direct textual contact: oral tradition and 'missing links' of other declaimers are undoubtedly present as well.

36 Nicholson (2013) 11.

37 Edmunds (2001) 12–13; cf. 134–35. On memes as a cultural (and potentially literary) phenomenon, see Knobel and Lankshear (2007).

(and even contentiously) through social practices'.[38] Seneca the Elder, once again, shows us this operation in action, providing many instances of phrases that became famous or infamous tags.[39] An inept *sententia* that Quintus Haterius used (apparently in a real court case), for example, turned into a popular source of innuendo:

> *Contr. 4.praef.*10: *Memini illum, cum libertinum reum defenderet, cui obiciebatur quod patroni concubinus fuisset, dixisse: inpudicitia in ingenuo crimen est, in servo necessitas, in liberto officium. Res in iocos abiit: 'non facis mihi officium' et 'multum ille huic in officiis versatur'. Ex eo inpudici et obsceni aliquamdiu officiosi vocitati sunt.*[40]

J.N. Adams points out that *officium* could have a sexual valence from Plautus onward; the Haterian 'meme' built on Haterius' *sententia* involved deliberately misconstruing non-sexual uses of the *offic-* lexeme as sexual ones.[41] Such 'allusions' will not be found in passages with an explicitly sexual meaning, but rather in places where there is a potential for the joke to be present for a receptive audience. For example, when a cuckolded husband, the 'fictive declaimer' of Latro's declamation 2.7, lays out the strictures for chaste uxorial behaviour, he charges his wife to be 'unkind rather than immodest' toward the greeting of an *officiosus:*[42]

> *Contr. 2.7.3* (Latro): *adversus officiosum salutatorem inhumana potius quam inverecunda sit.*[43]

---

38 Huelsenbeck (2011) 186 n.2.

39 A particularly well-known one is the 'Vergilian' collocation *plena deo* (*Suas.* 3.6) picked up by Gallio and applied to declaimers with an 'inflated' style, later used by Ovid in his *Medea* (*Suas.* 3.7). For these literary associations, but above all because the phrase does not appear in any surviving text of Vergil, this passage has attracted a great deal of attention: see Berti (2007) 282–90 with doxography.

40 'I remember he was once defending a freedman client who was alleged to have been the concubine of his patron; he said 'for a freeborn man, unchastity is a crime, for a slave, a necessity, for a freedman, an obligation.' The thing turned into a joke: 'You aren't fulfilling your obligations to me!' and 'He's very involved in his obligations to him.' From this, the unchaste and the perverted were for a while called 'obliging'.'

41 Adams (1982) 163–64; cf. the examples at *TLL* 9.2.5.20.30–40 (s.v. *officium*); Berti (2007) 182 n.2 cites Petronius 105.9 as a usage of *officiosus* potentially influenced by the joke found in Seneca. The word rarely has a negative connotation in ordinary usage: cf. Gellius 4.9.12.

42 For the distinction between the 'fictive declaimer' and the 'concrete rhetor/author', see van Mal-Maeder (2007) 41.

43 2.7.3: 'In response to the greeting of someone ingratiating, she ought to be unkind rather than immodest.'

Although this declamation precedes Haterius' *sententia* in Seneca's compilation, its actual date relative to Haterius cannot be known, and a double entendre on *officiosus* would be easily heard, especially given the overall theme of adultery and the fact that the potential suitor has just been termed an *impudicus*.[44] Although Haterius' inept sententia is the original target of subsequent 'allusions', their potential effect depends less on knowing the origin than on recognising a series of iterations and evaluating the newest element in the context of that series. This series, however, is itself made up of individual 'entries' like, perhaps, Latro's *officiosus salutator*; new entries respond to the existence of prior entries and not merely to the underlying meme.

This is the best model for thinking about the reception of declamatory 'intertextuality'. While there are places where Calpurnius seems to have been looking at an epigram or a treatment of a theme that we can also see in Seneca the Elder, the resulting adaptation is effective more because it is novel within a recurring field or fields of reference than because many or any members of the audience could identify its 'source'. At the same time, Calpurnius' declamations were not composed against undifferentiated fields of declamatory language and *loci*. Rather, they react to particular models within them.[45] This has implications in both directions: comparing the instances of a *locus* or a *sententia* reveals the 'meme' being built up over time, but the existence of that 'meme' is an indication that other specific versions of it – now lost to us – were being produced.

In the remainder of this paper, I consider three ways in which Calpurnius reuses Senecan declaimers by comparing his declamations with similar *controversia*-themes in other texts of declamation. First, Calpurnius' sententious habits come into focus through his adaptations of an epigrammatic binary with a

---

44 Two other places where the *officium* double-entendre may be in play, albeit on a subtler and meta-declamatory level, are *Contr.* 2.4.1 (Latro) and 10.5.16 (Gallio). In the first instance, an indulgent father praises a prostitute for her devotion to his dying son: '*ipsa fungebatur officiis*' ('She herself fulfilled those obligations'). Here the fictive declaimer's 'straight' usage would be overlaid with an allusion appreciable by the external audience. In the second, the speaker defends Parrhasius for torturing an Olynthian slave to death in order to paint a life-like Prometheus: '*Si quis tunc inter necessaria servilium officiorum ministeria percussit aut cecidit, iniuriarum accusabitur?*' ('So then, if someone strikes [the slave] in the course of the slave's ordinary duties, will he be charged with assault?') The subtext might have been audible in the context of servile necessity, the potential sexual meanings of *caedo* (and possibly *percutio*: cf. Adams 1982, 145–48), and knowledge of the typical controversia *topos* involving the capture of Olynthus: scenarios about a beautiful Olynthian youth preyed upon by his Athenian host or purchaser. (Seneca *Exc.* 3.8, *Decl. Min.* 292; cf. Kohl (1915) no. 205, 215–16 and Russell (1983) 119 on Olynthian themes in Greek declamation.)
45 Brescia (2004) 198–99.

long history. Second, Calpurnius' response to meta-declamatory discussions in Seneca that debate and evaluate popular and recherché *colores* shows continued relevance of such discussions for his declamatory community. Finally, a single *sententia* that is brought from a *controversia* about female adultery into a *controversia* about male rape contributes the associations of its original context to its force in a new declamation. In all of these cases, we have access to certain instantiations of a *locus*, a *color*, or an epigram in Seneca the Elder, in the *minor* and *major declamations*, and in Calpurnius. The comparison allows us to reconstruct the topoi that remained relevant to declaimers over time, and also to gage the effect of Calpurnius' particular adaptation against this tradition.

2 *Mendacium et venenum*: Adapting traditional *loci*

The *controversia* entitled *Veneficii Rea* is unique in occurring in near-identical form in three different corpora: Seneca *Contr.* 9.6, *Decl. Min.* 381, and Calpurnius 12. For this reason, it invites comparative study of the ebullient Tiberian *scholastici*, the late first or early second century *magister*, and Calpurnius, probably the latest of the three. Joachim Dingel has made the most detailed study of this *controversia*. He adduces parallels in expression and thought that show Calpurnius' familiarity with some of the material in Seneca, but argues that the *rhetor* of the *Minor Declamations* is only partially in the same tradition.[46] This is an opportunity to compare differences in technique and purpose among Latin declaimers in varied periods and environments; in the case of Calpurnius, it is a particularly fruitful example for seeing how he sharpens a *sententia* or repurposes a familiar antithetical pair.

The theme posits the poisoning of a boy by his stepmother, a classic declamatory villain;[47] when tortured, she claims her daughter as an accomplice. Her husband, the father of both children, defends his daughter in her trial. A favourite strategy among the Senecan declaimers, who, like Calpurnius and the rhetor of the *Minor Declamations*, speak almost universally on behalf of the daughter, is to draw and then exploit the parallel between what they portray as the stepmother's two crimes: poisoning her stepson and falsely accusing her daughter. The tropes associated with poisoning – underhandedness and secret plotting –

---

46 Dingel (1988) 26–32. Cf. the briefer analyses of Bornecque (1902) 30–31, Winterbottom (1984) 582–83, Sussman (1994) 130–32. There are some Greek declaimers in Seneca's treatment (more have probably fallen out), but the theme does not appear in any of the Greek treatises.
47 On declamatory stepmothers, see Mal-Maeder 2007, 128–36, Pingoud and Rolle 2016.

make it a commonplace metaphor for false accusations.[48] Seneca includes several examples of speakers linking the stepmother's poisoned words to literal poison. Votienus Montanus speaks of a *veneficio simile mendacium!* ('lie so like poisoning!': 9.6.3), and other declaimers extend this idea, so that the *noverca's* venomous words are not just 'like' her poison but are described as an instance of poisoning. So the declaimer Triarius describes the accusation as the stepmother's 'last act of poisoning' (*ultimum novercae veneficium*: 9.6.8), while Marcellus calls it a 'second act of poisoning' (*alterum veneficium*: ibid.).

Calpurnius 12 compresses this idea even further: *in uno utriusque mortem videtis: cum periit adulescens, et fratri venenum datum est et sorori* (Calp. 12, 12.14–15).[49] Where the Senecan declaimers assert a metaphor, in which one crime (a false accusation) is described as another (poisoning), Calpurnius' stretches the metaphor much farther: the same act of poisoning that killed the brother is killing the sister, and was perhaps always intended to. Also characteristic of what Weber termed Calpurnius' 'spitz, abgebrochen und lakonisch' style is the postponement of the second element of a pair beyond the verb, a hyperbaton of which he is extremely fond.[50]

Indeed, Calpurnius seems to have been so enamoured of this temporal syllepsis, in which an action on sequential objects is compressed into a single moment, that he used it again in Declamation 35, a *controversia* with a parallel theme: an estranged mother and a stepmother make mutual accusations when the son is found dead.[51] Here the father lays a similar accusation: *Totum noverca commisit, quae uno tempore et maritum miserae praeripuit et filium.* (Calp. 35, 30.9–10).[52] Logically, this is a much easier idea than the version in 12. This epigram gets most of its effect from its structure, which implies more paradox in the juxtaposition of the two objects achieved in one moment than it really delivers.

But Calpurnius can also expand a commonplace pair into a full period. Quintus Haterius, speaking on this theme in Seneca, has his 'fictive declaimer' deplore the stepmother's agency in the deaths of both of his children: *Liberos effero sem-*

---

48 Cf. slander figured as poison in Juvenal 3.123–24.
49 'In one you see the death of both: when the youth died, both brother and sister were given poison.'
50 Weber (1898) 20. Cf. Calp. 12: *et fratri venenum datum est et sorori*; 13: *quam et medicus confirmavit et tyrannus*; 25: *petitam mihi et veniam putavi pariter et nuptias*; 30: *et maritum miserae praeripuit et filium*; ibid.; *et in domo veneficae et in suppliciis docuit parricidae*; 37: *et amandam meretricem consentit et emendam.* (Some of these are more effective than others).
51 This *controversia* has a parallel in the Greek tradition: cf. Sopater 5 (Rh. 7.28.3–32.25) with additional Greek instances adduced by Innes and Winterbottom (1988) 36.
52 'The stepmother did it all: in a single moment she stole both the poor woman's husband and her son.'

per unius mulieris aut mendacio aut veneno. (Contr. 9.6.1).[53] Calpurnius picks this up very closely, but also expands it with an equally balanced second half: *Noverca filios nostros aut insimulatione persequitur aut veneno, quae scelus suum et in domo veneficae et in suppliciis docuit parricidae.* (Calp. 12, 12.11–12).[54] In spite of some vocabulary changes – *liberos* becomes the archaising *filios* and the *mendacium* the more lawyerly and suggestive *insimulatio* – the structure and point of the *sententia* are exactly as in the Haterian version.[55] Calpurnius even keeps the temporal reversal, so that stepmother's second crime (false accusation) precedes the first (poison); a pattern that is reversed in the second half of the sentence for the chiastic sequence *insimulatio... venenum/venefica... parricida.* The effect is also to set the speaker's words – and sententious formulation – against the stepmother's actions: with them she 'made plain' *(docuit)* her *scelus,* just as an orator might explicate a charge. The speaker figures the stepmother as a participant in the courtroom, attempting to 'prosecute' *(persequitur)* her child and step-child although she thereby in fact 'informs' the jurors *(docuit)* of her own crimes.[56]

In 35, Calpurnius repurposes the *sententia* again and brings on the stepmother plotting to herself: *Nonne hoc dicit: 'sola dominabor, cum et hic veneno meo perierit et illa mendacio'?* (Calp. 35, 30.16–18).[57] The outburst of a grieving father in Haterius' declamation is transformed into the soliloquy of an evil stepmother, and what is by now a trite binary pair with a familiar declamatory angle is given new life by being displaced into the *sermocinatio* of a figure internal to the declamation.[58] By using a semantic pair *(venenum/mendacium)* with such a long declamatory history, the fictive speaker gives the stepmother's soliloquy plausibility by grounding it in recognisable stepmotherly behaviour.[59] But with

---

53 'I keep burying my children because of this single woman – whether from her lies or her poison.'

54 'The *noverca* persecutes my offspring either with insinuation or poison; she revealed her crime to be poisoning at home and parricide during her execution.' The parallelism is related to a type of otiose anaphora that Winterbottom (1983) 75 identifies as particularly declamatory.

55 On this use of *filios* for *liberos,* archaic and sub-literary, see Weber (1899) 18, *TLL* 6.1.757.43–62.

56 *Persequitur* is common in Seneca the Elder in this judicial sense, e. g. *Contr.* 9.6.5, 7.5.3, 10.5.1, 15. Cf. *TLL* 10.1.1695.20–77.

57 'Is this not what she says: 'I shall be sole mistress, once he is dead by my poison and she by my lies'?'

58 For the technique, *ethopoiia* or *sermocinatio,* see *Rhet. Her.* 4.65, and Quintilian *Inst.* 9.2.30–31 with the survey of Naschert (1994) 1512–16. For its use in declamation, see van Mal-Maeder (2007) 52–55 and Hömke (2009). On the introduction of female voices in declamation, cf. van Mal-Maeder (2007) 98–99, 101–102.

59 Cf. the advice for *prosopopeia* at Quintilian *Inst.* 9.2.30: *His et adversariorum cogitationes velut secum loquentes protrahimus (qui tamen ita demum a fide non abhorrent, si ea locutos finxerimus*

this, Calpurnius also makes her into a declaimer who manipulates the key binary of this *controversia's* discourse, producing, in effect, a *sententia* against herself, just as in Declamation 12 the *noverca* was said to have 'demonstrated' (*docuit*) her crime. These stepmothers take on the role of the courtroom lawyer 'proving' the cases against them.[60]

It is tempting to say that these *novercae* even become *rival* declaimers of a sort, and so meta-declamatory models for the possibilities of imitation. The 'real' contest in a declamation is after all not the internal trial of the *controversia* but the contest between the present declaimer and other declaimers on the same theme. Imagined opponents who have already 'explained' their crimes or who formulate them in a sententious expression are pre-empting the speaker. While Calpurnius' *novercae* 'prove' the case against them themselves, do they also re-move the need for the present declaimer's skill and ingenuity? Quite the oppo-site. The fictive stepmother's self-damning *sententia* becomes her opponent's weapon, just as the reminiscence of a well-known commonplace or even a fa-mous *sententia* is an opportunity for the present declaimer to show his clever-ness in varying and refining it. The victory may be temporary (the stepmother will return the next time this *controversia* is declaimed, and the next speaker may have something even better to say), but it is still worth gaining – as indeed is shown by the very existence of Calpurnius' excerpts, which someone decided to record so that they could be competed against in turn.

3 Bad, good and best *colores*

The *Veneficii Rea* also lets us see that the technical disputes which Seneca repre-sents in detail were still alive or at least revivable a century or more later. The high-light of Seneca's treatment of this *controversia* is an excursus in declamation criti-cism that excoriates the logic of a popular angle taken on this theme: making the daughter so young that she is implausible as an accomplice. This is a *color* – ex-traneous details introduced by the speaker to make the fictitious 'facts' of the case conducive to his argument – that is disputed and ultimately rejected by discerning Senecan declaimers, wholeheartedly adopted by the declaimer of *Minor Declama-*

---

quae cogitasse eos non sit absurdum). ('[With *prosopopeia*] we bring forward the thoughts of our opponents as if in conversation with themselves (and yet they will only avoid straining disbelief if we contrive to have them speak things that it is not implausible for them to have thought.') **60** For this technique, where the speaker imagines the words of his opponent such that they constitute proof of his guilt, cf. Cicero imagining a letter of the tribune Rullus in *Agr.* 2.20.

tion 381, and conspicuously avoided by Calpurnius.[61] After giving examples from Cestius, a declaimer who favoured this tactic, Seneca introduces a polemic against it from the mouth of the Tiberian senator Votienus Montanus (the star of the Book 9 preface and a severe critic of declamation):[62]

> *Contr. 9.6.10: [Cestius]... Non servavit autem modum; nam et illum locum diu tractavit: non posse sororem in mortem fratris impelli, et interim tam puellam voluit videri ut nulli esset idonea ministerio. Itaque elegantissime deridebat Montanus Votienus in hac controversia ineptias rhetorum, quod sic declamarent tamquam haec quae nominata est infans esset, nec intellegerent si talis esset ne futuram quidem ream. Itaque hoc debemus, inquit, nobis proponere: puellam eius aetatis in qua est certe credibile scelus. Illud quidem intolerabile esse aiebat: induxerat Cestius matrem dicentem filiae: 'da fratri venenum', filiam respondentem: 'mater, quid est venenum?'*[63]

Montanus' criticism is in part a technical one: declaimers who posit a *filia* too young to be a legitimate defendant or even a conceivable suspect are breaking the rules in introducing a *color* that contradicts the conditions of the theme.[64] But his dismissal of the *ineptiae rhetorum* is also an opportunity for Montanus – a senator and a practicing orator as well as declaimer – to set himself apart from the *scholastic* by injecting 'real world' logic into the declaimers' 'Sophistopolis'.[65] Indeed Montanus, Seneca has informed us in the previous *controversia*, had conducted a centumviral case on behalf of the inheritance rights of a daughter whom the opposing side accused of poisoning. He may bring authority to this

---

61 Feddern (2013) 46 puts the function of *color* very nicely: '(...) die *colores* [füllen] die Leerstellen, die das skizzenhafte Kontroversienthema lässt.' For the meaning of *color* and its wide-ranging utility in declamation, see Calboli Montefusco (2007), Zinsmaier (2009), Feddern (2013) 44–59.

62 Although the preface to *Controversiae* 9 presents Montanus as someone who critiques but does not engage in declamation (9.*praef.*1), he appears regularly (and not always admirably) as a declaimer in *Controversiae* 7, 9 and 10, in contrast to comparable senatorial critics such as Cassius Severus or Asinius Pollio (Fairweather (1981) 47).

63 'Cestius... did not maintain proportion: he dwelt at length on the commonplace that a sister cannot be forced to kill her brother, but at the same time he wanted her to seem such a little girl that she would not be able to give any assistance. Votienus Montanus very neatly mocked the stupidity of the declaimers in this *controversia*, because they declaimed it as if the girl who was accused were a baby; they did not realise that if she were, she would not even have been charged. 'This is how we ought to set it up for ourselves', he said: 'a girl of an age in which criminality is at least believable.' The following, he said, was unendurable: Cestius brought on the mother saying to her daughter, 'Give your brother poison', and the daughter responding, 'Mother, what is poison?''

64 Cf. the criticisms at *Contr.* 2.4.12, 10.4.23 and Quintilian *Inst.* 4.2.28, with discussion by Fairweather (1981) 174–75, 226–27.

65 On the social posturing involved in criticizing declamation, see Bloomer (1997) 129–31.

declamation based on practical experience, having shown that one could defend an adult daughter against allegations of poisoning her father (*Contr.* 9.5.14).

On the other hand, Cestius's idea of the daughter innocently asking 'what is 'poison'?' proved a crowd pleaser. Seneca takes the reader through a series of increasingly outrageous riffs on the epigram, from Triarius' *'Mater, et mihi da'* (*Contr.* 9.6.11: 'Mother, give me some, too'), where the daughter innocently thinks that *venenum* is a special treat,[66] to Murredius' reapplication of the conceit to a scene where the father tries to explain to his child that she is going to be put on trial and she responds: *'Pater, quid est rea?'* (*Contr.* 9.6.12: 'Father, what is a 'defendant'?'). This last epigram brings even Cestius to his senses.

> *Contr.* 9.6.12 (Cestius): *'Ego nunc scio me ineptam sententiam dicere; multa autem dico non quia mihi placent sed quia audientibus placitura sunt.'*[67]

That the repudiation of this epigram and the *color* behind it was not universal, however, is demonstrated by the treatment of this theme in *Minor Declamation* 381. Here, the *magister* embraces the *color* that the *filia* was too young to have been an accomplice. He reuses conceits damned in Seneca's discussion, such as the presence of the girl's nurse, and finishes with the Cestian *'quid est venenum'* (381.4).[68]

Montanus' critique did make a significant impression on the *controversia* as it reached the Calpurnian excerpts, where it appears in two noncontinguous groups of *sententiae* (out of the five such groups identified by Sussman).[69] The fact that the age of the *filia* features so prominently in the excerpts suggests that this tactic intrigued the excerptor as well. The excerptor, his relationship to Calpurnius (if any) and the date at which he made his selections are unknown, but the excerpts reflect his interests as well as (or perhaps even more than) those of Calpurnius. Whether this was a student who took down notes or a later reader of Calpurnius' declamations, he imagined that his readers would still be interested in the presentation of *sententiae* that tackled a *filia* old enough to have committed the crime. Concern about the age of the *filia* is

---

66 Cf. Winterbottom (1974) 38.

67 'Now I realise that I spoke a stupid *sententia*. But I say many things not because they please me but because they will please the audience.'

68 Cf. *Decl. Min.* 381.1 and Seneca *Contr.* 9.6.10, 13; Dingel (1988) 27. The idea of the *filia* as too young to be an accomplice is so ingrained in the tradition that it is a point that must be addressed by the accuser, as we see in one of the few excerpts that Seneca gives of the *pars altera* (9.6.9, Triarius): *Quantum illi ad scelera aetatis adiecit quod illam noverca peperit* 'How much maturity for crimes she gains by the fact that a *stepmother* bore her!'

69 Sussman (1994) 42–44.

present even in the statement of the theme of Calpurnius 12, which has an extra stipulation that is not present in either Seneca or pseudo-Quintilian:

> Calp. 12.*praef.* (12.5–10): *Veneficii rea torqueatur, donec conscios indicet. Amissa uxore, ex qua habebat filium, duxit alteram et de ea suscepit filiam. Adoleverunt ambo infantes. Repente ambiguis signis perit adulescens. Pater uxorem accusavit et damnavit. Cum torqueretur, filiam sibi consciam dixit. Petitur puella ex lege ad poenam. Adest ei pater.*[70]

The crucial addition is that 'both children grew up'. Calpurnius' school or circle has adopted Montanus' rule and explicitly forestalls using the popular but questionable tactic of the infant daughter.[71]

The emphasis on the maturity of the *filia* in Calpurnius' declamation suggests a revival of Votienus' declamatory polemic. Cutting off a popular *color* allowed the declaimer to underline his own novelty and rigour: it is easy to argue that a child could not have been involved in a crime, but it takes more skill to defend an adult. The excerpts, moreover, show a speaker who revels in his ability to remain within the limits of the theme. To draw attention to this aspect of his treatment and the way that it accords with the revised theme, Calpurnius repeats the key verb *adolesco*, insisting on the *filia*'s maturity. In the first excerpt, probably from the *narratio*, the 'father' quotes this portion of the *controversia* theme while showing how the *filia* can still be established as an unlikely co-conspirator: *adolerunt ambo, sed minor filia et praeter sexum multo fratre simplicior* (Calp. 12, 12.13).[72] This seems like a precise response to the criticism present in Seneca, namely, that declaimers want to have the daughter both too young to be a plausible accomplice and old enough to be plausibly devoted to her brother. By specifying that, although the *filia* is mature, she is nevertheless younger, female, and

---

70 'Let a woman accused of poisoning be tortured until she names her accomplices. His wife, by whom he had a son, dead, a man took another wife and acknowledged a daughter by her. Both children grew up. Suddenly, the youth died with ambiguous indications. The father accused his wife and convicted her. When she was tortured, she said her daughter was her accomplice. The girl is tried for punishment according to the law. Her father defends her.'

71 The presence of the stipulation that the evidence for poisoning was ambiguous – something that is not used at all in the excerpts – is evidence that the theme was already attached to the declamation in this form when the excerpts were made, and probably preceded the original declamation, as there are no signs of the possibility encouraged by this addition, namely, that the stepmother herself is innocent, in the excerpts. (This same piece of information appears in the *Decl. Min.* 381 theme, where it is also ignored in the declamation; the theme in Seneca is silent on question of evidence, but no declaimer takes the tactic that the verdict on the stepmother was false.) Cf. the method for determining the priority of themes in the *Major Declamations* in Håkanson (2014) 6.

72 'Both grew up, but my daughter was younger and, even apart from her sex, far more naive.'

unusually naive, the declaimer shows his ability to manipulate the new rule and still, potentially, incorporate the standard *color* about the *filia*'s inability to act as an accomplice.[73]

Calpurnius brings up the age of the *filia* again in an excerpt that is probably a *prolepsis* of an argument to be put forward by the prosecutor: *Cur, postquam adolevit puella, est interemptus adulescens? Tamdiu ergo fuit novercae quieta crudelitas, quamdiu aetas illius ad persuasionem conscientiae perveniret?* (Calp. 12, 12.17–20).[74] Here we have precisely the argument that Seneca's declaimers and pseudo-Quintilian's speaker were trying to forestall when they insisted that the girl was too young to take part. Indeed, they make her young in order to make the contrary arguments: that she is too young to be of any use as an accomplice, too young even to know what poison is. Calpurnius, however, again recalling the words of the theme, reminds the audience that his defendant is both physically and mentally capable of committing the crime: the girl grew up (*adolevit*) and, once she was old enough to be affected by rational persuasion, the young man (*adulescens*) was killed. Not only is the daughter explicitly stated to be old enough to be a knowing accomplice, but the argument asserts a compelling causal relationship: after all, no one died until she was old enough to assist her mother – and old enough also, presumably, to be interested in an inheritance (which is the only *color in filiam* that Seneca gives (*Contr.* 9.6.15)).

The figure of *prolepsis*, Quintilian says, is 'remarkably effective' (*Inst.* 9.2.16: *mire valet*) because it allows the speaker to anticipate an opponent's arguments and then dismiss them on his own terms.[75] Given that there is little evidence that both sides of a *controversia* were regularly performed together, *praesumptio* is also an opportunity for the speaker to play both sides.[76] Pedagogically, this demonstrates the process of dividing an argument so as to take into account the likely arguments of a real opponent. On the side of entertainment, it allows the declaimer to introduce the semblance of such an opponent over whom his triumph is guaranteed. Indeed, Quintilian criticises declaimers for overindulging in the

---

73 Lacking the whole declamation, it is not possible to see how far this angle was pursued, although Calpurnius does seem to deal with sibling affection in a later excerpt (12.17).

74 'Why was it after the girl reached youth that the youth was killed? Are we to believe the stepmother's savagery was dormant for so long, until the girl's age had advanced enough to be persuaded to complicity?'

75 For a discussion of the figure in ancient rhetorical thought, see Lausberg (1998) §855 and Braun (2005) 197–98.

76 There are several places where Seneca notes that two declaimers treated the same theme on consecutive days (*Contr.* 1.7.13, 2.1.25–26); in both cases, however, the second speaker adopts the same side as the first one.

figure: *Id cum sit utile aliquando, nunc a declamatoribus quibusdam paene sem-*
per adsumitur, qui fas non putant nisi a contrario incipere (*Inst.* 4.1.49).[77] By rais-
ing a strong piece of circumstantial 'evidence', the very piece of evidence that
previous declaimers tried to circumvent, Calpurnius can then display his skill
in breaking it down.

In another *controversia* shared by Seneca and Calpurnius there is a similar
trace of earlier discussion about declamation in the *sententiae* that are borrowed
and reworked. Calpurnius 30, the *Nepos ex meretricio susceptus*, is a theme in
most respects identical to Sen. 2.4. In this declamation, a father wants to
adopt his disinherited dead son's child by a prostitute. He is accused of insanity
by his remaining son:

> Calp. 30.*praef.* (27.13 – 18): *Qui habebat filios frugi et luxuriosum, luxuriosum ob amorem me-*
> *retricis abdicavit. Abdicatus se ad meretricem contulit. Illic cum aegrotare coepisset, misit ad*
> *patrem et commendavit illi filium de meretrice susceptum rogans, ut eum in familiam recipiat,*
> *et obiit. Vult illum senex in familiam recipiere. Reus est alteri filio dementiae.*[78]

A comparison of Calpurnius' theme with the corresponding Senecan one
(2.*praef.*4.), where the sons are not characterised and no reason is given for
the father's disownment of the first son, shows that here, too, details have accret-
ed over time. In this case they merely spell out explicitly the implicit *personae* of
two sons: one dissolute and in love with a prostitute, and one prudent.[79]

Calpurnius' excerpts take the part of the son against his father, and they
show a wide variety of approaches. The speaker establishes his own character
as a pious son who grieves for his father's descent into insanity (30, 27.19 – 22)
but also indicates that his father's behaviour was misguided even when he disinherited the *luxuriosus* (30, 27.22 – 23). He attempts a definition of adoption, de-
cries the parentage of the supposed grandson, and claims that even his brother

---

77 'Although this is sometimes useful, these days it is introduced by certain declaimers almost
without fail; they don't think that it's legal unless one begins from the opposing side.' Cf. perhaps Seneca *Contr.* 7.*praef.*3 on the declaimer Albucius' mastery of a sub-type of this figure.
78 'A man who had sons, a sensible one and a dissolute one, disowned the dissolute one because of his love affair with a prostitute. Disowned, he went to live with the prostitute. When he
became ill there, he sent for his father and entrusted to him his son by the prostitute, asking his
father to accept the boy into the family, and then he died. The old man wants to accept the boy
into the family. He is accused of madness by his other son.'
79 Bornecque (1902) 75 compares Quintilian *Inst.* 7.4.20, but the latter is a simpler case of a father disinheriting a son who is in love with a prostitute, a theme that is built into the details of
Calpurnius' *controversia* and implicit in the version in Seneca. For the figure of the *luxuriosus* in
declamation, see Winterbottom (1984) 339.

did not truly intend to acknowledge the boy as his son. All of these moves have parallels among Seneca's declaimers, and a few are very common. Calpurnius' insinuation about the paternity of the prostitute's son, for example, is an idea used by every one of Seneca's declaimers who speaks on this side. Calpurnius' *In quo puero nescio quid sit indignius, utrum patris origo quod est dubia, an matris origo quod certa est* (Calp. 30, 29.3–4) has the same structure as Argentarius' '*Mulier, nescio an adversus patrem iniuriosior quod abstulisti illi heredem an quod dedisti*' (Sen. *Contr.* 2.4.5).[80] The thought, however, is identical with Latro's '*Quem honestius subiecit meretrix quam peperit. Pater istius incertus est; bene cum ipso ageretur si et mater*' (2.4.5) and Albucius Silus' '*cedo istum puerum nulli agnoscendum si mater adserat*' (2.4.6).[81] Equally common is the contrast between the father disinheriting his own son and now adopting the prostitute's son: '*Vos interrogo iudices, utrum sit sanus, qui et suos abdicat et adoptat alienos*.' (Calp. 30, 28.1).[82] Calpurnius puts into a characteristically compressed and gnomic antithesis an idea found in longer form in Albucius Silo's and Cestius' treatments of this theme:

> *Contr.* 2.4.6 (Albucius Silus): *Severissimus pater abdicavit etiam quem sciebat suum... Adoptavit eius filium propter quam etiam suum eiecerat.*[83]

> *Contr.* 2.4.6 (Cestius Pius): *Nullum genus iudicum recuso: si severi erunt, nocebit isti quod recepit meretricis filium; si clementes, quod abdicavit suum.*[84]

But Calpurnius' excerpts also show evidence of two *colores* that Seneca's discussion singled out as especially innovative and skilful, a mixture of *colores* that is perhaps all the more daring for being done in the *persona* of the son. Using multiple *colores* (*color mixtus*) introduced the danger of losing a consistent thread between parts of the speech, and, if the declaimer spoke *in persona* of one of the parties (rather than as an advocate), involved the risk of an inconsistent or

---

80 '[A boy] whom the prostitute snuck in more honourably than she bore. His father is unknown; it would be well for him if his mother were, too' (Latro). 'Give up this boy whom no one should acknowledge, should his mother claim him' (Cestius).

81 'I don't know what about the boy is worse: the fact that his paternity is doubtful or that his maternity is certain' (Calpurnius). 'Woman, I don't know whether you were more harmful to my father by taking away an heir or by giving one' (Argentarius).

82 'I ask you, judges, whether a man is sane who both disinherits his sons and adopts another's.'

83 'So strict a father disowned even the son he knew was his own... He adopted the son of the woman who caused him to throw his own son out.'

84 'I refuse no kind of judge: if they are strict, he will be harmed by the fact that he accepted the son of a prostitute; if they are lenient, by the fact that he disowned his own son.'

illogical *ethos*.[85] Seneca explains that different declaimers took different tactics in approaching the son's speech and presents four such angles of apparently increasing innovation: Hispo's harsh and severe personification that comes most naturally from the theme and insinuates that the father may be the real father of the prostitute's child (2.4.9), Cestius' *bella figura* of comparison that attacks the father with his own past actions (2.4.9), and then the unusually gentle filial *personae* presented by Latro and Fabianus, whose declamations were sympathetic to the father and the dead brother, respectively

> *Contr.* 2.4.10: *Latro patri pepercit; puerum pressit et dixit fratris filium non esse et ne fratrem quidem hoc fateri voluisse; illa verba aegro imperata. Fabianus ex omnibus istis colorem secutus est optimum, quo aiebat Messala posse non tantum bonam partem adulescentis fieri sed etiam honestam: obiecit patri quod fratrem abdicasset, non schemate, sed derecto... 'Abdicasti' inquit 'ut emendares? Vitia augeri vides. Nullum illius vitium: aetatis est, amoris est; recipe, antequam aliquid faciat cuius mox pudore moriatur'.*[86]

How a son can piously bring a charge against his father is a recurring concern of Latro's technique; Seneca explains in connection with another declamation concerning an allegedly insane father that Latro 'regularly blamed not the father's faults, but his affliction'. (*Contr.* 2.6.5: *non vitia patris accusari solere, sed morbum*). This emphasis appears in a series of excerpts from Calpurnius' declamation in which the son represents his actions as compassion for his father's affliction (30, 27.19–22): his task is not to give a speech (*dicere*) but rather to grieve (*dolere*); he is a good son in that he blames illness (*morbo*) rather than bad character (*moribus*) for his father's insanity, which is to be pitied (*miseranda*) rather than accused (*accusanda*).

Prima facie, absolving the father of blame ought to be incompatible with Fabianus' *optimus color* of directly challenging the rightness of disowning the brother in the first place. But the next set of excerpts does just this: *Multum potest ab-*

---

85 On the desirability of maintaining a consistent *color* throughout the speech, see Zinsmaier (2009) 263–64. At Seneca *Exc.* 4.6, Asinius Pollio critiques a *color mixtus* for compounding the faults of the individual *colores*, and at 1.7.17 Seneca explains that a declaimer speaks as an advocate so that he can have freer play to mix *colores*. On these passages, see Fairweather (1981) 173–74 and Feddern (2013) 47–48.
86 'Latro spared the father, attacked the boy, and said that he wasn't his brother's son and not even his brother had meant that he was: the sick man had been ordered to say the words. Fabianus pursued the best angle of all of these, by which, Messala said, the young man's case became not only good, but honourable. He charged the father with the fact that he had disinherited the brother, not through figures but directly... 'You disinherited him', he said, 'to reform him? You see his faults increasing. The fault isn't his; it belongs to his age, to his passion. Take him back before he does something the shame of which kills him.'

dicatio, cum timetur; post ex pudore iam liberius erratur. Vos interrogo, iudices, utrum sit sanus, qui et suos abdicat et adoptat alienos. (Calp. 30, 27.22–23).[87] Although there are no verbal similarities between the first *sententia* and Fabianus' argument, the sequence of thought is the same; moreover, as has been seen several times already, Calpurnius makes a typical move in rephrasing a *color* – that is, narrative and argumentative material invented to be specific to the *controversia* – so that it becomes a commonplace. Calpurnius repurposes Fabianus' idea to argue that the father was already *demens* when he disowned the brother. He then introduces the universal truth that disowning is not a cure for bad behaviour. As in the stepmother-poisoner *controversia*, Calpurnius imitates examples that are singled out for special praise in the authoritative voice of a noble declamation critic, here Messala.

The final excerpt from Calpurnius' treatment of this controversia returns to Latro's distinctive *color*, which denies that the brother really wished to acknowledge the child as his: *Dixit ille suum filium, dixit ut amator, dixit immo ipse iam parum sanus.* (Calp. 30, 28.5).[88] In keeping with the stance of sympathy toward the brother that this fictional speaker has adopted, he avoids direct blame. Whereas Latro had the brother dominated by his mistress, Calpurnius' speaker envisions him in the grip of an adolescent passion or even a mental disturbance akin to his father's. On the one hand, these traces of judgments passed by Senecan 'experts' on specific flawed and outstanding *colores* attached to particular themes suggest that Calpurnius did have access to the earlier discussions in some form, as Dingel already saw.[89] But the way in which Calpurnius incorporates these textualised critiques is also significant. By combining two celebrated *colores* in the *Nepos ex meretrice*, he outdoes the achievement of either of their originators, while his version of the *Veneficii Rea* draws attention to how it meets the challenge posed by Montanus' criticisms of Cestius. The stress that Calpurnius and his excerptor both put on this inclusion, moreover, is a telling sign of its effectiveness in his declamation. It is impossible to know whether these were novel *colores* or had become standard

---

87 'Disinheriting is very effective, when it is a threat; after the fact, one sins even more freely out of shame. I ask you, judges, whether a man is sane who both disowns his own children and adopts outsiders.' These are unlikely to have been contiguous in the original declamation (and they are distinguished by Sussman (1994) *ad loc.*). I would suggest, however, that they are both part of an argument to establish the father's insanity.

88 'He said it was his son, but he spoke as a lover, he spoke – indeed, already himself hardly sane.' Cf. Seneca *Contr.* 2.4.10: *Latro patri pepercit; puerum pressit et dixit fratris filium non esse et ne fratrem quidem hoc fateri voluisse; illa verba aegro imperata.* ('Latro spared the father, attacked the boy, and said that he wasn't his brother's son and not even his brother had meant that he was: the sick man had been ordered to say the words.')

89 Cf. Dingel (1988) 31–32.

in Calpurnius' circle, but in either scenario one can see not only the continuities of a declamatory 'tradition' but also the continued possibilities for recombining and innovating that tradition's stock tropes.

4 Intertextuality and manliness in the *Miles Marianus*

Sometimes, however, the original context of a *sententia*, at least loosely conceived, does seem to be an important part of the success of the adaptation. The theme of the *Miles Marianus*, the soldier who killed a superior officer who was attempting to rape him, was popular in antiquity; it appears as a rhetorical *exemplum* in Cicero's *De Inventione* (2.124), in Valerius Maximus (6.1.12) and in Quintilian (*Inst.* 3.11.14) and as a declamation in both Calpurnius (Declamation 3) and the collection of pseudo-Quintilianic *Declamationes Maiores* (*Decl. Mai.* 3).[90] Especially in this last version, a complete and elaborate speech from the soldier's advocate, the *controversia* has attracted attention in modern scholarship for the insights it provides into Roman discourses on homosexuality, masculinity and the intersection of both of these with structures of social hierarchy.[91] With the tribune's unwanted attentions, the soldier, the quintessential male, risks losing his masculine identity and becoming feminized, having been figured as the passive object of sexual penetration rather than in his proper masculine role as penetrator.[92] The soldier's advocate, the *persona* adopted by the declaimer of both Calpurnius 3 and *Decl. Mai.* 3, must counter this perception that even being considered a target for such a proposition has impaired his client's masculinity.[93] The tropes and language with which he can talk about fending off or avenging sexual advances, however, are coded with the femininity that must be kept far away from the soldier on trial. 'In the case of a soldier, I am ashamed even to praise his chastity,' says the speaker in *Decl. Mai.* 3. 'That virtue belongs to women.' (3.3, 45.2–3: *pudicitiam in milite etiam laudare erubesco: feminarum est ista virtus.*)

---

90 For a comprehensive list of instances of this anecdote, see Schneider (2004) 71, and for a discussion of the tradition, Brescia (2004) 36–38 and Schneider in this volume.

91 See Gunderson (2003) 153–90; Schneider (2000b), (2004) 25–34 (and *passim*) and (2005); Walters (1997) and Alston (1998); van Mal-Maeder (2007) 107–14; Bernstein (2013) 27–32.

92 For the normative Roman "rules" of masculine sexuality, see Richlin (1992), Williams (2010) 137–76. Gunderson (2003) analyses in detail the sexual anxieties expressed throughout Roman declamation.

93 Cf. Richlin (1992), 561–66, Gunderson 2003, 167–68.

A textual difficulty in Calpurnius can highlight what is at stake in reminisces of 'standard' topoi and particular *sententiae* in this declamation. One of the most striking *sententiae* under Calpurnius' treatment of this theme asserts that the soldier would have insufficiently protected his chastity with a mere verbal refusal: *non longe ab eo est* [*miles*], *ut promittat stuprum, qui rogatus tantummodo negat* (3, 3.12).[94] There is a consensus in modern scholarship that the word *miles* has crept into the text here, an easy scribal slip given that a form of *miles* occurs in four other of the seven excerpts under this theme and that '*miles est*' occurs in the *sententia* just preceding this one.[95] Whether one accepts the emendation, however, depends on whether one interprets the *sententia* as a maxim applicable to all people or as one particular to a soldier. So the textual problem in fact mirrors the dilemma faced by the soldier's advocate: is this a generalising sententious truth that aligns this soldier with all people (usually women) asked to submit to disgraceful sexual acts, or are there distinguishing features of this situation and this potential victim that set him apart?

The intertextual history of this *sententia* makes this tension quite clear. Calpurnius' *sententia* has both an extant ancestor, in a declamation preserved by the Elder Seneca on a different theme, and a cousin or even descendent, in the *Miles Marianus* of the *Declamationes Maiores*.[96] A comparison of the three shows the two later declaimers taking advantage of the associations of what appears to have become a well-known conceit about the force (or lack thereof) of 'no' as an answer.

Calpurnius' *sententia* is unusually close to two ideas put forward by Latro in a declamation against a possibly adulterous wife preserved apparently in its entirety at Seneca *Contr.* 2.7 (although the end of the declamation is lost in a lacu-

---

94 'One [a soldier] isn't far from promising sex if when he's asked, he merely says no.'
95 It would also be in keeping with Calpurnius' tendency to adapt *sententiae* so that they are more gnomic. Håkanson does not bracket in his text, but approves Winterbottom's suggestion in the apparatus. Sussman (1994) 101 also registers approval and reports the concurrence of D. A. Russell.
96 Neither *Decl. Mai.* 3 nor Calpurnius can be securely dated; both have been put as early as the end of the first century CE and as late as the end of the fourth century. For Calpurnius, see above, n.2. The speeches that make up the *Declamationes Maiores* transmitted under the name of Quintilian are dated to between the second and the fourth century CE, with *Decl. Mai.* 3 in a group that is traditionally put earliest (second century); Håkanson (1986) 2284–90 surveys the question, as do Brescia (2004) 23–31, with a convenient table of alternative dating systems on p. 25, and Stramaglia (2006) 555–564. Recently, certain scholars have argued for a late fourth-century date of compilation, based on subscriptions found in some manuscripts, and some have argued for placing the composition of *Decl. Mai.* 3 this late as well on thematic grounds: Schneider (2000a), (2000b) and (2004) 34–37. Against the late dating, see Cameron (2011) 446–48 and Stramaglia (2006) 556–64. Both the traditional and the later datings are compatible with a specific use of a Calpurnian *sententia*.

na).[97] The *controversia* has a woman repeatedly propositioned by a rich man while her husband is away on business. When the rich man dies, he names the wife as his heir, a reward, he says, for her proven fidelity. Her husband, upon his return, accuses her of adultery:

> *Contr. 2.7.praef.: Quidam, cum haberet formonsam uxorem, peregre profectus est. In viciniam mulieris peregrinus mercator commigravit; ter illam appellavit de stupro adiectis pretiis; <u>negavit illa</u>. Decessit mercator, testamento heredem omnibus bonis reliquit formonsam et adiecit elogium: 'pudicam repperi'. Adit hereditatem. Redit maritus, accusat adulteri ex suspicione.*[98]

Latro's fictional declaimer is the husband; his *argumentatio* attacks the central point of the wife's defence, enshrined in the details of the theme, namely that she refused the merchant's triple proposition (*negavit illa*).[99] This declamation's efforts to show that *negare* is a worthless strategy makes it an important predecessor to the argument implicit in the *tantum negare sententiae* in the *Miles Marianus* declamations. The husband undermines the value of his wife's refusal in a series of arguments that give further conditions for her behaviour, each of which culminates by echoing the theme's *negavit* to show the inadequacy of a merely verbal refusal. For ease of reference, I have broken down the components of this argument as (a) through (d). First, says the husband, a chaste wife would have dressed and comported herself in such a way as to repel an adulterer before he could imagine making the proposition:

> (a) *Contr. 2.7.3* (Latro): *Sic se in verecundiam pigneret ut longe ante inpudicitiam suam ore quam verbo <u>neget</u>.*[100]

---

97 In contrast to the other themes in Seneca's corpus, 2.7 is represented by one continuous declamation by one rhetor (Latro) rather than by snippets and summaries of multiple treatments, although the excerpts seem to show evidence that Seneca included some contrasting treatments at the end of the section. It has therefore attracted substantial attention: for technical analysis, see Fairweather (1981) 251–55 and Berti (2007) 44–78; for discussions of some of the thematic issues raised by the *controversia* see Polla-Mattiot (1990); Lentano (1998) 105–129; Brescia (2012) 38–46.
98 'A certain man, who had a beautiful wife, travelled abroad. A foreign merchant moved into the woman's neighbourhood; he propositioned her for adultery three times, adding bribes; she said no. The merchant died; in his will, he left as the heir to all his goods the beautiful woman and added praise: 'I found her chaste.' She accepted the inheritance. The husband returns; he accuses her of adultery on a suspicion.'
99 Berti (2007) 64–70; Brescia (2012) 42–43.
100 'She would pledge herself to modesty so as to deny her unchastity with her face long before she had to with her speech.' Cf. Lentano (1998) 120–23 notes that the wife's body, and not her voice, is the intelligible text in this declamation.

Next, the husband argues that his wife ought to have demonstrated her indignation at the merchant's proposition not by merely refusing it but by physically abusing his messenger to make her point clear. This section, too, is capped with a *sententia:*

(b) *Contr.* 2.7.4 (Latro): *Nemo sic negantem iterum rogat.*[101]

Finally, the husband turns to his wife's verbal responses themselves: why did she not complain to her family or write to her husband?

(c) *Contr.* 2.7.5 (Latro): *Abunde te in argumentum pudicitiae profecturam putas, si stuprum tantum negaveris, quod plerumque etiam inpudicissima, spe uberioris praemi, de industria simulat?*[102]

The husband develops this idea more strongly in the next punctuating *sententia*, in which he stretches the bounds of the theme to claim that the wife's refusal was silence, the next thing to consent:[103]

(d) *Contr.* 2.7.6 (Latro): *Quod proximum est a promittente, rogata stuprum tacet!*[104]

The *color* of unreliable 'no' was evidently popular in the declamation schools, but Latro's *sententiae* appear to have influenced the *Miles Marianus* of Calpurnius and the *Decl. Mai.* 3 declaimer in a more specific way.[105] The Calpurnian *sententia*, *Non longe ab eo est [miles], ut promittat stuprum, qui rogatus tantummodo negat*, is structurally identical to this last *sententia* of Latro. The correspondences are unusually close, suggesting that there is a closer dependence than merely a similar idea. Calpurnius appears to have combined two related

---

101 'No one asks someone who refuses thus a second time.' The manuscripts put this *sententia* in the middle of a series of apostrophes to the wife; editors since Wachsmuth have moved it to what seems to be a more appropriate place, although Håkanson's text does not make this transposition. For the argument in its favour, see Berti (2007) 69 n.1.
102 'You think that you will amply succeed in proving your chastity if you've merely said no to sex, something that an utterly unchaste woman will often pretend to do in hope of a richer bribe.'
103 Cf. Fairweather (1981) 253, Berti (2007) 70. In the context, *tacet* also refers to the fact that the wife did not write to her husband or make a public uproar about the merchant's proposition; Lentano (1998) 120 n.33 compares Lucretia's notification of her husband and father at Livy 1.58.5. Brescia (2012) 43 notes that this condemnation of silence reverses the association of silence with ideal feminine behaviour. Cf. Polla-Mattiot (1990) 260–62 on the thematics of silence throughout this declamation.
104 'The closest thing to promising it, when asked for sex she was silent.'
105 For the importance of this *color* throughout *Decl. Mai.* 3, cf. Brescia (2004) 224–25.

ideas from Latro, basing his new *sententia* on (d), which he matches almost phrase for phrase, but intensifying it by replacing the 'standard' declamatory dispute over the interpretation of silence with the conceit, present in Latro's (c), that verbal refusal is an ambiguous indicator as well.[106] So Calpurnius' *Non longe ab* matches Latro's *proximum a*; Latro's *a promittente* becomes *ab eo... ut promittat*, and Calpurnius' *stuprum ... rogatus tantummodo negat* combines the participial construction of Latro's *rogata stuprum tacet* with the preceding *si stuprum tantum negaveris*. Calpurnius' *sententia* thus pushes the antithesis much farther. Whereas Latro implies that *negare* may be a false 'no' and then that *tacere* is equivalent to *promittere*, Calpurnius asserts that *negare* and *promittere* are functionally equivalent. Instead of moving along a scale of responses (no, silence, yes), the new *sententia* pushes the *color* to its extreme and asserts that opposites are synonymous: saying no is essentially the same as saying yes. The paradox and the success of the *sententia* do not necessarily require the audience to be familiar with the exact source, nor, of course, can we be certain about the form in which Calpurnius had access to the earlier declamation.[107] They do depend, however, on familiarity with the constituent tropes of the sexual proposition and the inadequate or simulated refusal.

Graziana Brescia has noted that declamations about rape and seduction draw on a fairly consistent semantic field.[108] Moreover, there are far more declamatory themes about the rape or seduction of women than of men. As a result, in a declamation like *Decl. Mai.* 3 or Calpurnius 12, the terminology of the scenario, the common *colores*, the patterns of argumentation, and even the *sententiae* recall, and sometimes even derive from, previous declamations about women. The speaking *persona* of Calpurnius 3, for example, apologises that even the *exempla* of Lucretia and Verginia with which he is defending his client are feminising and inappropriate to a soldier: *Hanc vim Verginius parricidio fugit; propter hanc Lucretia pectus suum ferro fodit. Pudet me, imperator: feminae exemplis militem tueor.* (Calp. 3, 3.15).[109]

---

106 How to interpret silence is a common point of dispute in declamation themes: see Brescia (2012) 43–58 and, for examples from Roman oratory and law, Polla-Mattiot (1990) 268 n.30;. Usually it is a woman's silence, cf. e.g. Sen. *Contr.* 8.6.

107 These epigrams, however, do not appear in our excerpted tradition of Sen. 2.7. The fact that Seneca presents the declamation in its entirety might indicate that it already circulated as a discrete text.

108 On the typical terminology and treatment of these scenarios in relation to the *Miles Marianus* theme, Brescia (2004) 223–26; cf. the survey of rape declamations at Brescia (2012) 31–58.

109 'This is the assault that Verginius fled by infanticide; from this assault Lucretia buried steel in her own breast. I am ashamed, General. I am using precedents suitable to a woman to defend a soldier.' Cf. *Decl. Mai.* 3.11 (52.13–14) and Schneider (2004) 178; Brescia (2004) 136–38, who

This excerpt enacts a knowing play on the gendered nature of the *topoi* at his disposal. Initially, the fictional advocate tries to circumvent the threat of feminisation by flipping the *exemplum* of Verginia so that it is not a female victim but her father (a common soldier, in the tradition) who is threatened by *vis*.[110] Nevertheless, he must apologise for applying 'precedents suitable to a woman' to the case of a man. In a meta-declamatory move that is also found in the corresponding *Major Declamation*, the speaker argues that the conventions of discourse – and, as we shall see, especially of declamatory discourse – are working against his client: to talk about a soldier's right to defend his chastity is to talk about him in the feminised terms of his attacker.[111] The fictional advocate thus underlines the dire discursive situation in which he finds himself, but at the same time, the declaimer himself draws attention to the fact that he has repurposed an *exemplum* that was typically used to maintain the necessity of protecting female chastity. By having his speaker then complain that he has had to resort to 'precedents suitable for a woman', Calpurnius draws attention to his skilful recasting of the standard Verginia *exemplum* so that it presents a man and a soldier as its victim rather than a woman.

A similar move occurs in the *qui rogatus tantummodo negat* epigram. Whether or not the *miles* is excised, Calpurnius' *sententia* is not a fully generalised statement. Rather, it genders the sexual object as male. While the masculine is ordinarily the unmarked gender, in the context of being solicited for *stuprum*, with a *color* borrowed from a declamation about an adulterous wife in a *controversia* with so many anxieties over the expectations of gender, the masculine ending of *rogatus* becomes marked: 'A *man* who merely refuses when asked is not far from promising...' By resorting to a 'female'-coded maxim, Calpurnius' imaginary speaker underlines how inappropriate it is that he must even discuss the necessity of his male client's 'chastity'.

These intertextual possibilities come out more explicitly in the iteration of the *tantum negare sententia* in *Major Declamation* 3. The *Decl. Mai.* 3 speaker puts this epigram at a forceful place in his narrative, the moment when the trib-

notes that Lucretia's *virilis animus* in a *muliebre corpus* (the phrases are those of Val. Max. 6.1.1) reflects the same potential ambiguity of gender faced by the soldier.

110 Cf. Joshel (1992). For Verginius, see Cic. *Rep.* 2.63, Livy 3.54.1–58.9, Val. Max. 6.1.2, *Decl. Mai.* 3.11 (52.6–13). Further examples are collected by Schneider (2004) 173–75. Cf. the set of declamation themes in which a father prefers his handsome son to die rather than be put into the power of an enemy or a tyrant: Calpurnius 36 (*Speciosus desertor*), 43 (<*Speciosus filius peremptus*>), Seneca *Contr.* 9.1.11.
111 Cf. Gunderson (2003) 167–68, *Decl. Mai.* 3.6.

une makes his proposition, a proposition to which murder, the speaker argues, is the natural and only acceptable reaction:

> *Decl. Mai.* 3.6 (48.5–8): *Romano militi pro vallo excubanti meretriciam obscenae libidinis patientiam aliquis inperat? Suum quisque habeat fortasse iudicium; mea sententia non satis pudicus est* <u>*miles, qui armatus tantum negat.*</u>[112]

It is hard to be certain about a chain of influence between Calpurnius and the author of *Decl. Mai.* 3, especially as the dating of both are uncertain. *Decl. Mai.* 3 has its own set of verbal parallels with Latro's declamation,[113] but not only is the *Decl. Mai.* 3 *sententia* far closer to Calpurnius' version than it is to Latro's, it also introduces an innovation, the substitution of *armatus* for *rogatus*, that would be hard to imagine reversed. The result is a jarring, unbalanced *sententia* that is most effective in comparison to its previous iterations. Calpurnius' *sententia* operates through paired verbs of speaking: being asked (*rogatus*) is the circumstance to which saying no is a logical response, and thereby a response that needs to be interrogated. The version in the *Major Declamations*, however, puts together two ideas that do not naturally pair: being armed is not an obvious precursor to refusing; indeed it paradoxically asserts the opposite of what would be logically expected, as being armed is a condition under which a verbal 'no' would be enforceable.[114] The semantic inconcinnity of *armatus* and *tantum negat* is effective because it evokes and then breaks a more natural semantic pairing that was already in circulation in this very context. The novel disjunction reflects the argument: a verbal response has no place in the world of a soldier (i.e. someone who is *armatus*), and the soldier shows his masculinity by acting with his sword rather than with his word.[115] It's the fact that this soldier is armed, moreover, that distinguishes him from the kind of declamatory character who is habitually asked (*rogatus)* to submit to *stuprum*. This sword – figuratively, his penis as well as literally his weapon – makes the soldier a penetrator rather than someone liable to suffer penetration; indeed, he manages to become the

---

112 'Someone orders a Roman soldier on guard duty before the palisade to whorishly submit to his obscene lust? Everyone may make his own judgment, but in my opinion a soldier <u>is insufficiently chaste if he is armed and merely refuses.</u>'

113 Brescia (2004) 225.

114 Cf. Statius *Silv.* 3.5.10, where he imagines that his wife, 'armed' (with chastity?) would be thereby empowered to refuse. For the opposite idea, that it is difficult to refuse when the person asking is armed, cf. Lucan 1.348–49 (speech of Caesar) and *Decl. Min.* 281.4.2–3.

115 Cf. *Decl. Mai.* 3.7 (48.11–14): *ad primum statim obscenae libidinis sermonem..., gladium illum, quem a te pro pudicia nostrarum coniugum acceperat, per pectus infandi corruptoris exegit.*

penetrator in this scenario rather than the one penetrated.[116] By disrupting a familiar *sententia*, possibly even one already associated with this particular declamation, the fictional advocate of *Decl. Mai.* 3 restores his client's masculine identity, while the declaimer shows off his innovative skill.

5 Conclusion

Intertextual links between existing corpora of declamation show how certain ideas and even specific *sententiae* must have circulated within and between communities of declaimers. In some cases, as in Calpurnius' compression of *sententiae* from Seneca's declaimers and in the presence of Montanus' *color*-critique behind the innovations in Calpurnius' *Veneficii Rea controversia*, it may be possible to see how a later declaimer made use of existing declamatory texts and commentaries as models for still more concise or startling *sententiae* and as sources for recherché *colores*. More importantly, however, the context in which Calpurnius was a successful declaimer can be filled in with an intertextual approach that not only acknowledges his presence in a continuous tradition of declamatory techniques and *controversiae* treatments but also takes into account the reality that when declaimers emulated generic *loci* and tropes, they were also emulating precise versions of them produced by teachers, co-competitors, and even textualised predecessors. Seneca the Elder's collection shows this explicitly, but it is implicit in every preserved text of declamations or excerpts, especially where, as with Calpurnius, the selection seems to have been made for striking *lumina orationis*. When Calpurnius is set against the intertextual background of Seneca the Elder and the *Minor* and *Major Declamations*, the figures of his own contemporaries and the commonplaces that were still broadly relevant to them become, in the aggregate, more visible. Reconstructing the expectations of this audience is necessary for appreciating Calpurnius as an individual rhetor, one who was successful enough to have his declamations recorded, excerpted, passed down and who, in at least one instance, possibly became the model for a still more innovative *sententia*.

One might say that an excerpt by its very presence is some indication of what was rhetorically effective or interesting to contemporary and subsequent audiences. There is some evidence that our texts of declamation are the result of continual scholastic revision, which added to and emended its models to make them

---

116 Cf. Adams (1982) 19–22. Thanks go to Martin Dinter for this point.

more like the emulations that they could inspire.[117] While this potential for contamination makes any kind of intertextual reading provisional, it also reinforces the necessity of this approach. What we find in the declamations of any single speaker is always more than a single *ingenium*. Excerpts are a distillation not only of the declamations of an individual rhetor, but also of his models and rivals (both textual and contemporary) and his readers' judgments and even emendations. That texture, a continuous and diachronic community of active declaimers, can be found even in Calpurnius' fragmentary text.

---

117 The observations of Hagendahl (1936) 302–07 on the practices of the excerpter of Seneca the Elder are sobering: not only are epigrams compressed and words omitted in the interests of brevity, in the later books the word order is regularly altered to create metrical clausulae. Cf. Stramaglia (2006) 562–64, 568–71 on the 'fluidità testuale' that seems to have existed for the corpus that reaches us of the *Major Declamations*, as well as Santorelli in this volume.

Catherine Schneider
(Re)lire la déclamation romaine:
le *Soldat de Marius* par Calpurnius Flaccus

'C'est une immense recension dont la lecture est ardue et remplie d'énigmes puisque rien ne vient lier ces fragments les uns aux autres. À chaque phrase, l'esprit doit repartir à zéro et jouir d'une signification que rien ne précède et que rien ne vient assouvir en lui succédant ou bien en l'achevant. L'esprit s'applique tout entier à se pénétrer de la singularité de la forme d'une phrase unique. Aucun sens général ne se présente pour rassembler ces formes que plus aucun dessein ne guide'[1]. Rien ne paraît mieux définir les *Excerpta* de Calpurnius Flaccus, œuvre énigmatique s'il en est. Plus que tout autre texte déclamatoire, en effet, le florilège de Calpurnius Flaccus se signale par une tension extrême entre simplicité de la langue et complexité de la pensée, qui engendre des problèmes d'interprétation parfois insolubles. À cela, une exception peut-être: le *Miles Marianus*, dont la confrontation avec le plaidoyer analogue du pseudo-Quintilien et l'ensemble de la tradition conservée au fil des siècles, assez riche, nous renseigne sur son contexte et nous permet de ce fait d'en élucider bien des obscurités. À la différence de tous les autres 'morceaux choisis' qui composent ce recueil, la troisième série des *Excerpta* de Calpurnius Flaccus emprunte en effet à l'histoire romaine et prend pour prétexte l'épisode bien connu du jeune soldat de Marius, assassin de son tribun, qui tentait de le violer. En l'année 104 avant notre ère, Caius Lusius servait en qualité d'officier dans l'état-major de son oncle, le grand chef militaire Marius, qui faisait campagne contre les Cimbres et les Teutons coalisés. Plutarque nous raconte, dans sa *Vie de Marius*, que ce n'était pas un méchant homme, mais qu'il ne savait pas résister à la vue d'un joli garçon:

> 'Il s'éprit d'un tout jeune soldat placé sous ses ordres, un nommé Trebonius, et il essaya plusieurs fois de le séduire, mais sans succès. Enfin, une nuit, il l'envoya chercher par un valet. Le jeune homme vint, car, appelé, il ne pouvait refuser d'obéir. Quand il fut sous la tente de Lusius, celui-ci essaya de lui faire violence. Alors Trebonius tira son épée et le tua. Le fait avait eu lieu en l'absence de Marius. À son retour il fit passer Trebonius en jugement. Celui-ci, alors que beaucoup l'accablaient et que personne ne le défendait, fit front lui-même avec assurance, raconta l'affaire et produisit des témoins pour prouver qu'il avait souvent résisté aux tentatives de Lusius et que, malgré les grands présents que l'autre lui

---

1 Pascal Quignard, dans sa préface à Bornecque (1992[3]) 11, à propos du recueil de Sénèque le Père.

Catherine Schneider, Université de Strasbourg

https://doi.org/10.1515/9783110401554-005

offrait, il ne lui avait jamais abandonné son corps. Marius, plein d'admiration et de joie, se fit apporter la couronne qui récompense traditionnellement les grands exploits, la prit et la posa lui-même sur la tête de Trebonius pour avoir accompli une très belle action en un temps où l'on avait besoin de beaux exemples. Cette nouvelle, répandue à Rome, contribua beaucoup à l'élection de Marius à son troisième consulat'[2].

L'affaire était devenue si célèbre, dans l'Antiquité, que Plutarque la raconte deux fois; avant lui, elle avait déjà été évoquée à deux reprises par Cicéron, deux fois citée dans Quintilien et compilée dans Valère-Maxime; après lui, elle sera encore signalée par Iulius Paris, mentionnée dans la *Lettre à Octavien*[3], avant de traverser les siècles en donnant tour à tour matière à déclamation chez Calpurnius Flaccus[4], le pseudo-Quintilien[5], un auteur médiéval anonyme[6], Lorenzo Patarol[7], et, pour finir, matière à roman dans le fameux *Albucius* d'un célèbre écrivain, grand amateur du genre: Pascal Quignard[8].

Tel qu'il se présente à nous aujourd'hui, le *Miles Marianus* de Calpurnius Flaccus prend la forme de neuf répliques, inégalement réparties entre défense et accusation. Du jeu des voix signalées par les incises et les diverses marques énonciatives, on déduit par ailleurs que la pièce se distribue ici entre non pas quatre, mais cinq, rôles: deux rôles 'parlants' – ceux de l'avocat de la défense et

---

2 Plut., *Vit. Mar.* 14, 3–9 (éd. Flacelière – Chambry); l'anecdote est résumée dans ses *Apopht. reg.* 202 b-c. Sauf mention contraire, tous les textes sont traduits par nos soins d'après la Collection des Universités de France.

3 Cic., *Mil.* 9, cité et approuvé par Quint., *Inst.* V, 11, 15; Cic., *Inv.* II, 124; Quint., *Inst.* III, 11, 14; Val. Max., *Memor.* VI, 1, 12, résumé par Iul. Par., *Epit.* VI, 1, 12 ; Ps.-Cic., *Epist. Octav.* 10.

4 Calp. Flacc., *Exc.* 3 (*Miles Marianus*); le texte latin de Calpurnius Flaccus est cité d'après Håkanson (1978), à compléter par la traduction anglaise et le commentaire de Sussmann (1994) et la traduction française d'Aizpurua (2005); voir aussi Langlands (2006) 265–275. Nous préparons par ailleurs une édition avec traduction et commentaire des *Excerpta* de Calpurnius Flaccus pour la Collection des Universités de France, en collaboration avec Andrea Balbo.

5 Ps.-Quint., *Decl. Mai.* 3 (*Miles Marianus*); le *Miles Marianus* du pseudo-Quintilien est cité d'après le texte et la traduction, parfois retouchée, de Schneider (2004). Pour plus de détails, nous nous permettons de renvoyer le lecteur à Schneider (2004), à compléter, le cas échéant, par Dupont – Éloi (2001) 18–27; Gunderson (2003); Brescia (2004) et Bernstein (2013) 21–32.

6 Anon., *Trib. Mar.*; pour le texte latin et une traduction allemande de ce texte, voir Haye (1999) 191–211, à compléter désormais par Winterbottom (2015).

7 Pat., *Antil.* 3 (*Pro tribuno contra militem*), dans Patarol (1743) 137–153; pour une traduction française inédite, voir Schneider (2016). Pour une courte biographie de Lorenzo Patarol, on se reportera en particulier à sa biographie rédigée par l'abbé Natale dalle Laste en préface à Patarol (1743) vol. I, p. IX-XII et à son éloge funèbre paru dans le *Giornale de Letterati d'Italia*, 38, 2 (1733) 44–63; sur son œuvre, voir Bernstein (2013) 149–151 et 158–164.

8 Pascal Quignard, *Albucius*, Paris, 1990, chapitre XI, intitulé *Romans homosexuels et romans de débauche* (= Paris, 2004).

de l'avocat de l'accusation (les locuteurs), auxquels il faut ajouter trois rôles ici 'muets' – ceux du défunt tribun (le délocutaire-allocutaire absent), du jeune soldat accusé (le délocutaire-allocutaire présent), ainsi que du juge Marius (l'allocutaire). La présence d'un ou de plusieurs avocats contrevient à la procédure pénale militaire habituelle, qui s'applique en principe de façon expéditive et sommaire[9]: il est à peu près certain qu'un soldat prévenu de quelque infraction comparaissait libre de fers, que l'on faisait déposer les témoins à charge en sa présence et qu'il était autorisé à leur répondre, à les interroger et à présenter lui-même sa défense, comme dans le récit de Plutarque[10]. Elle s'accorde en revanche avec la pratique déclamatoire, qui autorisait presque toutes les libertés et où prévalait l'usage de se faire représenter en justice par un avocat, offrant ainsi un formidable espace de jeu aux déclamateurs. La jeunesse de l'accusé, la nature de la plainte et le contexte graveleux qui entourait l'affaire devaient par ailleurs les détourner de placer leur discours dans la bouche même du prévenu[11].

Afin de mieux cerner les enjeux du procès, il faut rappeler que tout individu mâle adulte et de naissance libre se définit en principe, dans l'éthique romaine, comme un 'impenetrable penetrator'[12] ; c'est particulièrement vrai du soldat romain, qui représente l'archétype du *vir* et de sa qualité correspondante, la *virtus*, le plaçant au sommet de la hiérarchie de la masculinité[13]. Les abus commis sur de jeunes soldats ou officiers par leurs supérieurs hiérarchiques constituent de ce fait, au regard de la législation romaine, des attentats d'une extrême gravité contre la *sanctitas*, autrement dit l'inviolabilité physique de l'individu libre[14], et entrent à ce titre dans la 'catégorie plus générale du *stuprum*, que l'on peut définir comme la violation du corps ingénu, qu'il soit masculin ou féminin'[15]. À l'époque républicaine, le *stuprum* ainsi défini tombait, dans la société civile, sous le coup de la *lex*

---

9 Pour le détail, voir Schneider (2004) 82 – 83 n. 17.

10 Plut., *Vit. Mar.* 14, 8; *Apopht.* 202b-c cités supra.

11 Quint., *Inst.* IV, 1, 46 – 47; ps.-Quint., *Decl. Min.* 260, 1, à compléter par Winterbottom (1984) 39 et 309; Sussman (1994) 100 – 101.

12 Pour reprendre les termes mêmes de Walters (1997) 30.

13 Voir notamment les gradations opérées dans ps.-Quint., *Decl. Mai.* 3, 2 ; 3, 7 et 3, 12. Sur le sens précis à donner aux termes *vir* et *virtus*, voir par ailleurs Schneider (2004) 78 – 80 n. 11 et 86 n. 23.

14 Pour reprendre les termes du ps.-Quint., *Decl. Mai.* 3, 17, qui désigne, au sens propre, l'inviolabilité physique du citoyen romain.

15 Dupont – Éloi (2001) 18, qui précise, p. 90 n. 11: La traduction de *stuprum* 'par *viol* ne rend pas bien compte du sens: le *stuprum* est une relation sexuelle avec un partenaire interdit et protégé par son *pudor*, un garçon, une femme mariée, une jeune fille libre et n'implique pas nécessairement la violence physique'; sur le viol dans l'Antiquité, voir aussi Doblhofer (1994) et sur le *stuprum* dans le *Miles Marianus*, voir Schneider (2004) 102 – 103 n. 50.

Sca(n)tinia[16]; l'armée, en revanche, appliquait des sanctions qui lui étaient spécifiques, les lois de la guerre étant exceptionnelles, à Rome comme partout ailleurs[17]. Il semble, en tout cas, que les abus de ce genre y aient été impitoyablement réprimés, à en croire Valère Maxime[18] et surtout Polybe, qui déclare dans son *Histoire romaine* que la bastonnade est réservée aux voleurs, aux faux témoins, aux récidivistes punis trois fois pour le même motif et aux 'jeunes gens dont les mauvaises mœurs sont avérées'[19].

En tuant son agresseur, le jeune soldat de Marius n'en commettait pas moins un crime contraire au droit universel, qui interdit de tuer un homme[20], et au droit militaire spécial, qui interdit à un soldat de porter la main sur son supérieur hiérarchique[21]. On en vient là au nœud du problème qui porte sur l'opposition, traditionnelle dans les écoles de déclamations, du droit (*ius*) à l'équité (*aequitas*): puisqu'il est impossible de nier l'existence des charges retenues, qui sont avérées, il s'agit pour la défense de démontrer que le jeune soldat était fondé à agir ainsi, parce que son officier l'agressait. C'est le principe même de ce que l'on appelle, en rhétorique, la *relatio* ou *translatio criminis*, dite 'transfert de responsabilité', qui confère au discours sa *qualitas iuridicialis adsumptiva* et c'est à ce titre précisément que l'exemple figure dans le traité cicéronien *Sur l'invention* ou dans l'*Institution oratoire* de Quintilien[22] – on évoquerait de nos jours un 'cas de force majeure' ou de 'légitime défense'. Comme toujours dans les exercices de ce genre, le sujet se corse par ailleurs de subtilités casuistiques, toute l'affaire se compliquant ici du fait que Marius soit à la fois juge et partie – c'est sans doute aussi ce qui a poussé les déclamateurs à s'emparer de cette cause célèbre.

C'est ici, conformément aux pratiques déclamatoires, l'avocat de la défense qui prend d'emblée la parole, pour rapporter l'une des attaques de la partie

---

16 Cette loi porte sur la 'régulation stricte des violences faites aux hommes libres', selon Dupont – Éloi (2001) 25. Sur cette loi énigmatique, voir Lilja (1983) 112–121; Cantarella 1987) 263–292; Dalla (1987) 71–99; Cantarella (1991) 159–171; Fantham (1991) 285–287; Richlin (1993) 569–571; Williams (1999) 119–124; Dupont – Éloi (2001) 24–25.
17 Cantarella (1991) 158–159.
18 Cf. Val. Max., *Memor.* VI, 1, 10–12.
19 Cf. Pol., *Hist. Rom.* VI, 37, 9 (éd. Weil – Nicolet); il s'agit du supplice bien connu du *fustuarium*, auquel un condamné n'avait qu'une infime chance de réchapper; voir Schneider (2004) 160–162 n. 163 et 168 n. 178.
20 Pour reprendre la formule même de Cic., *Inv.* II, 124, cité supra.
21 Voir notamment *Dig.* XLIX, 16, 6 [Menenius III *de re milit.*], avec le commentaire de Schneider (2004) 162–164 n. 169.
22 Cf. Cic., *Inv.* II, 124; Quint., *Inst.* III, 11, 14. Sur cet état de la cause, voir notamment Cic., *Inv.* I, 15; II, 78 et 124; *Rhet. Her.* I, 25; II, 22 et Calboli Montefusco (1984) 119–123; Schneider (2004) 166–167 n. 175; Brescia (2004) 37–47.

adverse: '*Propinquus*', *inquit*, '*imperatoris occisus est*', 'C'est un parent du général, nous dit-on, qui a été tué'[23]. Quintilien, dans son *Institution oratoire*,
évoque précisément pareils cas de figure, où le juge 'est soit un ennemi à nous,
soit un ami à nos adversaires' et où, pire encore, il peut avoir à juger de ses
propres affaires; l'avocat doit en ce cas, à l'en croire, proclamer hautement son
assurance et celle de son client[24]; c'est précisément la posture adoptée: *Macte
virtute, adulescens, et Marium vindicasti*, 'Magnifique, mon garçon, tu as même
vengé Marius!'. L'apostrophe signale ici un brusque changement d'allocutaire de
la part du plaideur, qui se détourne en apparence du juge pour s'adresser au
prévenu, selon une tactique connue pour ses effets percutants: un trait, nous dit
en effet Quintilien, est parfois 'plus piquant et plus vif, s'il est dirigé vers une
autre personne que le juge'[25]. D'emblée, le ton est donné: franc, viril et offensif, il
est parfaitement approprié au contexte militaire du plaidoyer[26]. Comme son
confrère fictif du pseudo-Quintilien, qui déclare de son côté: 'Je ne prendrai donc
pas la défense de l'accusé en niant qu'il ait commis ce meurtre', non seulement
l'avocat ne nie ici aucune des charges retenues contre son client[27], mais il les
assume pleinement, et il les assume *fièrement:* son client a fait justice et il a
même fait justice pour deux – *et Marium vindicasti*, dit-il. Ce trait, qui n'est pas
incompréhensible en soi, s'éclaire à la lumière des propos que le pseudo-
Quintilien prête à diverses reprises à son propre avocat de la défense, notamment lorsque celui-ci suppose le tribun en vie et l'affaire portée à la connaissance du général: 'Que feriez-vous?', lui demande-t-il alors, 'Que décideriez-
vous? On vous a rendu un grand service, Marius, oui, un grand service: vous
n'avez plus besoin de tuer votre parent'[28] – sous-entendu: comme vous auriez
besoin de le faire, s'il était encore en vie et je ne doute pas que vous le feriez,

---

23 Calp. Flacc., *Exc.* 3 (p. 3, 9 – 10).

24 Quint., *Inst.* IV, 1, 18 – 19.

25 Quint., *Inst.* IV, 1, 64... *hic acrior fit atque vehementior ad personam derectus alterius*, à
compléter par IV, 1, 63 – 64; IV, 2, 103 et 106; IX, 2, 38 – 39; IX, 3, 24 – 25; sur l'apostrophe, voir
aussi Lausberg (1998) §§762 – 765 et Franchet d'Espèrey (2006).

26 Quint., *Inst.* XI, 1, 31 – 34. Sur le sens de la formule *macte virtute*, voir par ailleurs Jonkers
(1949).

27 Ps.-Quint., *Decl. Mai.* 3, 8: *Reum ergo caedis non infitiatione defendam: viro, forti praesertim
et innocenti, nihil facere convenit, quod negandum sit. Non abnuo crimen, immo, si accusatores
tacerent, ipse narrassem*, avec le commentaire de Schneider (2004) 152 – 153 n. 141.

28 Ps.-Quint., *Decl. Mai.* 3, 14: *Age porro, si viveret tribunus, et hoc ad te factum, imperator,
deferremus, circumstaret universus exercitus, nec hanc militis contumeliam sed militiae putaret,
quid ageres, quid constitueres? Beneficium accepisti, Mari, beneficium: non habes necesse propinquum tuum occidere.*

vous aussi, étant donné la gravité des faits[29]. Un argument utilitaire, s'il en est, et des plus cyniques... Pour en revenir à Calpurnius Flaccus, ce *Macte virtute, adulescens, et Marium vindicasti* est donc une façon habile de défendre l'accusé et de piéger son juge: en félicitant l'un pour la noble action qu'il a accomplie, on félicite l'autre pour la noble action qu'il accomplira...sans aucun doute.

Le deuxième trait n'est pas destiné à un allocutaire précis, mais à l'ensemble de l'assistance: *Vbicumque periclitatur pudicitia, suam legem habet*, 'Partout où elle est en péril, la vertu a *ses* lois'[30]. La formule *suam legem habere* figure encore une fois chez Calpurnius Flaccus[31], mais aussi dans l'une des *Petites déclamations* du pseudo-Quintilien[32], et Michael Winterbottom explique à ce sujet: '*lex sua* normally would mean 'that favouring' someone'[sic] [33]. Il peut paraître paradoxal de parler de *pudicitia* à propos d'un soldat, car 'ce n'est qu'une vertu de femme'[34], nous dit le pseudo-Quintilien et c'est d'ailleurs l'un des 'paradoxes' dont il joue à plaisir dans son plaidoyer. En fait, la *pudicitia* peut se définir comme 'l'intégrité physique d'un homme (ou d'une femme) libre, intégrité qui relève de l'honneur'[35]; c'est cette vertu qui commande à la jeune fille de préserver sa virginité, à la femme mariée de se garder de l'adultère et à l'homme de s'interdire d'être l'instrument du plaisir d'autres hommes, car le sexe masculin a aussi sa *pudicitia*, qu'il peut perdre en s'abaissant à donner servilement du plaisir à autrui. L'adjectif *pudicus* renvoie ainsi, dans la société romaine, à la catégorie de celles et ceux qui respectent à la fois leur corps et leur honneur, par opposition à celle des *impudici*, déshonorés notoires à qui l'on peut demander un service sexuel[36]. La *pudicitia* revêt donc, dans l'éthique sexuelle romaine antique, un caractère presque 'sacré' et l'on

---

29 Voir déjà la glose de Badius Ascensius 1528, f. XIX^v-XX^r: ... *quid ageres, quid constitueres? Quasi dicat non dubito quin constitueres ultimum supplicium a tribuno sumendum, quod quia miles sumpsit: o Mari, tu accepisti beneficium, beneficium inquam accepisti, quia non habes necesse occidere propinquum tuum, ut haberes si miles non occidisset.*
30 Calp. Flacc., *Exc.* 3 (p. 3, 10–11).
31 Calp. Flacc., *Exc.* 43: *Habet quisque nostrum suam legem: rapta capitis, excaecatus oculorum.*
32 Ps.-Quint., *Decl. Min.* 341, 1: *Vnus furtum fecit duobus ; habet suam quisque legem.*
33 Winterbottom (1984) 556, à propos de ps.-Quint., *Decl. Min.* 350, 10.
34 Ps.-Quint., *Decl. Mai.* 3, 2: *At ego, si qua est fides, pudicitiam in milite etiam laudare erubesco: feminarum est ista virtus; aliter mihi laudandus est vir fortis: idoneus bello, promptus ad pericula, praestantis animi, libere dicam: dignior, qui tribunus esset.*
35 Dupont – Éloi (2001) 20, à la suite de Williams (1999) 172–174; voir aussi Meyer-Zwiffel-hoffer (1995) 197–211 et les travaux de Thomas (2005); Thomas (2006) et Thomas (2007). Tho-mas (2005) 60 définit plus précisément la *pudicitia* par les sèmes '/sentiment de retenue/ concernant la femme et l'homme dans leur vie intime/ qui vivent conformément à leur dignité/ et montrent une grande constance dans cette conduite/'.
36 Dupont – Éloi (2001) 140, à compléter par Schneider (2004) 25–34 (introduction) et 94–95 n. 38 (commentaire).

comprend mieux qu'en la matière 'nécessité fasse loi' – c'est l'opposition traditionnelle entre la loi écrite et la loi naturelle, qui reprend ses droits en cas de force majeure. C'est d'ailleurs en ce sens que légiférera l'empereur Hadrien, qui accorde précisément la relaxe au prévenu en pareille circonstance, si l'on s'en rapporte aux termes du *Digeste:* 'De même, le divin Hadrien a publié dans un rescrit que doit être relaxé l'assassin d'un agresseur imposant de force, à lui-même ou aux siens, une relation sexuelle illicite'[37].

Le trait suivant convoque les morts au tribunal des vivants, puisqu'il est directement adressé au tribun assassiné, selon une pratique connue du genre déclamatoire[38]: *Quid agis, tribune? Tibi nondum vir est, qui Mario iam miles est?,* 'Que fais-tu donc, tribun? Tu ne prends pas encore pour un homme celui que Marius prend déjà pour un soldat?'[39]. L'apostrophe, formellement remarquable, fonctionne comme une équation bâtie sur un strict isocôlon, *tibi nondum vir est – Mario iam miles est*, opposant terme à terme deux attitudes antinomiques (*tibi – Mario*) fondées sur une opposition temporelle (*nondum – iam*), autour d'un thème (la masculinité). Elle synthétise si l'on peut dire, de façon cinglante, une tirade de même nature que la défense adresse au défunt officier dans le pseudo-Quintilien:

'Mais enfin (car j'ai envie d'attaquer ce fou furieux comme s'il était là) est-ce que ce sont vraiment tes putains qui gagnent leur solde, des gigolos que tu attires sous les enseignes? C'est pour cela qu'on éloigne les prostituées de l'armée, qu'on interdit aux femmes d'entrer dans le camp? Vraiment, on n'en a pas besoin, je pense! Tu fais des avances à un soldat – un surhomme! – déjà prêt à se poster au front, en qui la patrie place son salut à la mesure de sa virilité? C'est peut-être pour cela que tu fais ta ronde quand sonne le clairon, c'est pour cela que tu patrouilles de guet en guet! Eh bien, quel tribun tu aurais fait, du temps où de jeunes garçons étaient soldats! Ce n'est pas un accès de folie, une attaque de démence? Tu as sous les yeux un homme au flanc protégé d'une épée, une cuirasse hérissée de fer, un visage enfermé dans un casque avec son panache menaçant pour semer la terreur à la guerre, le nom de Caius Marius inscrit sur un bouclier, un homme, enfin, dont toute la tenue de combat fait dresser les cheveux sur la tête: cela te paraît être une toilette de prostitué? Tu lui feras des avances? Tu l'agresseras? Comment t'attendre ensuite à ce qu'il te prenne, lui, pour un tribun, quand toi, tu ne le prends pas pour un soldat?'[40].

---

37 *Dig.* XLVIII, 8, 1, 4 [Marcianus XIV *inst.*, *Ad legem Corneliam de sicariis et veneficiis*]: *Item divus Hadrianus rescripsit eum, qui stuprum sibi vel suis per vim inferentem occidit, dimittendum*; sur ce point, voir notamment les commentaires de Dalla (1987) 56–62; Hermans (1995) 22.
38 Déjà signalée par Stramaglia (2002) 209 n. 354.
39 Calp. Flacc., *Exc.* 3 (p. 3, 11–12).
40 Ps.-Quint., *Decl. Mai.* 3.12: *Itane tandem (iuvat enim velut praesentis insequi furorem) scorta tua stipendium merentur, et sub signis exoletos trahis? Ideo meretrices ab exercitu summoventur, intrare castra feminis non licet? Ita puto, non opus est. Militem, hoc est plus quam virum, iamiamque in acie staturum, cui pro virili portione salutem suam patria commisit, appellas. Fortasse classico sonante ideo stationes circuis, ideo vigilias ambis. En quem tribunum faceres, cum praetextati militabant!*

Sur l'échelle de la masculinité, il y a donc situé au centre, le *vir* et, respectivement placés en-dessous et au-dessus, le *puer* et le *miles*; le *puer* est un peu moins qu'un *vir*, le *miles*, un peu plus; infliger pareil traitement à un soldat revient ainsi à le ravaler, du rang de *miles*, et donc de *plus quam vir*, c'est-à-dire de 'surhomme', comme dit le pseudo-Quintilien, à celui de *puer* et, sans doute, de *puer delicatus*, c'est-à-dire de 'sous-homme', incompatible avec le recrutement et, plus largement, l'univers militaire. La soumission sexuelle que le tribun impose à son subordonné, en même temps qu'elle est un abus de pouvoir, représente ainsi un acte, dont la défense sous-entend qu'il contrarie l'ordre civique et social, puisque, d'un *ingenuus*, il fait, pire qu'un *infamis*, un esclave: c'est en quoi l'attitude du tribun est ici stigmatisée comme transgressive. Mais la flétrissure de cet acte n'en rejaillit pas moins sur sa personne même, en ce qu'il contrevient à l'exemplarité normalement attendue d'un officier, dont le grade lui confère une autorité supérieure et laisse attendre de lui qu'il se comporte en guide, et non en corrupteur, des jeunes soldats placés sous ses ordres. Suivant un trait inhérent à la mentalité romaine, les vices de l'homme privé rejaillissent donc sur l'homme public, qui déshonore la position qu'il occupe dans la hiérarchie militaire et l'on sait combien 'l'exercice du *regimen morum* s'applique particulièrement quand il s'agit des conduites sexuelles et censure ce qui contrevient à la masculinité, exigée particulièrement des citoyens de l'élite'[41]. Cette pique vise donc à détruire l'honorabilité du tribun en le disqualifiant dans ses fonctions et lui forge une réputation incompatible avec sa dignité civique et militaire.

La *sententia* suivante a des tonalités plus 'gnomiques': *Non longe ab eo est miles, ut promittat stuprum, qui rogatus tantummodo negat*, 'Il n'est pas loin d'être consentant, le soldat qui, à des avances, se contente de dire non'[42]. Elle trouve là encore des échos dans le plaidoyer du pseudo-Quintilien, qui fait dire à l'avocat de la défense: 'Chacun peut bien se faire son propre jugement; à mon avis, il n'a pas assez d'honneur le soldat qui, tout armé qu'il est, se contente de dire non'[43]. Suit une violente diatribe contre la partie adverse, dont le plaideur fictif balaie une à une les objections dans un petit dialogue fictif:

Non hic profusus est furor, non manifesta dementia est? Vides munitum gladio latus, loricam ferro asperam, clausam galea faciem et ad terrorem belli cristas minantis, inscriptum in scuto C. Mari nomen, totum denique virum Martio habitu horrentem: hic tibi cultus prostituti videtur? Appellabis de stupro? Vim adferes? Quid deinde expectas, ut ille te tribunum putet, cum tu illum non putes militem? ; pour le détail du commentaire, voir Schneider (2004) 184–195.

41 Dupont – Éloi (2001) 87.

42 Calp. Flacc., *Exc.* 3 (p. 3, 12–13).

43 Ps.-Quint., *Decl. Mai.* 3, 6: *Suum quisque habeat fortasse iudicium; mea sententia non satis pudicus est miles, qui armatus tantum negat.*

'Mais vraiment, souillé par les propos indignes qu'on lui tient, n'opposera-t-il rien d'autre qu'un simple refus? Et qui ne le prendrait pas pour un prostitué, s'il pouvait s'exposer à recevoir encore des avances? – 'Qu'il se contente pourtant de dire non et sursoie à la réparation du préjudice subi'. C'est ainsi, j'imagine, qu'au lever du jour, il ira se plaindre… à son tribun! On empoigne un soldat et on l'arrache au poste qui lui est assigné pour lui faire subir un viol: je vous le demande, accusateurs, que doit- il faire? Laissera-t-il ces mains lubriques palper ses blessures? Rendra-t-il les armes ou les prendra-t-il? Car c'est un homme. – 'Mais le tribun a toute autorité, c'est un officier de haut rang qui en donne l'ordre; un soldat doit légitimement obéissance à son tribun'. Il peut même en espérer de l'avancement, peut-être bien qu'il recevra en récompense de ce service le grade de cen- turion, qu'il dirigera une compagnie et que d'autres serviront sous son commandement! Si tel est l'état de la cause, si on ne lui accorde aucun moyen de défense, dites-le, déclarez-le! S'il est interdit de frapper son agresseur, il assumera les conséquences; car il n'est pas possible de le repousser à mains nues: souvenez-vous, son agresseur est armé'[44].

Le participe *rogatus* renvoie chez Calpurnius Flaccus à une forme d'agression sexuelle qui revient comme un leitmotiv chez le pseudo-Quintilien sous son appellation juridique et se trouve ainsi définie dans le *Digeste:* 'Draguer, c'est attenter à la vertu d'autrui par un discours racoleur: il ne s'agit pas, en effet, d'insulte, mais d'atteinte aux bonnes mœurs'[45]. Le verbe *appellare* et, dans une moindre mesure, son synonyme *rogare* sont régulièrement attestés chez les dé- clamateurs au sens de 'faire des avances', 'faire des propositions honteuses', 'apostropher – une femme ou un garçon – en termes obscènes'[46]. Dès l'époque d'Ulpien, l'*interpellatio de stupro*, qui inclut toutes sortes d'incitations à la dé- bauche, est insérée parmi les *iniuriae in corpus*, que le législateur assimile dès lors aux atteintes à l'honneur, retenant comme critère de son classement la seule intentionnalité[47]. C'est dire toute la gravité que revêt cette forme d'incitation à la

---

44 Ps.-Quint., *Decl. Mai.* 3, 9: *Indignis vero vocibus contaminatus nihil amplius aliud quam renuet? Et quis non illum inter prostitutos habeat, si commiserit, ut possit iterum appellari?* 'Neget tamen, et ultionem iniuriae suae differat'. Ita puto, cum inluxerit, tribuno queretur! Inicitur manus, et ab adsignata statione miles abducitur, ut stuprum patiatur: vos interrogo, accusatores, quid fa- ciet? Feret libidinosas manus vulnera sua tractantes? Deponet arma, an opponet? Vir est enim. '<At> auctorem habet, ho<mo> primi ordinis iube[n]t; aequum est tribuno militem parere'. Inde sperare etiam processus potest, pro hoc merito accipiet fortasse vitem, ordines ducet, et sub illo alii mili- tabunt. Si haec condicio causae est, si defensio sui non permittitur, indicate, praedicite. Si cor- ruptorem non licet feriri, feret; non enim potest nuda manu repelli: mementote, corruptor armatus est.
45 *Dig.*, XLVII, 10, 15, 20 [Vlpianus LXXVII ad ed.]: *Appellare est blanda oratione alterius pu- dicitiam attentare : hoc enim non est convicium, sed adversus bonos mores adtemptare.*
46 Voir notamment Ps.-Quint., *Decl. Mai.* 3, 2; 3, 3; 3, 9 et 3, 12 et, avant lui, Sen., *Contr.* II, 7; VIII, 6; IX, 1, 7; Quint., *Inst.* IV, 2, 98; ps.-Quint., *Decl. Min.* 279, 18; 363, 1.
47 Desanti (1990) 129–142; Cantarella (1991) 173.

débauche aux yeux de la société romaine, qui la considère comme l'équivalent verbal de la pénétration sexuelle[48]. Voilà sans doute pourquoi le législateur met un soin particulier à protéger indistinctement l'honneur des *matresfamilias* et des *pueri* 'des dragues insistantes et fastidieuses. Les deux catégories de personnes qui devaient être 'pudiques' étaient ainsi défendues, de manière identique, du célèbre comportement méditerranéen: comportement provoqué, en fin de compte, à la fois par le désir réel de séduire et par la nécessité pour le mâle de donner grossièrement la preuve évidente de sa virilité. Un jeu, en somme, où chacun tient son rôle: le mâle celui de chasseur, la femme – et, à Rome, les garçons – celui de la proie'[49]. Un soldat, qui est plus qu'un *vir*, et que l'on place au sommet de la hiérarchie de la masculinité, ne saurait donc réagir autrement que par les armes pour défendre son honneur d'homme: c'est la seule réponse adéquate pour un homme en armes et l'on comprend dès lors combien la mention *miles* est importante en la matière[50], car l'on en revient de ce fait à la stratégie du 'transfert de responsabilité'[51]. La violence appelle la violence et l'on ne peut s'exposer, en fait de sexualité, ne serait-ce qu'au soupçon d'*impudicitia*.

Le cinquième trait est directement adressé à Marius, en sa qualité de chef d'armée et donc, de juge: *Crede, imperator, male de te iudicasset miles tuus, si tribuno pepercisset*, 'Croyez-moi, général, votre soldat vous aurait mal jugé, s'il avait épargné le tribun'[52]. En dépit de sa jeunesse et de sa relative inexpérience, le soldat 'n'ignorait pas', nous dit-on chez le pseudo-Quintilien, 'à quels risques il s'exposait alors qu'il se dégageait, à coups d'épée, des étreintes obscènes d'un agresseur fou furieux'[53]. Il savait qu'il était légalement passible de la peine capitale pour le meurtre d'un officier; il a donc agi en parfaite connaissance de cause, pariant sur l'impartialité, l'honorabilité et la clémence du juge dont il espérait une relaxe au bénéfice de la légitime défense. Le raisonnement est retors et se place davantage sur le plan moral que sur le strict plan juridique: seule la pensée que le général condamnerait et le meurtre et l'auteur du meurtre aurait pu retenir la main du soldat. Or condamner le meurtre revenait dans son

---

48 Walters (1997a) 36–37.

49 Cantarella (1991) 174.

50 Il faut donc la maintenir, contre l'avis de Sussman (1994) 101: 'The person … (*non longe ab eo est* [*miles*] … H 3.12–13): W. as reported in H. app. suggests deleting *miles*, as does D. A. Russell (*per litt.*). I concur; the expression would seem to be a generalized statement, with *miles* easily slipping in from the surrounding context, supplied by an early scribe'.

51 Sur la *relatio* ou *translatio criminis*, voir supra n. 22.

52 Calp. Flacc., *Exc.* 3 (p. 3, 13–15).

53 Ps.-Quint., *Decl. Mai.* 3, 2: *Neque ignoravit quae manerent eum pericula, cum obscenos furiosi corruptoris amplexus gladio divelleret*, etc.

esprit à excuser d'une certaine façon le geste du tribun. Toute indulgence en la matière revenait par ailleurs à 'autoriser' en quelque sorte ce harcèlement sexuel à l'armée et, donc, à jeter le soupçon sur la moralité même du juge. C'est d'ailleurs en ce sens que plaide l'avocat fictif du pseudo-Quintilien: 'Quant à vous', dit-il à Marius, 'dites-vous bien que les hommes sauront ce que vous avez pensé de cette affaire. Cet exemple ne peut rester muet ni dans un sens, ni dans l'autre; chacun, c'est certain, se dit qu'il approuve, quand il juge, ce qu'il aurait fait lui-même dans un cas semblable'[54]. Ayant à juger du soldat, Marius juge de ce fait aussi du tribun à titre posthume: l'acquittement de l'un vaut forcément condamnation de l'autre, et vice versa.

Le trait suivant est toujours adressé à Marius et convoque ces deux figures féminines légendaires de la Rome républicaine que sont Lucrèce et, au travers de son père ici nommé, Virginie: *Hanc vim Verginius parricidio fugit, propter hanc Lucretia pectus suum ferro fodit. Pudet me, imperator: feminae exemplis militem tueor*, 'Voilà la violence que Verginius a évitée au prix d'un infanticide, voilà pourquoi Lucrèce s'est enfoncé un fer dans la poitrine. Honte à moi, général: citer des femmes en exemple pour défendre un soldat!'[55]. Il ne faut évidemment pas se laisser abuser ici par la 'honte' de l'avocat à l'évocation de précédents féminins, car ces exemples 'tirés des inégalités ont', d'après Quintilien, 'une force particulière. La vaillance est plus admirable chez la femme que chez l'homme. Par conséquent, s'il s'agit de pousser quelqu'un à l'héroïsme, Horace et Torquatus n'auront pas autant d'influence que la matrone de la main de qui Pyrrhus a été assassiné, et s'il s'agit de pousser à la mort, Caton et Scipion n'en auront pas autant que Lucrèce; c'est précisément un exemple du plus au moins'[56]. L'association de ces deux noms était depuis bien longtemps devenue un stéréotype auquel les auteurs romains antiques ont eu fréquemment recours et ces exemples figurent d'ailleurs, ainsi développés, chez le pseudo-Quintilien:

---

54 Ps.-Quint., *Decl. Mai.* 3, 10: *Tu cogita, quid te sensisse homines sciant. Hoc exemplum in neutram partem potest taceri; cogitare certum est id quemque, cum iudicat, probare, quod in re simili ipse fecisset.*

55 Calp. Flacc., *Exc.* 3 (p. 3, 15 – 17).

56 Quint., *Inst.* V, 11, 9 – 10: *Ad exhortationem vero praecipue valent inparia. Admirabilior in femina quam in viro virtus. Quare, si ad fortiter faciendum accendatur aliquis, non tantum adferent momenti Horatius et Torquatus quantum illa mulier, cuius manu Pyrrhus est interfectus, et ad moriendum non tam Cato et Scipio quam Lucretia ; quod ipsum est ex maioribus ad minora.* L'*exemplum* compte parmi les preuves logiques et objectives de la démonstration rhétorique (Lausberg (1998³) §410 – 426): s'apparentant à l'argumentation syllogistique, il consiste en un raisonnement inductif permettant de saisir, par une intuition directe, l'universel dans le singulier, répété ou isolé; sur les *exempla* dans la tradition déclamatoire, voir en particulier Van der Poel (2009).

'Dois-je dire à présent que la morale romaine a toujours témoigné d'un souci particulier de la vertu? Rappeler Lucrèce, qui se planta une épée dans les entrailles, pour expier les exigences qu'elle avait dû satisfaire, et qui, pour détacher au plus tôt son cœur de femme vertueuse de son corps souillé, se frappa elle-même, parce qu'elle ne pouvait tuer son agresseur? S'il vous plaît à présent que je cite l'exemple d'un soldat, pourquoi ne pas vous raconter celui de Virginius, qui préserva la virginité de sa fille par l'unique moyen en son pouvoir – la mort! – et se saisit d'un couteau à portée de main pour le plonger dans le cœur de la jeune fille, sans résistance de sa part? Il laissa Appius se sauver sans le frapper, mais le peuple romain le poursuivit pourtant en justice et le fit jeter aux fers, en menaçant les Pères d'une sécession et presque d'une guerre civile, et rien, alors, ne souleva davantage l'indignation de la plèbe, que le fait qu'il eût tenté de prendre sa vertu à la fille d'un soldat. Voilà de nobles exemples, voilà des exemples de femmes à raconter – quant aux hommes, de quelle vertu font-ils preuve, sinon de ne pas agresser?'[57].

À la différence du pseudo-Quintilien qui présente ces deux *exempla* par ordre chronologique, Calpurnius Flaccus les classe par ordre d'importance, du plus grave, le parricide – ou plus exactement l'infanticide –, commis par Verginius[58], au moins grave, l'homicide commis par le soldat, en passant par le suicide de Lucrèce. Les rapports charnels illégitimes 'souillent' en effet le sang de celui ou celle qui s'y est soumis, volontairement ou non; ainsi, même lorsqu'elle n'est pas consentante, une personne souillée est-elle irrémédiablement déchue[59]. Dans tous les cas, il s'agit donc de laver son honneur dans le sang: pour les femmes, cela passe par la mort que l'on reçoit ou que l'on se donne, pour les hommes, par la mort que l'on donne.

---

57 Ps.-Quint., *Decl. Mai.* 3, 11: *Dicam nunc ego praecipuam semper curam Romanis moribus pudicitiae fuisse? Referam Lucretiam, quae condito in viscera sua ferro poenam a se necessitatis exegit, et, ut quam primum pudicus animus a polluto corpore separaretur, se ipsa percussit, quia corruptorem non potuit occidere? Si nunc placet tibi miles, quid ego Virginium narrem, qui filiae virginitatem, qua sola poterat, morte defendit raptumque de proximo ferrum non recusanti puellae immersit? Dimisit illaesum Appium, quem tamen populus Romanus secessione a patribus et prope civili bello persecutus in vincula duci coegit, neque ulla res tum magis indignationem plebis commovit, quam quod pudicitiam auferre temptaverat filiae militis. Haec sunt honesta, haec narranda feminarum exempla – nam virorum quae pudicitia est, nisi non corrumpere?*

58 Le *parricidium* se définit anciennement comme tout 'homicide commis contre un homme libre quelconque', puis le 'meurtre d'un proche parent, tel qu'un ascendant ou un descendant' (Monier (1948[4]) 230); voir désormais Langer (2007) 87–90 et Pasetti (2011) 13–20). Il s'agit, aux yeux des anciens, de l'un des crimes les plus abominables qui soient et qui, de ce fait, appelle un châtiment spectaculaire : jusqu'à l'époque de Justinien, un individu convaincu de parricide était battu de verges, puis enfermé dans un sac avec un chien, un coq, une vipère et un singe et jeté à l'eau; voir *Rhet. Her.* I, 23; Cic., *Rosc. Am.* 70–71; Val. Max., *Memor.* I, 1, 13; *Dig.* XLVIII, 9, 9 [Modestinus]; *Cod. Iust.* IX, 17, 1.

59 Bernay-Vilbert (1974) 444; Grimal (1979) 124–125.

Le septième et dernier trait lancé à l'appui de la défense fonctionne également sur une comparaison *ex maioribus ad minora;* il joue en outre, au plan formel, sur l'homéoarchon en *mi(n)-,* qui le rend difficilement traduisible en français[60]: *Stuprum minatus est militi tuo: minus est quod nobis Cimbri minantur,* 'Il a menacé de viol ton soldat? Les Cimbres nous menacent de moins!'[61]. Il s'éclaire à la lecture de l'indignation que l'on prête aux troupes dans le pseudo-Quintilien sur le motif bien connu du 'Tout plutôt que le déshonneur'; voici en effet ce que l'avocat de la défense fait dire aux frères d'armes du soldat de Marius:

'Non, nous ne pouvons pas obéir aux ignominies des tribuns. Aucun d'entre nous ne refuse l'épreuve des marches, ni le paquetage énorme en plus de nos armes, pas plus que l'ardeur du soleil d'été ni l'hiver passé sous la tente. Doit-on, harassé de fatigue, creuser un fossé, veiller en avant des portes et des retranchements, soit! C'est en braves que nous marcherons vers des batailles incertaines, que nous compenserons nos blessures par la gloire. La mort sera préférable à l'ignominie. Tout ce que nous subissons au combat est épreuve d'hommes. Que le tribun impose des expéditions périlleuses, s'il faut débusquer l'ennemi de la crête d'une montagne, s'il faut partir en reconnaissance au travers de bois infestés de guerriers en armes; qu'il s'acharne enfin sur notre dos à coups de trique, exige une soumission d'esclave sous les coups: la loi stipule que les esclaves aussi sont la propriété de leur marchand; peut-être s'autorisera-t-on de cette loi pour nous mettre en vente comme prisonniers de guerre! Mais si l'on nous donne l'ordre de satisfaire comme des prostituées à de telles exigences, si, contre les sévices sexuels d'un violeur, nous n'avons plus les armes que pour nous humilier, il vaut mieux que le camp tombe aux mains de l'ennemi et que ce soit au Cimbre à s'opposer aux sévices du tribun. Les Germains ne connaissent rien de tel, et l'on vit plus chastement au bord de l'Océan'[62].

On reconnaît, chez le pseudo-Quintilien comme chez Calpurnius Flaccus, une trace de cette déformation rhétorique que l'on a pu désigner, à l'exemple de la

---

60 On notera au passage la dimension ludique de ce trait, qui transparaît dans d'autres *sententiae* du recueil, comme dans le jeu sur les comparatifs qui se lit en Calp. Flac., *Exc.* 26 (*Tria praemia sacerdotis*): *Melior quidem fama seniorum, spes tamen minoribus maior est,* ou encore l'anagramme figurant en *Exc.* 52 (*Infamis non militet*): *gladiatorem me fecit non pirata, sed patria.*
61 Calp. Flacc., *Exc.* 3 (p. 3, 17–18).
62 Ps.-Quint., *Decl. Mai.* 3, 16: '*Non ignominia tribunis parere possumus. Nemo nostrum recusat itinerum laborem nec iniustum super arma fascem, non aestivi solis ardorem nec sub pellibus actam hiemem. Ferienda sit fatigato fossa, pro vallo portisque vigilandum. Fortiter ancipites inibimus pugnas, vulnera laude pensabimus. Mors erit ignominia potior. Quicquid in pugna patimur, virorum est. Imperet asperas tribunus expeditiones, si quo vertice montis hostis pellendus est, si inter infestos armatis saltus speculandum; saeviat denique in terga verberibus, exigat servilem plagarum patientiam: leno etiam servis excipitur; fortasse hac lege captivos vendes. Si meretricia imperatur necessitas, si adversus obscenam vim corruptoris arma tantum contumeliae causa habemus, potius castra capiantur, et vim tribuni interpellet Cimber. Nihil tale novere Germani, et sanctius vivitur ad Oceanum*'.

littérature du Siècle des Lumières, sous le nom de mythe du 'bon barbare', et qui consiste à opposer, dans une intention satirique ou moralisatrice, la pureté morale des peuplades étrangères à la dépravation des habitants de l'Empire. La *Guerre des Gaules* n'en est pas exempte, ni la *Germanie* de Tacite, qui fait tout particulièrement honneur aux peuples germains de ce que leurs mœurs ont de plus fruste et primitif[63]. Mais cette observation est aussi à mettre au compte des lieux communs de l'amplification oratoire, qui permettent de soulever l'indignation de l'auditoire, et dont Cicéron nous dit: 'Le huitième lieu est celui grâce auquel on démontre que le crime dont il est question n'est pas courant ni perpétré habituellement même par les gens les plus téméraires; qu'il est également étranger aux sauvages, aux peuples barbares et aux bêtes féroces'[64]. Sur l'échelle de la barbarie, le tribun se place donc plus haut que le Cimbre qui représentait pourtant, dans l'imaginaire romain, la quintessence de la barbarie[65].

Venons-en à présent à la riposte de l'accusation, dont le premier trait souligne bien la position délicate, puisqu'elle se voit en quelque sorte contrainte d'endosser l'*impudicitia* de son client: *Miles tuus, imperator, iam aliquid impudici habet quod ad impudicitiam placet*, 'Votre soldat, général, a déjà ceci de vicieux qu'il plaît au vice'[66]. L'*impudicitia*, dont le sens exact a été longtemps controversé, peut se définir comme le déshonneur physique et, plus particulièrement, l'atteinte sexuelle portée au corps libre, masculin ou féminin[67]. Elle représente, pour un citoyen romain de condition libre, le comble de la déchéance: renoncer à son honneur d'homme, c'est se ravaler, on l'a vu, au rang des *impudici*, ces déshonorés notoires à qui l'on peut demander un service sexuel[68]. La stratégie mise en œuvre relève donc, là aussi, du 'transfert de responsabilité': puisqu'il est impossible de nier la tentative de 'séduction' de l'officier, il s'agit pour l'accusation de démontrer que le tribun s'est comporté ainsi, parce que son jeune

---

63 Caes., *B. G.* VI, 21, Tac., *Germ.* 17, 5; 19, 1; ces réflexions préfigurent notamment les paradoxes soutenus au Ve siècle de notre ère par Salvien de Marseille au sujet du barbare candide et doué de toutes les vertus (Salv., *Gub. Dei* VII, 6, 23; 7, 26; 16, 64).

64 Cic., *Inv.* I, 103: *Octavus locus est per quem demonstramus non vulgare neque factitatum esse ne ab audacissimis quidem hominibus id maleficium de quo agatur; atque id a feris quoque hominibus et a barbaris gentibus et inmanibus bestiis esse remotum.*

65 Sur les Cimbres et des Teutons perçus comme métaphore par excellence de la barbarie septentrionale, voir notamment Callies (1971) 341–350; Dauge (1981).

66 Calp. Flacc., *Exc.* 3 (p. 3, 20–21).

67 Dupont – Éloi (2001) 14, à compléter notamment par Thomas (2005) 65, qui définit l'*impudicitia* par les sèmes '/absence du sentiment de retenue/ concernant la femme et l'homme dans leur vie intime/ qui ne vivent pas conformément à leur dignité/ et montrent une grande constance dans cette conduite/'.

68 Voir Dupont – Éloi (2001) 140, cités supra.

soldat a affiché une forme de disponibilité sexuelle. C'est d'ailleurs exactement ce que l'avocat fictif du *Tribunus Marianus* médiéval reproche avec véhémence au jeune soldat accusé:

> 'Pourtant, vénérable général, votre soldat avait, dans sa vie, une attitude et une tenue telles qu'il a pu faire croire qu'il se prostituait, même à l'armée. Je n'apprécie guère de la part d'un soldat ni une peau soignée de femme, ni des œillades aguicheuses, ni des regards furtifs en coin, ni une coiffure artistement arrangée, ni des manières affectées ou un langage sensuel, ni, enfin, une démarche langoureuse, absolument rien de ce qui peut être une invitation à la débauche. Après l'avoir en effet attiré et pris à ce piège, il aurait pu subjuguer sans tarder n'importe quel gaillard, s'il était de ceux qui couchent avec des hommes. Votre soldat s'est laissé, sans en rougir, couvrir de cadeaux, sans les décliner, attendrir par des compliments, sans y répugner, dispenser de corvées, en tout cas il a fait concurrence, et par ses tarifs et par ses talents, à la courtisane qui est d'ordinaire bien aise de se cramponner aux riches et de tourner le dos aux pauvres. Et si vraiment j'ai présenté cet individu-là sous un jour trop ou assez vertueux, je reconnais de moi-même avoir menti'[69].

Les Romains étaient particulièrement attentifs aux détails physiques ou vestimentaires susceptibles de trahir toute forme de dépravation morale et donc de disponibilité sexuelle. Cette disponibilité, en plus de valoir à celui qui la subissait, ou l'acceptait, le titre peu envié d'*impudicus*, se doublait d'une sorte de dégradation civique, que l'on appelait *infamia*[70] et qui signait, en quelque sorte, la 'mort sociale' de celui qui en était frappé: il entrait ainsi dans la catégorie des prostitués notoires, mais aussi des esclaves et des affranchis, avec lesquels on pouvait avoir des rapports sexuels non seulement licites, mais encore tout à fait acceptés. Ce qui est, en effet, le plus souvent dénoncé par les historiens, moralistes ou satiristes, c'est 'l'asservissement volontaire, l'*impudicitia* voulue. En somme, il y a un crime, le viol de l'homme libre, et il y a une infamie, l'asser-

---

69 Anon., *Trib. Mar.* 5, 3 – 4, d'après Winterbottom (2015) 68: *Eo tamen, imperator piissime, miles tuus et actu vixit et habitu, ut et inter arma prostitisse credi potuerit. Non amo femineam cutis curam in milite, non petulantiam oculorum, non furtivos et oblicos intuitus, non crines arte compositos, non affectatam gestuum seu verborum mollitiem, non denique remissiorem incessum, nichil omnino quod ad lenocinamentum spectare possit lasciviae. His enim implicitum quempiam et illectum, si quis masculorum erat concubitor, sine cunctatione subegisse potuerat. Miles tuus non erubuit invitari muneribus, non refugit emolliri blanditiis, non despexit remissionibus sublevari, meretricis utique caritatem et ingenium aemulatus, quae libenter et adhaerere divitibus et a pauperibus solet recedere. Quem profecto si pudicum nimis praedicavero sive satis, ipse me mentitum esse confiteor.*
70 Il tombait ainsi au statut d'*infamis*, c'est-à-dire de ceux à qui, selon Rousselle (1998) 268 – 269, 'Rome ne reconnaît pas la pleine capacité civique, personnes privées des noces légitimes et donc de descendance légitime, privées de la faculté de représenter autrui devant un tribunal, privées de la capacité de se présenter aux magistratures des cités'.

vissement volontaire du corps libre'[71]. C'est le sens de l'anecdote que Sénèque le Père rapporte à propos de Quintus Hatérius; ce rhéteur, 'à force de ne vouloir rien dire que d'élégant, que de brillant, versait souvent dans des formulations qui ne pouvaient échapper aux railleries'. Sénèque nous dit 'qu'un jour où il défendait un affranchi à qui l'on reprochait d'avoir couché avec son patron, il dit: 'Perdre sa vertu est un crime pour l'homme libre, une obligation pour l'esclave, un service pour l'affranchi'. Le mot tourna à la plaisanterie: 'Tu ne me rends pas service?' et: 'Il est fort serviable pour untel'. Aussi appela-t-on quelque temps 'serviables' les vicieux et les libidineux'[72]. C'est donc, pour ainsi dire, dans la catégorie de ces 'serviables' que le tribun a rangé son soldat, à tort – selon la défense – ou à raison – selon l'accusation.

Le trait qui conclut cette série est en revanche directement adressé au jeune soldat accusé et remet en cause le principe même de légitime défense qu'il fait valoir pour sa protection: *Tu gladium commilitonis tui cruore tinxisti, quem satis fuit minari*, 'Tu as trempé ton épée dans le sang de *ton* frère d'armes, alors qu'il suffisait de l'en menacer!'[73]. Même s'il est dépourvu de toute dénomination propre en latin, ce principe est énoncé de bonne heure dans le droit romain antique. Cicéron expliquait déjà dans son plaidoyer *Pour Milon* qu'il existe des circonstances où il est justifié, voire inévitable, de 'se défendre par la violence d'une violence qu'on vous fait', car 'au milieu des armes, les lois se taisent' – c'est le fameux *vi vis illata defenditur*, qu'il illustre précisément en citant l'exemple du soldat de Marius[74]. Le juriste Cassius écrit de même 'que l'on peut repousser la violence par la violence: c'est une disposition du droit naturel. Il est évident, dit-il, que l'on peut repousser les armes par les armes'[75]. Il est intéressant, afin d'en mieux cerner les enjeux, de faire un détour par l'article 122–5 du Code pénal actuellement en vigueur en France où il est stipulé, concernant la

---

71 Dupont – Éloi (2001) 27.

72 Sen., *Contr.* IV, *praef.* 10: *Hoc exempto nemo erat scholasticis nec aptior nec similior, sed dum nihil vult nisi culte, nisi splendide dicere, saepe incidebat in ea quae derisum effugere non possent. Memini illum, cum libertinum reum defenderet, cui obiciebatur, quod patroni concubinus fuisset, dixisse: 'Impudicitia in ingenuo crimen est, in servo necessitas, in liberto officium'. Res in iocos abiit: 'Non facis mihi officium' et 'multum ille huic in officiis versatur'. Ex eo inpudici et obsceni aliquamdiu officiosi vocitati sunt.*

73 Calp. Flacc., *Exc.* 3 (p. 3, 21–22).

74 Cic., *Mil.* 9: *Atqui si tempus est ullum iure hominis necandi quae multa sunt, certe illud est non modo iustum, verum etiam necessarium cum vi vis illata defenditur.* Sur ce principe et sa réception chez le juriste Cassius, voir notamment en dernier lieu Tarwacka (2012) et Varvaro (2013).

75 *Dig.* XLIII, 16, 1, 27 [Ulpianus]: *Vim vi repellere licet, Cassius scribit: idque ius natura comparatur. Apparet autem, inquit, ex eo arma armis repellere licet;* voir aussi *Dig.* IX, 2, 45, 4 [Paulus]: *vim enim vi defendere omnes, omniaque iura permittunt.*

légitime défense: 'N'est pas pénalement responsable la personne qui, devant une atteinte injustifiée envers elle-même ou autrui, accomplit, dans le même temps, un acte commandé par la nécessité de la légitime défense d'elle-même ou d'autrui, sauf s'il y a disproportion entre les moyens de défense employés et la gravité de l'atteinte'[76]. La légitime défense y est classée sous les causes d'irresponsabilité pénale: elle dégage l'auteur d'un crime ou délit de toute responsabilité pénale, même lorsque l'infraction est légalement constituée. En l'état actuel de la jurisprudence, il s'agit d'un acte de défense exceptionnel, uniquement reconnu lorsque l'agression est à la fois réelle, injustifiée et que le danger couru est imminent; la riposte doit être en ce cas instantanée, nécessaire et, surtout, proportionnelle à l'agression commise[77]. C'est ici sur la disproportion entre les moyens de défense employés et la gravité de l'atteinte, somme toute présentée comme mineure, que porte le trait. L'antilogie composée par Lorenzo Patarol pour la défense du tribun joue précisément de ce déséquilibre entre défense et attaque (supposée): 'Je pensais', dit en l'occurrence l'avocat de l'accusation, 'que le tribun s'était rué sur son soldat en grondant des menaces horribles, qu'il lui avait sauté à la gorge et provoqué de sa part une riposte désespérée; et qu'il était ensuite arrivé – puisqu'il est permis de repousser la violence par une égale violence – que le soldat avait pris l'avantage à la pointe de l'épée. Mais tout ce qu'on lui reproche, ce sont des galanteries!'[78]. Il poursuit son argumentation sur le même ton ironique et indigné:

> 'Je me félicite, C. Marius, que le soldat n'ait pas toléré d'élans pervers, qu'il ne se soit pas laissé déshonorer; mais est-il admissible de se dégager d'une caresse à coups d'épée? Était-ce là le seul recours qui restait à la morale et ne pouvait-on se satisfaire du sentiment d'avoir repoussé le 'violeur' par un refus? Tout homme qui oppose une mine vraiment revêche à des avances obscènes et contre-attaque par des menaces, par de l'intimidation, enlève à un agresseur pervers toute envie de l'aborder une seconde fois. Elles se brisent en effet tout net, les pulsions qui restent sans réponse et c'est dans les scrupules et la honte que bascule d'un seul coup un sentiment déshonorant. Rien ne triomphe mieux de ce genre

---

[76] Code pénal (Version consolidée au 28 mars 2015), Titre II: De la responsabilité pénale, Chapitre II: Des causes d'irresponsabilité ou d'atténuation de la responsabilité, Article 122–5, disponible en ligne sur www.legifrance.gouv.fr.

[77] L'apologie du soldat de Marius est d'ailleurs bâtie en réponse à ces différents critères dans le pseudo-Quintilien.

[78] Patarol (1743) 141: *Putabam terribili irruisse minarum fragore Tribunum, juguloque Militis imminentem desperationis excitasse concilia; indeque factum, ut, cum vim repellere vi pari liceat, valuerit gladio plus Miles. Quidquid objicitur blanditiae sunt.*

de vices que de renoncer à toute lutte, à toute résistance, que de ne pas trop montrer ses capacités de vaincre'[79].

Il suffisait donc, aux yeux de l'accusation, d'opposer un simple refus à une offense qualifiée de mineure et de se plier ensuite au protocole prévu par le règlement militaire; voilà pourquoi le défenseur du tribun conseille pour finir au jeune soldat incriminé de produire les témoins de son héroïsme et de sa fermeté:

'Tu dois forcément prouver qu'on t'a fait des avances. J'estime donc la fuite préférable dans ton cas; je te demande à toi, l'agressé, de promener à la ronde ta personne à travers les légions, à travers le camp, d'accuser publiquement le tribun de violence, de lui reprocher son vice aux yeux du monde. Souviens-toi, personne d'autre ne peut, dans ta cause, être plus crédible que toi. Cherche recours auprès de Marius; dénonce l'acte du neveu. Défends-toi finalement, fais-toi justice de façon à démontrer ton innocence, à prouver qu'on t'a vraiment 'agressé', à nous faire entendre, si possible, l'aveu du crime de la bouche même du pervers sexuel. Toi, bien sûr, tu déclares avoir tué un homme qui te faisait des avances; toi, tu accuses le tribun, alors qu'il a perdu, avec la vie, tout moyen de défendre sa propre cause'[80].

Comme les précédents traits examinés, cette dernière *sententia* atteste de la permanence et de la vitalité d'une tradition rhétorique, et de ses enjeux argumentatifs notamment, qui se perpétue d'un millénaire à l'autre, de Calpurnius Flaccus à Lorenzo Patarol, en passant par le pseudo-Quintilien et l'anonyme médiéval. La confrontation de ces neuf traits avec le reste de la tradition déclamatoire conservée nous permet par ailleurs de mesurer combien leur interprétation dépend de la stratégie argumentative adoptée: pour comprendre la *sententia*, il faut en somme connaître le *color*, ce qui suppose un formidable travail d'investigation et de reconstitution de la part du traducteur et/ou du commentateur. C'est ici, plus que partout ailleurs peut-être, que le philologue

---

79 Patarol (1743) 144: *Laudo, C. Mari, quod impudicos Miles non sustinuit occursus, quod se foedari non passus est; at quis ferre possit amplexus gladio divelli? Hoccine restabat unum castitati refugium; neque satis erat neganti conscientiae repulisse corruptorem? Quicumque sane severa facie, & graviori execrationum, minarum impetu conatibus occurrit obscoenis, praestat ne velit iterum tentator impudicus accedere. Frangitur enim statim libido, cui non redditur blanditiarum aequalitas, & in formidines, pudoremque subito labitur foeda conscientia. Nullo melius vincitur genus hoc turpium, quam si renuas luctari, contendere, si minus praestes, quo possis vincere.*
80 Patarol (1743) 147: *Profer fortitudinis, & constantiae tuae testes; interrogatum te probes de stupro necesse est. Malo igitur fugias; postulo ut tentatum pectus per Legiones, per Castra circum feras; ut violentum palam accuses; ut omnium oculis impudicum objicias. Memento, nulli minus in tua causa credi potest, quam tibi. Confuge ad Marium; facinus Nepotis enuncia. Sic demum tuere te, sic te vindica, ut innocentiam praestes, ut tentatum te vere probes, ut, si fieri possit, ab ipsius etiam obscoeni voce accipiamus sceleris confessionem. Tu scilicet interpellantem de stupro occidisse te dicis; tu Tribunum accusas, postquam ipse omnia cum vita causae suae perdidit patrocinia.*

peut ressentir à quel point, comme le dit si bien J.-R. Ladmiral, 'nous ne tra-
duisons pas tant un en-soi du texte original que la lecture que nous en faisons;
et notre traduction se situe toujours en aval de notre compréhension du texte. Ou
encore, pour le dire d'une formule: on ne traduit pas ce qui est écrit, mais ce
qu'on pense qu'a pu penser celui qui a écrit ce qu'il a écrit, quand il l'a écrit – on
ne peut pas être plus clair!'[81].

---

81 Ladmiral (2009) 219–220.

Alfredo Casamento
Colorem timere peius quam sanguinem. Paintings, family strife and heroism

Within the framework of declamatory studies, the *vir fortis* (*brave man*) character plays a pivotal role and can be found in every collection of Roman declamations. One aspect of the themes involving a *vir fortis* that deserves further analysis concerns family relations during wartime, with a particular focus on family conflicts between father and son, or among brothers. In this regard, the oeuvre of Calpurnius Flaccus represents an interesting field of study. Through an analysis of Calpurnius' *excerpta*, I will outline the process through which *argumenta* are built, and I shall also highlight the originality of Calpurnius' work. Moreover, I will focus on *excerptum* 21 in particular, where the dispute between two brothers for a reward due to the *vir fortis* takes an unexpected turn because of the presence of a declamatory law that allows painting the deeds (*facta*) of a hero. I will also analyse *excerpta* 32 and 36, which showcase the themes of desertion and cowardice in a novel way.

When reading your way through the corpus of Roman declamations, it is quite common to come across a quotation such as the following: "If you had ordered me to go across the sea, I would have led the ship through the storm; if you had asked me to travel, nothing would have appeared to me as hard, if only you had ordered me to. But now you command me to do something which is too difficult for a *vir fortis:* to be defeated."[1]

The character who utters these words is a son who has had the privilege of sharing the battlefield with his father. In the course of battle, father and son fought against a common enemy. They were, however, involved in a fight on two different levels. Besides the warfare fought against an actual enemy, another duel was taking place: father and son were involved in a battle to achieve the title of *vir fortis*. In other circumstances and with other participants, this could have been considered as admissible or even desirable. But the fact that the two duellists are father and son adds a further layer of friction.[2]

---

[1] Sen. *Contr.* 10. 2. 13: *Si navigare imperasses, per hibernos fluctus egissem ratem; si peregrinari, nihil fuisset iubente te durum. Hanc rem imperabas difficilem forti viro, vinci.*
[2] Lentano (1998) 56–60 highlights the significance of this theme showcased by ps.-Quint. *Decl. Min.* 258, where a father and his son fight with weapons rather than trial (cf. now Casamento

---

Alfredo Casamento, University of Palermo

https://doi.org/10.1515/9783110401554-006

This passage taken from Seneca's *Controversy* 10. 2 perfectly introduces my chapter on the work of Calpurnius Flaccus. In fact, it shows a tendency particular to all collections of Roman declamations to relate warfare by mapping it closely onto a family environment.[3] This mapping of private life onto public life, sometimes conducted in a paroxysmal way, illustrates how declamation schools attempted to develop new situations and new strategies.[4] Something similar can also be found in the work of Calpurnius Flaccus.[5] For this reason, I shall here focus on three *excerpta* that, despite their differences, show a similar approach to the subject.

The first text that I will discuss is *excerptum* 32. This is the *thema* (28, 19 – 21 H.):

> *Qui filios habebat unum oratorem, alterum militem, reus proditionis factus est. Pendente iudicio miles fortiter fecit. petit praemio abolitionem iudicii. Contradicit frater orator.*

> A man who had two sons, one an orator, the other a soldier, was accused of treason. While his trial was pending, the soldier fought heroically. He seeks as his reward the cancellation of the trial. His brother, the orator, speaks in opposition.[6]

Here the military theme is based upon two particular elements. The first one is clearly expressed and concerns the status of one of the two sons as *miles* (soldier), while the second element, which links to the military, regards the charge of treachery. The *proditio* is common in the *corpus* of Calpurnius: it can be found in several texts, such as *Exc. 7*, where a rich commander gives the order to torture to death the sons of his personal enemy.[7] Another example is

---

[2016]). Furthermore, the case of *Decl. Min.* 317 is remarkable, where a father, who is head of an army, is challenged by his son, who betrayed him changing armies, cf. Brescia (2006).

3 See Lentano (1998) 51–77 and recently (2014) 40: "come forma di giuridicizzazione si possono interpretare le numerose norme che in declamazione afferiscono all'ambito militare." On Seneca *contr.* 10.2 see now Casamento (2016).

4 About the rhetorical trend, practised by the declamation schools, to push the boundaries of human experience in their cases, see Hömke (2007) esp. 123–27, who, paraphrasing a famous quotation by Votienus Montanus (*qui declamationem parat, non scribit ut vincat sed ut placeat*, Sen. *Contr.* 9.*praef*.1), states: "declamation offered an opportunity to continuously recreate new paradox constellations within a constant framework, introduce their protagonists in personal situations at boundaries, and to illuminate them argumentatively, emotionally and psychologically". See also Pianezzola (1981); Berti (2007); Lentano (2009); Bernstein (2013) 3–6.

5 For the text of Calpurnius, Håkanson's (1978) edition undoubtedly is fundamental and preferable to the old text by Lehnert (1903a); for commentary, cf. Sussman (1994), and now Balbo (2016) particularly on Calpurnius' language.

6 Here and throughout the translations of Calpurnius' text are adapted from Sussman (1994).

7 Concerning the importance of torture in the rhetorical tradition, Bernstein (2012) 176 states: "The number of *controversiae* involving torture that appear in each of the extant declamatory

Exc. 15; here, a man who won the title of *vir fortis* three times asks to be exempt-
ed from fighting in the new battle by virtue of a declamatory *lex* (*ter vir fortis militia vacet*[8]), but since this is denied, he decides to desert. His commander, mind-
ful of the previous accomplishments of the soldier, calls for the impunity of the
desertion, justifying his request with the title of *vir fortis* that the soldier had
gained in the past. In this particular case then, as indicated by the internal struggle of the hero who has become a deserter we are dealing with a *disertio*, rather
than with a *proditio*.[9] The hero's internal struggle consists in the opposition between the heroism of the hero's juvenile years and the prospect of having to
spend old age in infamy in case he lives on after having accepted the reward
(*cur enim dubitem per infamiam senex emori qui etiam iuvenis optavi saepe per
gloriam?*). *Exc.* 15 suggests that the soldier could use his past victories as atone-
ment for the crime he has committed, but also concedes that he might refuse for
fear of losing his status of *vir fortis*.

Through the juxtaposition of these two declamations we can observe the
presence of traditional themes in *Exc.* 32, such as the amalgamation of treachery
and desertion, and a discourse on guilt and reward. Moreover, the originality of
the new situation lies precisely within the latter discourse. In addition, *Exc.* 32
also showcases solidarity within a family. Two sons try to help their father
who has been charged with treason. In this simple framework, based upon the
elementary duty of a son to support his father whenever he faces a harsh situation,[10] we also find an important change; although the two sons share the same
aim of saving their father, they pursue their goal in two different ways. While one
son wants to save his father through a regular trial, the other son, referring to his
own military successes, tries to save his father by calling for the *abolitio iudicii*.[11]

---

collections suggests that developing the capacity to rhetoricise torture may have been a pedagogical priority". Cf. also Danesi Marioni (2011–12); Bernstein (2013).

8 The law is also present in Sen. *contr.* 1.8: cf. Bonner (1949) 88–89. The Greek concept, the τρι-
σαριστεύς, is also present in Hermogenes' exercises.

9 The *disertio*, by the way, belongs to the *proditio* cases: see Bonner (1949) 109–111.

10 We must stress that the topic is a recurrent one in Latin culture and that solidarity among male
descendants, and fathers and sons in particular, is fundamental and occurs with some frequency in
Roman declamation. In Sen. *Contr.* 1.4, for example, a father, unable to punish his adulteress wife
and her lover, because he has no hands, asks his son to do this on his behalf. About the Senecan
controversy see Gunderson (2003), 75–9; Casamento (2004) and (2013). About the relationships between fathers and sons in declamatory culture see Richlin (1997); Bloomer (1997); Lentano (1998),
(2007), (2009) 15–43, 45–79, (2015); Vesley (2003); Fantham (2004); Corbeill (2007).

11 A variation on this topic is provided by Iul. Vict. 17. 12 Giom.-Celent., where two brothers,
both *viri fortes* whose father is charged with betrayal, ask for different rewards: one asks for
the trial to be cancelled, the other asks for the trial to take place (*vir fortis praemium accipiat:*

Furthermore, this particular narrative setting contains many traits from the wider literary tradition.[12] Michael Winterbottom has examined this aspect in depth with reference to *Decl. Min.* 268, in which an orator, a doctor and a philosopher compete for the inheritance that their father left to the one who, among them, had offered the best service to their community.[13]

Coming back to the analysis of *excerptum* 32, we find the orator strongly supporting the necessity of a trial in his speech as the only means to save the father (28.22–29.8 H.):

> *Quemadmodum vixerit pater, apparet in liberis. Publicae utilitatis est omnium reorum iudicari causas, ne aut nocens evadat poenam aut innocens patiatur infamiam. Gloria quantum nobis honoris attulerit, tantum virtutis exposcit. Innocentiam patris dum liberare quaeris, infamas. Homini verecundo in eiusmodi crimine longe gravior est fama quam poena. Vetus, iudices, dictum est, ut aurum igni, itidem innocentiam iudicio spectari solere. Melius est patri virtutum tuarum argumento te prodesse quam praemio.*

> It is obvious from my father's children how he concluded his life. It is conducive to the public interest for the cases of all defendants to go to trial so that neither does any guilty party escape punishment nor does an innocent one suffer infamy. His glory will confer as much respect on us as it demands of our steadfastness. While you are seeking to have the charges dropped, you are smearing our father's innocence with suspicion. For a man with any self-respect, in a charge of this sort his reputation weighs more in the balance than any punishment. There's an old saying, gentlemen, that just as gold is customarily tested by fire, so is a man's innocence by a trial. It is more fitting for you to help father by a proof of your merits than by the reward.

The most prominent aspect of this speech is the unity of its thought: from beginning to end, the most suitable way to preserve the honour both of the father and his offspring is juridical. Therefore, if we follow the interpretation of the case that the orator has chosen, the trial is also a matter of family honour. This read-

---

fratres, qui patrem habebant proditionis reum, fortiter fecerunt: petunt alter ut aboleatur iudicium, alter ut agatur, "a brave man shall receive a reward; brothers, who had a father accused of treason, fought heroically; one seeks the abolition of the trial, the other asks for the trial").

12 On the cultural background of these themes, based on the comparison between military and civil achievements as practised in the *forum*, see the Cic. *Mur.* (Bianco [2010] in particular). For the presence of this theme in the declamatory *corpus* see also Quint. 2.4.24, where the comparison between situations as *rusticane vita an urbana potior* ("which is preferable, town or country life?" or *iuris periti an militaris viri laus maior* ("which deserves the greatest praise, the lawyer or the soldier?") is considered a suitable thesis for young students.

13 For Winterbottom (1984) 358–9, the comparison between different professions represents a common subject of the declamation schools, and further proof lies in the interest that Quintilian shows in this theme, giving it a prominent outing in 7.1.38, where he mentions a further version of it. Other versions in Fortun. (*RLM* 87, 24 = 1, 10 Calb. Mont.; 97, 7 = 1, 22 Calb. Mont.) and Walz 8.412, 21.

ing is supported by a metaphor which says that "as the quality of gold is tested with fire, the innocence of the accused is proved through the trial". This metaphor, which finds its origins in the biblical tradition,[14] is often used in Latin as a means to express the ability to recognise true friendship. Used in this way, this expression can be found in three times in Cicero and Ovid.[15] On the other hand, in the *Octavius* of Minucius (36, 9: *usque ad extremam mortem voluntatem hominis sciscitatur, nihil sibi posse perire securus. itaque ut aurum ignibus, sic nos discriminibus arguimur.* "Even to death at last, he investigates the will of man, certain that to him nothing can perish. Therefore, as gold by the fires, so are we declared by critical moments"), the fire becomes a metaphor of the harsh difficulties that man has to face and that allow him to discover gold, in other words: his own strength. This passage probably refers to Seneca's *de providentia* (*ignis aurum probat, miseria fortes viros*, Prov. 5. 10 "fire tests gold, misfortune brave men")[16], which conveys the idea that a *vir bonus* who went through several challenges deserves redemption. It seems, however, that Calpurnius uses the image in a new way here, since he connects the fire with the trial as a means to discover the *aurum* – meaning the innocence of the hero.[17]

Resultingly, the speech of the orator gives great importance to the trial as the only means to prove his father's innocence, insisting that the defensive strategy suggested by his brotherwould be completely ineffective. In his views, using his

---

14 Detailed lists can be found in Otto (1890) 170 s.v. *ignis* 2 and in Tosi (1991) 817; nevertheless, our quotation from Calpurnius is lacking. See Balbo's article in this book.

15 *Red. in Sen.* 23: alio *transferenda mea tota vita est, ut bene de me meritis referam gratiam, amicitias igni perspectas tuear* ("All my life is to be devoted to a different object: to that of showing my gratitude to those who have deserved well of me; to preserving those friendships which have been tried in the fire"); and *Fam.* 9.16.2: *tametsi non facile diiudicatur amor verus et fictus, nisi aliquod incidit eius modi tempus ut quasi aurum igni sic benevolentia fidelis periculo aliquo perspici possit, cetera sunt signa coomunia* ("for though it is not easy to discriminate between true and false affection, unless some such crisis occurs as may enable the sincerity of a friendship to be tested by some special danger, just as gold is tested by fire, yet there are all the ordinary indications of goodwill"). *Trist.* 1.5.25 – 26: *scilicet ut fulvum spectatur in ignibus aurum, / tempore sic duro est inspicienda fides* ("'Tis clear that as tawny gold is tested in the flames so loyalty must be proved in times of stress").

16 The metaphor of the suffering man became very popular in the Christian tradition: apart from the paragraph of Minucius, see also Aug. *Civ.* 1.8 p. 13, 27 Dombart-Kalb: *nam sicut sub uno igne aurum rutilat, palea fuma... ita una eademque vis irruens bonos probat, purificat, eliquat; malos damnat, vastat, exterminate* ("exposed to the same fire gold grows red but chaff smokes... just so one and the same force assailing the good tries, purifies and purges them clean but condemns, ruins and destroys the wicked"). About the Senecan text cf. Traina (2000) 18 – 9 and Lanzarone (2008) 370.

17 On paremiography in Calpurnius, and this passage in particular, see Balbo in this volume.

reward to save their father would not solve anything, because bad reputation could follow the final verdict.[18] In this case, the *praemium* is not perceived as something that may lead towards a solution, but conversely as the wrong way to achieve the status of innocence. The pivotal aspect in the interpretation offered by the orator is how the guilt or innocence of the father affect his sons' lives. It seems to me that this aspect may clarify the ambiguity of the expression *gloria quantum nobis honoris attulerit, tantum virtutis exposcit*, which has attracted various interpretations. In fact, on the one hand Sussman translates it as "His glory will confer as much respect on us as it demands of our steadfastness", but on the other, he airs his doubts whether to assign *gloria* to the soldier or to the father in the commentary.[19]

For a correct interpretation of this expression I consider it necessary to refer back to the introductory sentence of the orator's speech: *quemadmodum vixerit pater, apparet in liberis*. Here we find a principle well-established in Latin culture and ideology, the expectation to find stable patterns of behaviour among members of the same paternal line. According to this idea, the honour gained by one of the male members of the family through his heroism is passed to his descendants, unless they degenerate. Accordingly, as described in the well-known eulogy of Gnaeus Cornelius Hispanus, a son will always be able to boast that he has followed the paternal path if he performs similar heroic actions and adopts the same behaviour.[20] From this perspective, we understand why the orator, in the initial part of his speech, creates a strong link between his and his brother's successes, and their father's *facta* (deeds). In accordance with this statement, I believe

---

18 See Dinter (2016) on the workings of *Fama* in Roman Declamation.

19 Sussman (1994) 192: "Whose *gloria* is it? [...] if it refers to the father, accused of treason, it would either be ironical, or refer to his being declared innocent in a trial, and also his pride in his sons' display of virtue in defending him". Aizpurua (2005) assigns *gloria* to the other son: "Autant la gloire de mon frère nous a apporté d'honneur, autant elle exige de lui de courage", but the explanation he gives is not convincing: "La gloire doit être celle du soldat, qui rejaillit sur toute sa famille, mais qui lui impose aussi, à lui-même, d'avoir le courage d'assister au procès de son père, au lieu d'utiliser à contretemps le privilège des héros et d'interrompre prématurément un procès destiné en toute certitude à faire éclater l'innocence de l'accusé" (233).

20 Cf. the *elogium* of Gnaeus Cornelius Scipio Hispanus (CIL I² 15= ILS 6) in which the dead person shows that he has enlarged the *virtutes* of his *genus* through his *mores* by fathering children and following his father's deeds (*Virtutes generis mieis moribus accumulavi/progeniem genui, facta patris petiei./Maiorum optenui laudem, ut sibei me esse creatum/laetentur: stirpem nobilitavit honor,* "by my good conduct I heaped virtues on the virtues of my clan; I begat a family and sought to equal the exploits of my father. I upheld the praise of my ancestors, so that they are glad that I was created of their line; my honours have ennobled my stock"). On this text, cf. Till (1970); Courtney (1995) 228–29; Massaro (1997); Lentano (1998) 71–2; Hölkeskamp (2004) 187; McDonnell (2006) 384–86.

that the quotation *gloria quantum nobis honoris attulerit, tantum virtutis exposcit* can be interpreted neither as an ironic expression nor as a proverb. Here, the term *gloria* refers to the *pater,* and its sense should be understood in the following way: "His glory provided us with much honour; our virtue is what glory requires now."

This statement mirrors the words of the orator at the beginning of his speech: if the distinction of paternal *virtus* appears in the social prestige and the accomplishments of the sons, it is now up to the sons to reply with just as much *virtus.* This is what the orator reaffirms to his brother, who acted bravely during the war, stating at the end of the *excerptum* that *melius est patri virtutum tuarum argumento te prodesse quam praemio* ("It is more fitting for you to help father by a proof of your merits than by the reward"), and underlining that it is far better to help their father through heroic and honourable behaviour than to employ the reward to ask for the acquittal. As in *excerptum* 15, the reward becomes less important, since it might be used to obtain an acquittal for their father, but would not erase their father's shame and bad name. Both texts refer to this shame in a telling way:

> *Exc. 32: Innocentiam patris dum liberare quaeris, infamas. Homini verecundo in eiusmodi crimine longe gravior est fama quam poena* (29. 3–6 H.)
>
> While you are seeking to have the charges dropped, you are smearing our father's innocence with suspicion.
>
> *Exc. 15: Cur enim dubitem per infamiam senex emori qui etiam iuvenis optavi saepe per gloriam?* (16. 6–7 H.)
>
> For why should I hesitate to die as an old man during the period of my disgrace, I, who even as a young man often desired to die during my period of glory?

In both cases, the *praemium* and the shame would be at the same level. However, in our *excerptum* the situation is worse, because it would be the son who, using the reward to acquit his father, might bring shame on him.

We now move on to the second *excerptum* under consideration, *Exc.* 36. It shares some traits with the previous text: the military setting, where a father and his son represent the main actors, a new case of desertion, and the use of the reward. The subject suggests turning to the *status* known as *leges contrariae* since it deals with two *leges* upon which the discussion is based:[21] *desertor duci*

---

[21] This case, also known as *leges contrariae,* belongs to the so-called *status legales.* This *excerptum* takes into consideration *cum inter se duae videntur leges aut plures discrepare* (Cic. *Inv.* 2. 144, "when two or more laws seem to disagree"). This format is very old and dates back to Aristoteles (*Rhet.* 1375b8) who, however, did not give a specific name. Cf. Calboli Montefusco (1986) 166–78.

serviat ("a desertor shall become his commander's slave") and *viro forti praemium* ("a brave man shall receive a reward"). While the latter is well known in the rhetorical tradition, the former is not found in any other declamation. It seems to represent a variation of the capital punishment that was usually inflicted on deserters.[22] In this regard, it could be useful to analyse *Exc.* 27. Here, too, there are two men who, following two different strategies, intend to use the *praemium*. The dichotomy of these two *excerpta* appears to be simple, characterised by two main actors and two similar situations: on the one hand the heroic behaviour and the reward that comes with it, and on the other hand desertion and punishment.

However, the two *excerpta* also show some significant differences. In *Exc.* 27 the poor man, who has fought bravely, asks for using the prize, obtained for his heroism, to save the rich deserter. But in this case, the *praemium* is used as a kind of punishment, since the rich man shall be forced to keep living with the burden of his shame (26. 3–9 H.):

> *Sero coepit hic miles, iudices, mortem contemnere. Ego tacui cum peterer, hic vivere iubetur et queritur. Expectavi diu divitem, ut ille potius quod promisit, impleret. Ab ipso quoque divite inire debeo maximam gratiam: quod ille debebat, ego solvi. Idem in praemio facio quod in proelio: servo civem, commilitonem meum protego. Idem eris in aevum, qui semper adhuc fueris.*

> Gentlemen, it was too late for this soldier to start despising death. As for me, I kept silent when his assault was being directed against me; this man is being commanded to live and yet he complains about it. I waited too long a time for the rich man to fulfil his promise instead of me. I also ought to win special gratitude from the rich man himself: yes, I fulfilled that man's obligation. I am doing the same thing in the matter of the reward that I did in the war: I am saving the life of a fellow citizen, I am protecting my fellow soldier. You will forever be the same kind of person, you who have always been so up to now.

In this case, the act of rescuing a fellow citizen from capital punishment, rather than being a noble duty that all *cives* should fulfill (*idem in praemio facio quod in proelio: servo civem, commilitonem meum protego*), becomes a means to condemn the deserter to a punishment worse than death, namely a life marked by shame.

Contrary to *Exc.* 27, *Exc.* 36 features a third character, whose presence is of particular importance for our analysis (30. 21–31. 8 H.):

---

22 Cfr. Lanfranchi (1938) 430–31: "come potrebbe spiegarsi questo asservimento del disertore al *dux*? Si può pensare ad una sua responsabilità diretta verso il supremo responsabile della disciplina militare in tempo di guerra? [...] Molto più semplice pensare ad una *servitus poenae*: il disertore cioè sarebbe asservito al *dux*, che ha pronunciato in base ai suoi poteri la sentenza di morte, fino al momento dell'esecuzione".

DESERTOR DUCI SERVIAT. VIRO FORTI PRAEMIUM.

Pauper et dives inimici. Dives creatus est imperator. Pauper sub illo cum filio specioso adulescente militavit. Pauper fortiter fecit, adulescens deseruit. Dives iure erit, pater praemio petit, ut occidatur. Filium meum si liberare non licet, saltem liceat occidere. Creditis, iudices, quod filio meo bene inimicus velit, pater nolit? Profiteor mortem me filii mei non quidem velle, sed malle. Vos cogitate, quanto sint mala illa graviora, quorum sunt etiam remedia crudelia. O fili, morere constanter! Fac hoc saltem quasi meus filius.

(1) A deserter shall become his commander's slave. (2) A war hero shall receive a reward. A poor man and a rich were enemies. The rich man was appointed commander of the army. The poor man served as a soldier under his command along with his handsome young son. The poor man fought heroically, but the young man deserted. The rich man institutes a proceeding according to the law, while the father seeks as his reward that his son be executed.   (Speech of the father)

If I may not free my son, please at least allow his execution. Gentlemen of the jury, do you suppose that my enemy wishes my son well, but that his father doesn't? I hereby declare that I certainly do not desire my son's death, but I do prefer it. Imagine, yes you, how much more serious those misfortunes are whose remedies are likewise so savage. Oh my son, die resolutely! Do this at least as though you are my son!

Two elements explain the peculiarity of *Exc.* 36: the first refers to the different attitudes and personalities of a father and his son. While the former is brave and honourable, the latter is a coward and acts as a deserter: *pauper fortiter fecit, adulescens deseruit.*[23] The declamatory law according to which a deserter must become the slave of his commander provides a second element of originality. In the case under discussion, the beauty of the son links to the theme of *miles Marianus*, which implies sexual subjugation of a soldier by another *miles* of higher rank.[24] Here, this particular theme is probably less evident in comparison to other texts such as Calp. 39 or 45, in which a *tyrannus* threatens to attack a city if its citizens refuse to give him a young man; but the use of the term *speciosus* to identify the young man in *Exc.* 45[25] seems to confirm my interpretation of *Exc.* 36.

---

23 This is a common theme among the surviving declamations, as in *Decl. Min.* 315 where a father, who holds the title of *vir fortis*, refuses to kill his son for being a deserter.

24 On homosexuality in Calpurnius, see 3.3.45. The theme of *Miles Marianus* is very common in the declamation schools (cf. Gunderson [2003] 153–90; Schneider 2003 and in this book).

25 *INDEMNATOS LIBEROS LICEAT OCCIDERE. Tyrannus finitimae civitatis sub minis belli adulescentem speciosum postulavit. Civitas decrevit. Pater illum lege indemnatorum peremit. reus est laesae rei publicae* ("One may execute children without a trial. The tyrant of a neighbouring state, subject to the risk of war, demanded a handsome young man. The state consented. His father executed him in accordance with the law concerning those who can be condemned without a trial. He is then accused of harming the state"). Here "the subject of homosexuality is again

Nevertheless, an element that plays a pivotal role in the narrative development of the text is the fact that the father himself asks, as a reward, that his son be killed. It is an unusual situation, and only in *Decl. Min.* 304 can a similar case be found, where a *vir fortis* asks to be granted as reward to be allowed to kill his son for his faults. This very son had already been rescued three times by a *sacerdos* through the use of his own prizes.[26]

Although the request may be unusual, it should be understood within the privileges that ancient Roman law granted a father over his son. These privileges can be linked to the concept of *patria potestas,* which implied the *vitae necisque potestas* (power over life and death).[27] It is interesting to note that, although this right was hardly ever used,[28] it was well established in Roman imaginary culture. In fact, it is often used in declamation schools,[29] and in Calpurnius it is also identified with the *lex indemnatorum* (Calp. *Exc.* 24, 44, 45, 46, 53).[30] In the case under scrutiny, the father's request should be understood as an attempt to rescue the young man from the sexual attention of the *dux* and, above all, as a means to reaffirm his *patria potestas.* Therefore, killing his own son represents, in fact, the only way to save him from slavery and keep him under his own *patria potestas.* In this regard, the Latin expression (31. 7–8 H.)

> *O fili, morere constanter! Fac hoc saltem quasi meus filius!*
>
> Oh my son, die resolutely! Do this at least as though you are my son!

underlines that one way of confirming to be part of one's *genus* (*meus filius*) was through an honourable death.

---

very delicately handled" (Sussman (1994) 219). On *speciosus* in Latin and especially in declamatory literature see Pasetti (2013).

26 *Tria praemia divitis sacerdotis. Sacerdos tria praemia accipiat. Viro forti praemium. Dives sacerdos inimici panperis filium sacrilegum uno praemio liberavit* ("Three rewards of a rich priest. Let a priest receive three rewards. Let there be a reward for a hero. A rich priest with one reward freed the son of a poor man, his enemy, who had committed sacrilege"). See Winterbottom (1984) 434–35.

27 About this topic cf. Breij (2006); but cf. also Sussman (1995); Vesley (2003); Lentano (2015).

28 Breij (2006) 3 notes that "research into the *vitae necisque potestas* is hampered by the fact that throughout Roman history there are but very few cases known in which fathers actually made use of this right".

29 Breij (2006) 1 identifies "twenty-two extant Roman declamations in which fathers have killed, or wish to kill, their sons".

30 The *lex indemnatorum* refers to a father's power of life and death over his children under the terms of *patria potestas:* Sussman (1994) 168. See also Lanfranchi (1938) 251–54. According to Lentano (2014) 65 this is the only case in the entire *corpus* of declamations in which we can find a law that "'giuridicizza' la possibilità per un padre romano di mettere a morte i propri figli".

There is a final aspect that deserves to be mentioned; it concerns the particular role the reward plays in this context. In fact, as it happens in *Exc.* 36 as well as in *Decl. Min.* 304, the father, rather than using the *ius vitae necisque* to legitimise the right to kill his son, evokes his reward. In this regard, the appropriation of the prize in place of applying the *ius vitae necisque* to claim rights over a son challenges the legitimacy of this ancient legal and social institution. On the other hand, there are no doubts about the details of the son's crime and about its punishment: in fact, treachery cases had customarily been punished by death since the times of the Twelve Tables.[31]

Furthermore, challenging paternal *officia* represents a common topic in Calpurnius' work, as for example in *Exc.* 24, where a father, after having asked and obtained the death sentence for his son on the base of the *lex indemnatorum*, hesitates to execute the punishment personally (22. 22–23. 2 H.):

> *Lege indemnatorum interficiendum pater filium carnifici tradidit. Ille vult manu patris interfici. pater ipse, qui fuerat offensus, ultro se non posse facere quod coeperat, confitetur.*

> A father handed over his son to be killed, in accordance with the law concerning those condemned without a trial, to a professional executioner. The son wants to be killed by his father's hand. The father, for his part, who had been met with ill-success in this, freely admits that he is unable to finish what he had begun.

However, in this text, the son does not object to the paternal privileges. On the contrary, he demands that his own father be the executor of the punishment, while the son wants to be killed from his father's hands[32] (23. 15–17 H.):

> *Nemo umquam magistratum fecit vicarium nec in alio militavit nec sacra gentilicia insitiva stirpe corrupit. Vita mihi tollitur, sed manus paterna debet<ur>.*

> Nobody ever acted as a substitute magistrate or performed military service in another person's name or tampered with a family's sanctity of inheritance through grafted on stock. Life is taken from me, but my father's hand is owed to me.

We discuss now the last text, *Exc.* 21 (19. 21–20. 1 H.):

> *VIRORUM FORTIUM FACTA PINGANTUR. VIRI FORTES DE PRAEMIO ARMIS CONTENDANT. Fratres fortiter fecerunt. pater a minori petit, ut maiori cederet. non impetravit. proelio interfecit maiorem minor. petit praemio, ne facta pingantur. pater contradicit.*

---

31 Marcian. *Digest.* 48.4.3: *Lex XII Tabularum iubet eum qui hostem concitaverit, quive civem hostem tradiderit capite puniri.* ("The Law of the Twelve Tables directs that anyone who stirs up an enemy, or who delivers a citizen to him, shall be punished capitally"). Cf. Bonner (1949) 109–10.
32 About the topic of the hands see Citti-Pasetti 2015.

(1) The brave deeds of heroes shall be painted in pictures. (2) Heroes shall contend in combat over a reward. [Two] brothers fought heroically. Their father requests that the younger give way to the elder. His request was unsuccessful. The younger son killed the elder in the combat. He seeks as his reward that his exploits not be painted. The father objects.

As with the previous *excerpta*, *Exc.* 21 deals with two different laws, the second of which appears more frequently in other declamations, as for example in *Decl. Min.* 258; the first one, on the other hand, is found in no other text,[33] although a similar idea is used in Seneca's *Controversy* 10. 2.[34]

In this *excerptum*, there are two main elements: two brothers who fight to gain a reward, causing the death of one of them, and the fact that the brother who obtains the prize uses it to prevent his heroic *facta* from being depicted.

We possess only a small part of this text, in which the father commands his son to allow the depiction of his deeds. As in the previously mentioned texts, here too the main subjects are warfare, heroism and family strife; but in comparison to Seneca's *Contr.* 10. 2, Calpurnius' *excerptum* seems to attenuate the conflict. In fact, in the Senecan controversy as well as in *Decl. Min.* 258, the conflict between father and son could be defined as generational: while the son fights to assert his superiority, the father aims at reaffirming his paternal privileges. This fight symbolises the social concern of a generation – the fathers' generation – who fears a premature change of the family leadership.[35] This concern can be clearly grasped from the following passages (Sen. *Contr.* 10. 2):

---

33 Cf. Lanfranchi (1938) 389. But see *Decl. Min.* 282, where a man who killed a tyrant in women's clothes, accused the magistrate of injuries who had put up a statue representing him dressed in those very same clothes. (*Tyrannicidae praemium. Tyrannus cum in arcem duci iussisset cuiusdam sororem, frater habitu sororis ascendit et occidit tyrannum. Eodem habitu magistratus illi praemii nomine statuam collocavit. Iniuriarum reus est:* "Let there be a reward for a tyrannicide. When a tyrant ordered that somebody's sister be brought to the castle, the brother went up in his sister's clothes and killed the tyrant. By way of reward the magistrate put up a statue to him dressed in the same clothes. He is accused of injuries". On this text, cf. Winterbottom (1984) 396, according to whom "the speech gives hardly more than hints towards possible colours in an extravagantly unreal case". A variation on the same topic is given by declamation 11 of Choricius of Gaza (about whom cf. Penella [2009] 222), dealing with a war hero who defeated his enemies by putting on female clothes and asked that he not be represented as he had been at that moment.

34 In this case, however, a son, fighting with his father to gain the title of *vir fortis*, makes a promise to build a statue to honour his father if he gets the reward.

35 On the other hand, according to Lentano (2009) 49 "la declamazione sarà tanto più pedagogicamente efficace quanto più le istanze che si confrontano appaiano entrambe dotate di una forte legittimità culturale".

Vidi patrem iam senem loricam induentem: multum est pugnare cum exemplo [...]. Ego vici, sed omnes patri gratulati sunt. (Contr. 10. 2. 2)

I saw my father, now an old man, putting on a breastplate; it is a great thing to fight with an example at one's side [...]. I won – but everyone congratulated my father.

Quis te felicior? tu omnes vicisti, te filius... avidus sum gloriae: hoc si vitium est, paternum est. (Contr. 10. 2. 5)

Who is luckier than you? You have overcome all – and your son has overcome you. I am greedy for glory; if that is a vice, it is one I have inherited from my father.

Novi generis res accidit: filius vicerat; omnes aiebant: o felicem patrem! (Contr. 10. 2. 10)

Hence a novelty: the son had won, but everyone said: Lucky father.

Vici te, pater, sed nempe vici tibi. (Contr. 10. 2. 14)

I defeated you, father – but in fact it was for you that I won.

In this regard, the following quotation, mentioned by the Greek rhetor Nicetes, is particularly interesting. The passage is taken from Homer *Od.* 24.514–515, where Laertes declares his happiness for having the privilege to witness the bravery of his son and his grandson, fighting together against a common enemy (*Contr.* 10. 2. 18):[36]

τίς νύ μοι ἡμέρη ἥδε, θεοὶ φίλοι. ἦ μάλα χαίρω
<υἱός θ' υἱω>νός τ' ἀρετῆς πέρι δῆριν ἔχουσιν;

What a day is this for me, dear gods! I rejoice indeed
My son and grandson quarrel over bravery.

In *Decl. Min.* 258, however, we find on the one hand the reassertion of the virtues of the son, caused by paternal "imprinting", and on the other the fear that the son could kill the father in order to inherit all paternal property:

Animus iste ad contemnenda pericula paratus ex meo fluxit (1).

This courage ready to despise danger flowed from mine.[37]

Hoc tibi praemio maius videbatur, committi cum patre et parricidium facere iure (6).

It meant more to you than the reward to duel with your father and commit parricide under the law.

---

36 According to Guérin (2010), "le projet auquel répondent les *Controuersiae* fait de la citation le fondement même du discours mémoriel, didactique et critique que tient Sénèque le rhéteur". On quotations from Greek orators in Seneca the Elder, see Citti (2007).

37 Translation by Shackleton Bailey (2006).

Discede de domo mea. Non iam ultionis gratia facio, sed etiam securitatis: insomnes noctes ago et ad omnes terreor strepitus (8).

Leave my house. I am not doing it just for revenge now, but also for security. My nights are sleepless and I am afraid at every sound.

Therefore, if we want to compare the three texts we have just analysed, the *excerptum* of Calpurnius appears to be the least dramatic among them. Here, the main actors of the conflict are not a father and his son: they are two brothers. Accordingly, the reward and, above all, its social and symbolic implications become ever more prominent. In fact, while the son looks at the prize as a means of deleting the memory of a heroic but sad exploit, the father, on the contrary, conceives the reward as the only way to do justice to a son killed by his brother. In this case, by denying permission to depict his deeds, the son deprives his brother of the possibility of being remembered – this would make him a criminal. However, an important role is also held by the father, since he openly claims that the heroic *facta* of his two sons should not only be depicted, but also represented in bronze or carved in stone (§ 10):

Simuletur hoc factum non tantum colore, sed aere, si possit, et lapide et quaecumque nostrorum corporum materia vel ars aemula est.

Let this deed be represented not just in paint, but in bronze, if possible, also in stone, and in whatever medium artistic skill also rivals our actual flesh.

The character of the *pater* is once more fundamental because he participates in the conflict between his sons and so keeps his important leading role. I would like to illuminate this concept through another text, *Exc.* 48, which deals with a man who gives his wife to his brother, sick of love, at the suggestion of his father. But the generous brother keeps seeing his ex-wife in secret, and is killed by his love-sick brother.[38] In these circumstances the father uses *abdicatio* to condemn the guilty son; but in our controversy, on the contrary, the father asks for the full fulfilment of the reward. For having the entire event depicted is the only solution for the father to avenge his dead son.

In conclusion, I think it is possible to highlight how in a survey on the mechanism of constructing the declamatory arguments a significant place is occupied

---

38 This is one of the various versions of the tale of Antiochus and Stratonice in declamatory culture (see Sen. *Exc.* 6.7 and *Decl. Min.* 291, about which cf. Winterbottom (1984) 408–09). The topic is widely discussed by Brescia-Lentano (2009) 13–48. On the law concerning the death penalty for adulterers caught in the act, see Sussman (1994) 226. On the *lex Iulia de adulteriis coercendis* and, in general, on adultery in Rome, see Rizzelli (1997) and now Lentano (2016).

by those themes in which the contexts of war provide further points of view and further focus on the theme *par excellence* of declamatory literature, the relationships between father and son. The three *excerpta* of Calpurnius' collection taken into consideration (*exc.* 21, 32, 36) are, in this respect, a testimony of particular importance as they allow us to observe how the war background with its topical elements (heroism, prize, rivalry as well as desertion or betrayal) generates an interesting tension in the parent-son relationship, particularly suited to the fantasy of declamators.

Andrea Balbo*
Problems of Paremiography in Calpurnius Flaccus

1 Proverbs and *sententiae*

In Classics, paremiography is a complex and difficult research subject. Since Otto's edition of *Die Sprichwörter und sprichwörtlichen Redensarten der Römer*, scholars have tried to collect proverbs in order to understand the role of this folkloric element in literature and, most of all, in genres such as satire and epistolography. As Otto's title shows, one of the main difficulties consists in understanding the precise nature of the proverb and in constructing a theoretical grid that separates proverbs from other similar texts which, for various reasons, cannot be classified in the same way. Despite progress in scholarship, a precise definition is yet to be found.[1] In 1949, Otto and Rupprecht made a clear distinction between a proverb in its strict sense (*Sprichwort*) and a paremiographic expression (*sprichwörtliche Redensart*), defined respectively as a brief, coherent and clear sentence connected with folk wisdom, and a longer sentence, less concise, involving words and ideas related to the meaning of a proverb. Other scholars have studied the relationship between proverbs and their contexts, and have underlined the low level of authorship that is usually typical of paremiographic material.[2] Yet others, such as Nosarti (2010), have tried to analyse content and form alongside each other, and to link proverbs with other Latin writings characterised by their brevity: Nosarti thus classified proverbs among the "very short forms" of Latin literature.[3]

It is equally difficult to draw a firm conceptual boundary between proverb and *sententia*: the research of Biville (1999), Hallik (2007) and Tosi (2009) have allowed the study of this topic to move forward, but scholars have yet to agree on a universally accepted definition. All the studies quoted above have highlighted, albeit from different perspectives, how close these two forms of expression are, and how difficult it is to introduce a strict division between them.

---

* I wish to thank Biagio Santorelli for his helpful advice on several occasions.
1 Cf. Tosi (1991; 1995 and 2009), Biville (1999), Lelli (2006), Hallik (2007).
2 Tosi (2009) 13–14.
3 Nosarti (2010) 38–40.

Andrea Balbo, Università degli Studi di Torino

https://doi.org/10.1515/9783110401554-007

This as well had already been underlined by ancient sources, especially from Late Antiquity; as the two following examples will show:[4]

> Donatus, Comm. Andr. 426 – 427: *VERUM ILLUD VERBUM EST VOLGO QUOD DICI SOLET, OMNIS SIBI MALLE MELIUS ESSE QUAM ALTERI. Id est proverbium et sententia. Et sic veteres verbum pro sententia.*[5]

> Macrobius, Sat. 5.16.6 – 7: *Homerus omnem poesin suam ita sententiis farsit ut singula eius* ἀποφθέγματα *vice proverbiorum in omnium ore fungantur* [...] *et alia innumerabilia quae sententialiter proferuntur.*[6]

This close connection, already found in the ancient tradition, clearly shows that we must avoid any abstract classification that would map modern mindsets onto ancient phenomena. Moreover, the features of every literary genre call for a distinct analysis, as the relationship between *sententia* and proverb strongly de-

---

4 Apart from the passages quoted here – which I think represent material enshrined in ancient thought –, this proximity appears, for instance, in Cic. *De Or.* 2.258 and Quint. *Inst.* 5.11.41; 6.3.98; 8.6.55 – 58. The passages give us important statements, even if they are not original assertions but owe a lot to the Peripatetic and Stoic traditions. In particular, in the *excursus de ridiculis* in *De Or.*, Julius Caesar Strabo underlines the comic function that proverbs can sometimes assume; see Cic. *De Or.* 2.258: *Atque haec omnia verbo continentur.* [...] *In hoc genus coniciuntur etiam proverbia, ut illud Scipionis, cum Asellus omnis se provincias stipendia merentem peragrasse gloriaretur: "agas asellum" et cetera; qua re ea quoque, quoniam mutatis verbis non possunt retinere eandem venustatem, non in re, sed in verbis posita ducantur.* "Now all such jests hinge upon a word [...]. Old sayings fall into this category, that for instance is applied by Scipio, when Asellus was bragging that his military service had taken him all over every province; whereupon Scipio quoted 'You may drive the ass's colt,' and the rest of it [see Hor. *Sat.* 1.1.90 – 91]. It follows moreover that such jests, since they must lose their charm when the terms of expression are varied, should be regarded as depending on language, not on facts." (Tr. E. Warmington). Quint. *Inst.* 5.11.41: *Ea quoque quae vulgo recepta sunt hoc ipso, quod incertum auctorem habent, velut omnium fiunt, quale est: 'ubi amici, ibi opes', et 'conscientia mille testes', et apud Ciceronem: 'pares autem, ut est in vetere proverbio, cum paribus maxime congregantur'; neque enim durassent haec in aeternum nisi vera omnibus viderentur.* "Generally received sayings also become common property owing to the very fact that they are anonymous, as, for instance, "Friends are a treasure," or "Conscience is as good as a thousand witnesses," or, to quote Cicero, "In the words of the old proverb, birds of a feather flock together." Sayings such as these would not have acquired immortality had they not carried conviction of their truth to all mankind." (Tr. H. E. Butler).
5 "That is a true proverb, which is wont to be commonly quoted, that "all had rather it to be well for themselves than for another". This is both a proverb and a sentence. And, in a similar way, ancients used *verbum* instead of *sententia*." (Tr. H. T. Riley with some additions).
6 "Homer stuffed all his verse so full of epigrams that his individual sayings have the status of proverbs and are on everyone's lips." (Tr. R. Kaster). Then he quotes some examples from Homer and Vergil.

pend on the genre of the texts in which they appear. Precisely for this reason, we need to take into account the specific features of the declamatory genre.

2 Proverbs in declamation[7]

We have very little information about the use of proverbs by declaimers. Otto (1890²) identifies thirty proverbial expressions in Seneca, but his findings cannot, in my opinion, be accepted *in toto*, as I tried to show in Balbo (2011): he leaves aside a number of texts that I think should be considered paremiographic, while listing as proverbs other texts that are simple metaphors or idioms. At the same time, he counts only 14 entries in the ps.-Quintilianic corpus and none in Calpurnius Flaccus. In Häussler's additions, declaimers are scarcely present: Seneca the Elder is quoted only on rare occasions[8] and ps.-Quintilian and Calpurnius Flaccus are cited no more than 10 times. In the entries collected by Tosi (1991) the two authors feature also very scarcely.[9] Moreover, if we leave aside these collections and pay attention to secondary literature, we realise the absence of papers on the subject: what I have demonstrated in Balbo (2011) about Seneca the Elder also rings true for Quintilian and Calpurnius Flaccus.[10] The scarcity of this material seems to be caused by several factors. First of all, the nature of the corpus is an obstacle by itself. Declamations consist, in fact, largely of *sententiae* and this is true in particular of the surviving text of the *excerpta* of Seneca the Elder and in Calpurnius Flaccus. Very often these *sententiae* express general concepts, sometimes pseudo-philosophical ones, and are

---

7 I have dealt with the problem of the definition of proverbs and their boundaries in depth in Balbo (2011) and in Balbo (2015): I refer to them for a summary of my views.

8 The authors collected by Häussler (1968) include other proverbial cases: Weyman (1893) 26 (= Häussler (1968) 54) s.v. *certus* quotes Sen. *Suas.* 1.10, *hic dixit incerta peti certa deseri*; Weyman (1893) 29 (= Häussler (1968) 57) s.v. *flumen* cites Sen. *Contr.* 1.5.2 *retro amnes fluant*; Weyman (1904) 258 (= Häussler (1968) 255) has s.v. *homo* ibid. 7.1.9: *haec est condicio miserrima humani generis, quod nascimur uno modo, multis morimur* and *quam facile erramus homines* ibid. 7.1.5; Szelinski (1903–4) 475 (= Häussler (1968) 235) suggests ibid. (exc.) 3.5 *in securem incurris* s. v. *crus*. Nonetheless, I do not treat these texts as paremiographic because they are deeply connected with the content of the controversy.

9 Only the *Institutio Oratoria* is quoted for Quintilian.

10 On Seneca, Bonner (1949) 54–55, Fairweather (1981) and Berti (2007) only touch on the issue briefly. On ps.-Quintilian only Becker (1904) 64–66 is helpful: Di Capua (1946) 75–87 is of no use and Bernstein (2013) does not pay attention to the problem. The only specific works concerning *sententiae* are Delarue (1979) and Breij (2006a), with some additions in Berti (2007) 155–182; van Mal Maeder (2007) does not deal with the topic. Contributions to the problem are absent in Calpurnian studies.

usually brimming with ethical content, mostly without any authorial identification. As a matter of fact, recent monographs about declamation do not distinguish between *sententia* and proverb. See for instance the following statement
of Berti (2007: 164), who writes that *sententia* in Seneca the Elder "indica solo
le massime di carattere proverbiale e moraleggiante, che danno voce a una
norma etica o a una verità generale, e corrispondono alle *gnomai* greche".

The external appearance of *sententiae* with their vivid character, small scale
and highly condensed and conceptualised content poses a further challenge.
These traits make them particularly suitable for reuse in declamations in ever
different contexts and situations. Because of this feature, *sententiae* were called
translaticiae by ancient rhetoricians: they constitute "una sorta di 'corredo' o
'bagaglio' (*supellex*) cui il declamatore può attingere ogni volta che voglia arric-
chire il discorso con un elegante detto sentenzioso".[11] Consequently, every mark
of authorship is erased from the text, and *sententiae* morph into a form of expression that often involves proverbial content. Accordingly, in the declamatory
corpus, *sententiae* and proverbs are strictly connected and sometimes simply express *loci communes* that are the basis of the argumentation, as, for instance, the
locus de fortuna.

Consequently, when researching proverbs, the genre of declamation merits
specific attention; this 'merging' of sententious and proverbial content is showcased by the relatively rare occurrence in the declamatory corpus of the Latin vocabulary used by Biville (1999) for defining proverbs:

---

11 Definition in Sen. *Contr.* 1.*praef.*23. *Solebat autem* [scil. Latro] *et hoc genere exercitationis uti,
ut aliquo die nihil praeter epiphonemata scriberet, <aliquo die> nihil praeter enthymemata, aliquo
die nihil praeter has translaticias quas proprie sententias dicimus, quae nihil habent cum ipsa controversia inplicitum, sed satis apte et alio transferuntur, tamquam quae de fortuna, de crudelitate,
de saeculo, de divitiis dicuntur; hoc genus sententiarum supellectilem vocabat.* "He practiced another sort of exercise: one day he would write only "exclamations", one day only *enthymemes*,
one day nothing but the traditional passages we properly call *sententiae*, that have no intimate
connection with the particular *controversia*, but can be quite aptly placed elsewhere too, such as
those on fortune, cruelty, the age, riches." (Tr. M. Winterbottom).

Words	Seneca the Elder	Ps.-Quintilian	Calpurnius Flaccus
Dictum	Sen. *Contr.* 1.7.14 (*illud Homeri <in> Priamo dictum:* <καὶ κύσε χεῖρας δεινάς, ἀνδροφόνους>), *Contr.* 7.3.8 (*illum de eadem re dictum: desunt luxuriae multa, avaritiae omnia*).[12]	Both in the *Maiores* and in the *Minores* we do not find the words *proverbium* or *dictum*; *verbum* does not appear to define proverbial expressions.	*Decl.* 32 *Vetus, iudices, dictum est, ut aurum igni, itidem innocentiam iudicio spectari solere.*[13]
Proverbium	Sen. *Suas.* 2.13: *quasi proverbii loco*[14]		
Verbum	No occurrence		No occurrence

To this list I would add some other words or expressions:

- *Sensus*: Sen. *Contr.* 1.8.9, in connection with *vetus* (*illum sensum veterem*); *Contr.* 2.6.13 with *vulgaris* (*Barbarus dixit vulgarem sensum satis vulgariter*)[15]
- *Sapientes* (as a source of paremiographic expression): ps.-Quint. *Decl. Mai.* 9. 14 (*voluere sapientes*)
- *Quod aiunt*: Sen. *Contr.* 2.7.7; *Decl. Mai.* 6.14 and 12.11.

A quick lexical search shows that the terminology used by Biville does not cover all possibilities for denoting a proverb. Thus it does not suffice for explaining the presence and the meaning of the proverbs in the *corpus declamatorium*, both because of its incompleteness and of its insensibility to the features of this particular literary genre. Therefore, paremiography in Calpurnius deserves further investigation.

---

12 We can also quote some periphrasis, such as *ut transeam innumerabilia quae Cicero in orationibus aut in sermone dixit ex <ea> nota, ut non referam a Laberio dicta* (*Contr.* 7.3.9: "I may pass over innumerable things said by Cicero in that vein, in both speeches and conversation, and also over sayings of Laberius", tr. M. Winterbottom). We find also *sensus*, but it mainly means "thought" or "idea": cf. OLD s. v. *sensus*, 8–10.

13 "There's an old saying, gentlemen, that just as gold is customarily tested by fire, so is a man's innocence by trial" (tr. L.A. Sussman).

14 As demonstrated in Balbo (2011) 13–14, *Suas.* 2.13 is very important because Seneca speaks about a phrase used *quasi proverbii loco*.

15 On Greek declaimers see Citti (2007); on Barbarus cf. Echavarren (2007) 85.

3 Paremiographic material in Calpurnius

It is impossible to apply the rigorous categories of Biville to Calpurnius or to Seneca the Elder; nonetheless, Calpurnius' text is rich in *sententiae* that share the features of popular character, of moral teaching and of easy memorization and shortness that are very close to those of proverbs. Moreover, the nature of the *excerpta* forces us to pay particular attention to stylistic considerations and to every individual case. Consequently, it seems reasonable to apply to Calpurnius as well the general category of "paremiographic" or "proverbial material" – a term Hallik (2007) suggests, that I have already used for Seneca – in order to avoid the risk of applying too strict a definition that could cause the omission of some data. At the same time for pointing out "proverbial material" I will use the same formal criteria that I have already applied to Seneca the Elder and which have been highlighted by Emanuele Lelli: "la brevità della formulazione, spesso resa più efficace mediante accorgimenti retorici e fonici; la riconosciuta tradizionalità e condivisibilità del contenuto; la funzione didascalica, etica, morale, in altri termini 'di ammaestramento/giudizio' sociale e umano del messaggio".[16] To these let me add some further elements already pointed out by several scholars: a) clear and unambiguous meaning; b) autonomy (mainly in terms of content) from the theme of declamation; c) the possibility of remembering the text easily.[17]

We can thus move on to the analysis of Calpurnian proverbial material. In the table on the following page I list the most important and obvious paremiographic expressions that one can find in the declamations. There is obviously very little paremiographic material dealing with the most common proverbial themes: *amor* (*Decl.* 2 and 33), *fortuna* (*Decl.* 8, 44), man (*Decl.* 8), *voluntas* (*Decl.* 29 and 37). The criteria quoted above help us to avoid the inclusion of an excessive number of expressions; still, some of the texts we retained have a doubtful status. Calpurnius' *excerpta* seem to connect the paremiographic material strictly with the subject of the declamation in which it appears and thus deprive it of its peculiar general meaning. Nonetheless, as deeper analysis will show, these rare examples demonstrate that the declaimer can use this material competently and consciously.

---

16 Lelli (2006) 11.
17 In Calpurnius, there are also *loci communes* that do not create paremiographic phrases, mainly when they are developed in long sentences or are strictly connected with the argument or the characters of the declamation.

Order	Place	Text	Presence in the main repertories
1	*Decl. 2*	*expers iudicii est amor*	Otto (1890²), 99 – 100; Tosi (1991), 1418 (they both omit this occurrence)
2	*Decl. 6*	*plus quam civilia*	
3	*Decl. 8*	*omnium calamitatum materia est homo diu felix*	
4	*Decl. 25*	*interdum praestat ad gloriam non certare quam vincere*	
5 – 6	*Decl. 29* and 37	*velis enim nolis*	Otto (1890²), 1852; Tosi (1991), 891 (they both omit this occurrence)
7	*Decl. 32*	*aurum igni*	Otto (1890²), 843; Tosi (1991), 1325; Weyman (1893), p. 385 (= Häussler (1968) p. 274)
8	*Decl. 33*	*crimen aut error*	
9	*Decl. 44*	*o fortuna crudelis*	Otto (1890²), 705 – 709; Tosi (1991) 838 – 841 (they both omit this occurrence)

3.1 A proverb identified by Calpurnius

In *Decl.* 32, a man who is the father of an orator and a soldier is accused of treason; the soldier, having fought as a hero, asks for the case to be dismissed, but the orator objects to this. The surviving fragment probably comes from the latter's speech: **Vetus**, *iudices*, **dictum** *est, ut* **aurum igni**, *itidem innocentiam iudicio spectari solere.*[18] Otto (1890² n. 843) quotes the proverb, but not Calpurnius as its source. He points out that the idea goes back to Menander and finds instances of the proverb in Cicero and Seneca. The concept is that fire can test gold in the same way as difficulties can test *fides*. Tosi (1991 nn. 1325 and 1835) adds some passages to Otto, in particular referring to medieval versions of the proverb, and does not quote Calpurnius either. Sussman (1994: 192) refers to Cic. *Fam.* 9.16.2; *Off.* 2.38; Ov. *Tr.* 1.5.25; Sen. *Prov.* 5.9 – 10; Plin. *Nat.* 33.62 and stresses the importance of the commonplace in its moral sense in the Vulgate Bible. It is interesting to take a closer look at Cicero, who is the oldest Latin source of the

---

18 Tr. above, n. 13.

dictum, and in particular at the text of *Ad familiares* that seems closer to Calpurnius's version than the one from *De officiis*:

> Cic. *Fam.* 9.16.2 *tametsi non facile diiudicatur amor verus et fictus, nisi aliquod incidit eius modi tempus ut* **quasi aurum igni sic benevolentia fidelis periculo aliquo perspici possit;** *cetera sunt signa communia.*[19]

Cicero addressed this particular letter to L. Papirius Paetus in 46 BC,[20] insisting that he was making every effort to survive politically. In Cicero, the *dictum* appears in a *similitudo* that highlights the proverbial content of the phrase: as Forbes (1971) 177 and 249 explains, the gold was mixed with lead in a special porous container. Then it was oxidised with a strong air stream that separated the two metals and freed the gold from any impurity. Accordingly, the proverb means that it only is possible to identify friends in difficult times by exposing them to harsh treatment similar to that experienced by gold and lead. In Cicero's correspondence, the *dictum* underlines his strong belief that in the final years of the Civil Wars Caesar's friends appreciated him. In Calpurnius, the word *dictum* underlines the connection between orality and textual transmission, popular knowledge and communicative pattern. The adjective *vetus* highlights the connection of the saying to tradition which imbues these words with an authoritative role. Nonetheless, the structure *ut... itidem* seems more interesting, because it parallels Cicero's *ut... sic*:[21]

> Calpurnius: *ut* **aurum igni**, *itidem* **innocentiam** *iudicio* **spectari solere**

> Cicero: *ut* **quasi aurum igni** *sic* **benevolentia fidelis** *periculo aliquo* **perspici possit**

There is only a slight *variatio* in the syntax: Cicero uses a clause with subjunctive, while in Calpurnius we find an infinitive clause; nonetheless, the position of the words is substantially the same and the structure is perfectly balanced and corresponds to that of Cicero. Therefore, we can observe a strong proximity to Cicero that I do not consider accidental. Moreover, if we pay attention to the

---

19 "For, though genuine love is not easily distinguished from feigned, unless some crisis occurs of a kind to test faithful affection by its danger, as gold in the fire, there are other indications of general nature" (tr. E. S. Shuckburgh).

20 On this letter see Shackleton Bailey (1977) 334–339 (in particular 335); Leach (1999); Garbarino, Tabacco (2008) I: 824–833.

21 Although *ut* in connection with *itidem* appears later than *ut... sic* (not until the time of Fronto and Gellius).

rhetorical structure, the apostrophe to *iudices* creates a strong hyperbaton and the *dictum* confers solemnity to the words of the orator son.

As Sussman (1994) 191 writes, "to support his contention that their father should stand trial, the orator son argues that he [the father] is innocent, but that by cancelling the trial, this innocence would never be put to the true test of a trial, thereby impugning their father's reputation". In this strategy, the *dictum* plays an important role, explaining that a trial is the right way to prove innocence – and, in fact, that there is no better way to do it –, just as gold can only be tested with fire. The orator's statement confirms that the main issue of the declamation is virtue and that virtue can be achieved only through personal risk and sacrifice. In Calpurnius, this *dictum* serves to underline the concept of purity of *virtus*. Calpurnius reuses and adapts Cicero's arrangement of the proverb, charging it with significance.

3.2 Forgotten proverbial material?

In both *Decl.* 29, which deals with the hostility between a poor and a rich man,[22] and in *Decl.* 37, where the theme concerns a struggle between father and son about matters of money and love,[23] we find the expression *velis nolis*: *Decl.* 29: **velis enim nolis**, *suspecta res est amator inimicus*;[24] *Decl.* 37: *<im>paria sunt nobis in amore tormenta: primum quod amor,* **velis nolis***, in senectute frigidior est.*[25] The phrase *velis nolis* is already listed by Otto (1890^2 n. 1852 s.v. *velle*), and quoted also by Tosi (1991 n. 891). Its meaning is "anyway", "at any rate" and it takes its force from the oxymoronic contrast between two verbs with the same root and opposite meaning. The expression appears in all the singular forms of the present subjunctive and, sometimes, of the perfect. In the second person, it is attested in ps.-Quint. *Decl. Mai.* 5.18 and *Decl. Min.* 315.18, as well

---

22 "The poor man had two daughters. In war time the rich man guaranteed that he would fight heroically if one of the poor man's daughters was given to him in marriage. While the poor man kept his silence, the state so decreed. The rich man fought heroically. The girl committed suicide. The rich man asks for the hand of the other daughter. The poor man speaks in opposition." (Theme, tr. L. A. Sussman).
23 "A father and a son were conducting love affairs with different mistresses. The father gave his son money to buy the release of the one loved by the father. The son bought the release of his own mistress. He is disinherited." (Theme, tr. L. A. Sussman).
24 "Of course, whether you like it or not, the situation reeks with suspicion when her father's personal enemy is her ardent suitor" (tr. L. A. Sussman).
25 "We have <un>equal torments in love: in the first place because, whether you like it or not, your sexual passion is more frigid in old age" (tr. L. A. Sussman).

as in Sen. *Brev.* 8.5 and Mart. 8.44.16. Similar clauses in Terence and Cicero are not entirely comparable: accordingly, the presence of the second person could be interpreted as a feature proper to our literary genre. It is called *proverbiale* (in the third person) by Donatus, Ter. *Eun.* 1059. In Calpurnius, the proverb highlights the hostility of the poor man who is speaking. Its position at the opening of the sentence is rhetorically very strong, thus enhancing the emotion expressed and strengthening the statement of the poor man. In 37, the force of the proverb is even greater as it interrupts the closing sentence of the son's speech. Even if we should be careful with stylistic statements, we must observe that the proverbial material seems to have been deliberately used in key passages of the text.

A second example of proverbial material is found in *Decl.* 44, where brevity once more prevents us from comprehending the plot.[26] Here the speaker uses the theme of the cruelty of fate – which he similarly used in a previous case – in order to separate two sentences that contain specific arguments: *o fortuna crudelis! abstulisti mihi filium: relinque vel filiam. Partiamur vel saltem liberos meos.*[27] The characterization of *Fortuna* as *crudelis* is common. Otto (1890[2] nn. 705 – 709) and Tosi (1991 nn. 838 – 841 [mainly 840]) have several examples, even if neither of them records the Calpurnian occurrence. Nonetheless, it appears at Hor. *Sat.* 2.8.61 – 62, Sen. *Tranq.* 16.1; *Cons. Polyb.* 3.4; *Cons. Helv.* 15.2[28] and in late antique literature, as at Serv. *Aen.* 11.42.[29] Calpurnius has reused it along with a personification that improves the pathos of the speech.

3.3 Reuse of literary expressions

Famous literary expressions can be reused in the following centuries, when the connection with their author loses its relevance. Sometimes they also are misinterpreted, as Nosarti (2010:39 – 40) explains. Initially, Nosarti seems to think that a proverb cannot change in this way, while the *sententia* can; later he concedes,

---

26 Sussman (1994) 83: "A man was suspected of misconduct with his maiden sister. He was executed […]. A plague arose. An oracle gave the advice that a maiden had to be sacrificed. The woman who was suspected of misconduct with her brother volunteers. Her father opposes this."
27 "Oh cruel fate! You have taken a son away from me; leave me at least a daughter. If you like, let us at least share my children!" (tr. L. A. Sussman).
28 About this concept in Seneca see Balbo (2014).
29 *Videtur autem dolere quod queri non potest de Fortunae crudelitate, quae ei uno eodemque tempore et tanta contulit beneficia, et tale intulit damnum.* ("He seems to suffer because he cannot complain about the cruelty of destiny, that at the same time gave so many benefits and damaged him so much").

upon the authority of A. Jolles, that "alcune sentenze o detti di scrittori o di poeti possono assumere per il proprio contenuto e la particolare elaborazione formale una tale universalità da divenire detto popolare e quindi proverbiale".[30] I share this idea – see also Macr. *Sat.* 5, quoted above – and I would like to suggest that this feature appears twice in Calpurnius Flaccus.

The first example is found in *Decl.* 6, concerning the case of a rich young man who is accused of having killed his guest. The one who speaks against the rich man says: *Sceleratis ingeniis et plus quam civilia cupientibus, non dominari instar servititis est.*[31] Tabacco (1985:46) and Sussman (1994:11) have already considered the rich texture of literary references in this passage that starts with Ov. *Met.* 12.583,[32] continues with Luc. 1.1,[33] Tac. *Ann.* 1.12[34] and goes all the way to Isid. *Or.* 18.1.2.[35] In another paper, I once more reconsider this passage from a linguistic point of view, adding a new *locus* to the dossier.[36] Despite the Ovidian model, the text parades its closeness to Lucan's *exordium* and it is evident that, in this declamation, the passage has lost all connection to its author and has acquired a general meaning, connected with the idea of fighting against tyranny that is the main theme of the passage.[37] It is probable that the authority of Lucan has given way to a scholastic reuse as, for instance, in the following passage of Fronto *Aur. Orat.* 7, who quotes this part of the verse as an *exemplum*:

---

30 Nosarti (2010) 40. See also endnote 271 (p. 177).

31 "For minds that are criminal and desire more than what is suitable to one's status as a citizen, not to be a despot is the equivalent of slavery" (tr. L. A. Sussman).

32 *Exercet memores plus quam civiliter iras.* "[The god] indulged his unforgetting wrath excessively" (tr. F. J. Miller).

33 *Bella per Emathios plus quam civilia campos.* ("Of war I sing, war worse than civil, waged over the plains of Emathia" (tr. J. D. Duff).

34 *(Asinius Gallus) nec ideo iram eius lenivit, pridem invisus, tamquam ducta in matrimonium Vipsania M. Agrippae filia, quae quondam Tiberii uxor fuerat, plus quam civilia agitaret Pollionisque Asinii patris ferociam retineret.* "He failed, however, to soothe the imperial anger: he had been a hated man ever since his marriage to Vipsania (daughter of Marcus Agrippa and once the wife of Tiberius), which had given the impression that he had ambitions denied to a subject and retained the temerity of his father Asinius Pollio" (tr. J. Jackson).

35 *Quattuor genera sunt bellorum: iustum et iniustum, civile et plus quam civile* "Now there are four kinds of war: just, unjust, civil, and more than civil" (tr. S. A. Barney et al.).

36 Aur. Vict., *Caes.* 39.3: *Quae quamquam plus quam civilia tumidique et affluentis animi, levia tamen prae ceteris.* (referred to Diocletian: "although these things went beyond good taste and betrayed a vain and haughty disposition, they were nevertheless trivial in comparison with the rest", tr. H. W. Bird). I am referring to Balbo (2016).

37 This is confirmed by the example of Manlius in the following lines: see Tabacco (1985) 68 and Sussman (1994) 112.

*Vnum exempli causa poetae prohoemium commemorabo, poetae eiusdem temporis eiusdem-
que nominis: fuit aeque Annaeus. Is initio carminis sui septem primis versibus nihil aliud
quam "bella plus quam civilia" interpretatus est.*[38]

The scholastic nature of the phrase is confirmed also by its presence in the *Com-
menta Bernensia* to Lucan, which quote and explain it three times, using Lucan
to explain and comment on Lucan. In my opinion, the process of generalisation
and the erasure of authorship that characterise the use of this text in declamations allows us to include it in the paremiographic material used by Calpurnius.

In *Decl.* 33 we have a similar case. Here a slave, who is in love with his prostitute mistress, is going to be crucified by her and addresses the tribunes because
he thinks that the punishment is unjust. The slave speaks and, at the end of the
fragment, says: *esset meum crimen aut error, si te solum adamassem.*[39] Sussman
(1994) 193 comments: "The phrase is reminiscent of Ovid's cause for banishment:
perdiderint cum me duo crimina, carmen et error (*Tr.* 2.207); Ovid also likes the
direct conjoining of *crimen et error*; cf. *Ep.* 17.48; *Met.* 3.141–142; *Pont.* 3.3.75".
The phenomenon is slightly different from the case of *Decl.* 6: here we have
an echo of Ovidian wording, not a real quotation, but it seems probable that
the result is almost the same. The reuse is interesting from three perspectives:
it seeks to create a literary allusion easy to detect in schools through its paronomastic effect; it demonstrates that some literary phrases were quite widespread,
at least in a scholastic context; and it thus documents the continued relevance of
Ovid in declamations even after Seneca the Elder.

3.4 Other cases

Finally, I will deal with some further occurrences. The first comes from *Decl.* 2,
which discusses the case of the *natus Aethiops*, *i.e.* of the woman who gave
birth to a black son and is accused of adultery. The declamation is extremely interesting and involves many problems (family, racism, natural law), but these
topics are beyond the scope of the present inquiry.[40] The passage that includes
proverbial material is the following: *Expers iudicii est amor; non rationem habet,*

---

38 "One prelude of a poem I will quote by way of example from a poet of the same time and of
the same name, an Annaeus like the other. In the first seven verses the beginning of his poem he
has done nothing but paraphrase the words *Wars worse than civil*" (tr. C. H. Haines).
39 "It would be a crime on my part, or a moral lapse, had I been the only man to fall passion-
ately in love with you" (tr. L. A. Sussman).
40 On this declamation, see especially Sussman (1999).

non sanitatem.[41] In Calpurnius, the phrase *expers iudicii amor* belongs to an argument that highlights the madness of love, a very common theme at least since Euripides 161 N.[2], and underlines the lack of healthy *ratio* of the lovers, with a final part that needs some explanation.[42] Here, the proverbial material could refer also to the topics of *amor amens* and *caecus* that are widely attested in Otto (1890[2] n. 79 and 99–100 s.v. *amare* and *amor* 1), but has also been commonplace both in Greek literature and in Cicero, as is shown by Tosi (1991 n. 1399 and 1418). The pairing of *amor* and *iudicium* is very rare in Latin literature and particularly prominent at Cic. *Pis.* 31; *Brut.* 331.5; *Fam.* 10.23.7 and 10.24.1.[43] Moreover, the opposition between *ratio* and *amor* has frequently been emphasized in the rhetorical tradition, as in the section about *concessio* at *Rhet. Her.* 2.24.5[44] or at Fronto *Ad Aur. Caes.* 1.4: *Nec omnino mihi amor videtur qui ratione oritur et iustis certisque de causis copulatur. Amorem ego illum intellego fortuitum et liberum et nullis causis servientem.*[45] In the fragment, the function of the proverb is significant: it perhaps occupied the opening position of the speech against the wife and fits perfectly into an *exordium*. Calpurnius, with consummate skill, probably used the *dictum* to create the hostile background that serves to develop the discussion.

We find a further relevant instance in the very short fragment of *Decl.* 8. It concerns a highly successful man who has tried to hang himself and was rescued by his sons, who subsequently charge him with madness. In the first speech, in

---

41 "Love is blind. It has neither rhyme nor reason" (tr. L. A. Sussman).

42 The declaimer continues: *alioquin omnes idem amaremus.* Sussman (1994) 97 translates "otherwise, we would all love in the same way", but *idem* seems to define the object of love, not the way to love. Aizpurua (2005) writes: "sinon nous aurions tous les mêmes amours". That is literally correct, but does not explain the idea that "in the absence of unreason, we'd all (he implies) love white Indo-Europeans" (M. Winterbottom *per litteras*). I suspect that here the declaimer could feel the influence of Cic. *Tusc.* 4.76, where *amor* is criticised: *etenim si naturalis amor esset, et amarent omnes et semper amarent et idem amarent, neque alium pudor, alium cogitatio, alium satietas deterreret.* ("For were love a matter of nature all men would love, as well as always love and love the same object, nor should we find one discouraged by shame, another by reflection, another by satiety", tr. J. E. King). Calpurnius could have summarised the Ciceronian phrase, yet referring it to nature and not to *ratio*.

43 Less important is the connection at Vell. 2.83.1.

44 *Nam qui se propter vinum aut amorem aut iracundiam fugisse rationem dicet, is animi vitio videbitur nescisse, non inprudentia.* ("For a person who declares that his reason fled because of wine or love or anger, will appear to have lacked comprehension though fault of character rather than ignorance", tr. H. Caplan).

45 "For what seems to me no love at all which springs from reason and depends on actual and definite causes: by love I understand such as is fortuitous and free and subject to no cause" (tr. C. R. Haines).

defence of the father, the declaimer starts with a *locus communis* about the un-stable nature of luck: *omnium calamitatum materia est homo diu felix.*[46] Sussman (1994:118) underlines the commonplace nature of this passage, also referring to the index of *loci communes* in Winterbottom (1974). Nonetheless, the content of the passage also echoes proverbial expressions such as *levis est Fortuna* (see Tosi 1991 n. 838), and in this case the distinction between commonplace and prover-bial material is unhelpful. It is also possible that the *sententia* belongs to the aforementioned *translaticiae* type, but this fact does not annihilate its proverbial content.[47] The structure of the *sententia* is not uncommon: after an initial geni-tive there is a sequence nominative – verb *esse*, followed by another nominative. Sussman (1994:118) underlines the proximity of the passage to *Rhet. Her.* 2.34: *Omnium malorum stultitia est mater atque materies.* The structure of the Calpur-nian expression is indeed very similar and shares a common rhetorical origin.

Decl. 25 offers a further case, which refers to a disagreement between two brothers. One of them has raped a woman who wants him to be sentenced to death. The young man is not executed immediately and his brother, who has fought in battle as a hero, asks for two rewards for his actions: the salvation of his brother and the death of the woman; but his brother refuses. In the speech for the rapist, the *sententia* probably refers to the fact that his brother's victory saves his life but threatens the life of the girl: *interdum praestat ad gloriam non certare quam vincere.*[48] In this instance, too, the brevity of the fragment makes it hard to understand.[49] In this context, the proverbial material consists of the idea, found already in Livy 22.39.20[50] and Sen. *Ben.* 5.1.4,[51] that for obtaining glory it is not compulsory to seek it. His brother's glory poses a problem for the rapist, and

---

46 "A man fortunate for too long a time is fertile ground for the full range of calamities" (tr. L. A. Sussman).

47 In *Decl.* 26 we find another example of a *translaticia: facilius fuerat amittere filios quam eli-gere.* This does not seem to carry any proverbial material, because of its close connection to the context of the declamation, which refers to a priest of Mars whose three sons had deserted.

48 "To achieve praise and glory sometimes it is better not to fight than to win a victory" (tr. L. A. Sussman).

49 The collocation *praestare ad gloriam* does not appear anywhere else in the Latin corpus, while the structure with the two infinitives connected in comparison by *quam* with the verb *praestare* is frequent: see Cic. *Phil.* 14.34 *quos laudare quam lugere praestabit* ("it will be more fitting to praise than to mourn", tr. D. R. Shackleton Bailey, rev. J. Ramsey and G. Manuwald); Cic. *ad Brut.* 24 *non esse quam esse per illum praestat* ("and indeed it would be better not to exist than to exist on his sufferance", tr. D. R. Shackleton Bailey, rev. J. Ramsey and G. Manu-wald).

50 *Gloriam qui spreverit veram habebit* ("Who will despise glory, will get it in its fullness").

51 *Gloria fugientes magis sequitur* ("Glory chases more people who avoid it").

to surrender to the brother's suggestion would perhaps have resulted in a better solution for him, but not for the woman. Glory is not always good and useful for everyone, as Sussman rightly notes.[52] In this situation, the proverbial sentence also plays a role in the argumentation: first of all, it divides two sentences that refer to the personal experience of the *persona loquens*[53] and also creates suspense; secondly, it elevates the speech on a more general level for a moment, reinforcing the strength of the rapist's words.

4 Conclusions

In Calpurnius we have found limited traces of paremiographic material, and only a single case where the declaimer states that he is using a proverb. The use of this material is obvious in Calpurnius' declamations; it is established in a cultural background that is rooted in the world of education and schooling, as we can see from the cases listed under 3.2. We can also observe the phenomenon of the paremiographic reuse of famous *sententiae* of authors (such as Lucan: see section 3.3) and in some places we perceive proximity to Cicero's texts, as in example 3.1.

If we pay attention to the functions of the proverbial material in Calpurnius, we can identify three major purposes a) to strengthen the argumentation or to close it with an epigrammatic point; b) to enhance the pathos of the situation; c) to create a pause between two important clauses.

As Jacqueline Dangel stated, a proverb can be considered as an "outil rhétorique ou poétique, apte à conférer un niveau de style, *ornamentum orationis*. Agrément du discours, il fonctionne alors à l'exemple d'un bon mot ou d'une construction intercalée en vue d'égayer, en particulier, une démonstration aride".[54] Accordingly, in Calpurnius the use of proverbial material is strictly related to the argumentative and rhetorical strategies used by the declaimer in order to persuade. At the same time, it works also as a literary element to give *ornatus* to the speech.

---

52 Sussman (1994) 173.
53 In the first, the orator is wishing that the divinity forbid the transformation of the young woman from plaintiff to defendant. In the second, he declares his love for the raped.
54 Dangel (1999) 55–56.

Biagio Santorelli
Metrical and accentual *clausulae* as evidence for the date and origin of Calpurnius Flaccus

Whether he was a professional rhetorician, an amateur declaimer, or a mere collector of *sententiae* from the works of other orators, Calpurnius Flaccus is a figure destined to remain obscure to modern readers. All we know about him is that, at some point in late antiquity, a collection of excerpts from his declamations was deemed worthy to be preserved in an anthology of ten "minor" orators. The so-called *Corpus decem rhetorum minorum*, about which we have only indirect information, must have been a collection of extracts from ten rhetoricians, *minores* in comparison to Cicero, and apparently is the archetype of our tradition of the *Lesser Declamations* ascribed to Quintilian, as well as the excerpts from Seneca the Elder and Calpurnius Flaccus.[1] The compiler of this collection, however, did not even record the *praenomen* of our author, condemning later scholars to fluctuate between fanciful hypotheses[2] and discouraged resignation.[3] The aim of this paper is to contribute to our understanding of Calpurnius Flaccus by proposing a hypothesis on his probable date and provenance.

The basis for the present investigation is provided by a seminal work of Lennart Håkanson,[4] mainly devoted to the study of the metrical *clausulae* in the

---

1 See the helpful surveys in Sussman (1994) 19–20; Sallmann (1997); Stramaglia (2006) 572 n. 7.
2 For an overview of the hypotheses propounded so far see Sussman (1994) 6–9.
3 See e. g. Aizpurua (2005) 15: "Calpurnius Flaccus n'est pour nous qu'un nom: on ne peut dire avec certitude à quelle époque il vécut, ni dans quelle région de l'empire".
4 Håkanson (2014d). This monumental essay was arguably composed as a preparatory study for his Teubner edition of the *Major Declamations* (1982), but the author's death in 1987 prevented its publication. Håkanson's *Nachlass* then languished at the Uppsala Universitetsbibliotek until 2011, when the combined efforts of Francesco Citti, Gerd Haverling, Antonio Stramaglia and Michael Winterbottom made it available to the scholarly community. A first volume of Håkanson's unpublished writings appeared in 2014, bringing together four essays devoted to the *argumenta* of the pseudo-Quintilianic *Declamationes maiores* (Håkanson 2014a), their major literary models (2014b), the history of their transmission (2014c) and, what is most relevant for the purposes of the present contribution, the rhythms of their *clausulae* (2014d). In 2015 and 2016 the other studies that Håkanson had prepared for publication have been published, namely an edition with commentary of the *Tribunus Marianus* (Håkanson-Winterbottom 2015) and a commentary on the first book of the *Controversiae* of Seneca the Elder (Håkanson 2016); the rest of Håkanson's

Biagio Santorelli, University of Florida

https://doi.org/10.1515/9783110401554-008

Major Declamations ascribed to Quintilian.[5] By means of a systematic analysis of the *clausulae* in the corpus of the extant *Maiores*, Håkanson recognised 19 recurring rhythmical patterns, listed in the table below (p. 140).[6]

This table shows a clear predominance of three forms, namely the dicretic (form 9, making up 10.2% of the total), the ditrochee (form 15 = 17.2%) and the cretic-trochee (form 18 = 25.8%). The sum of these three forms amounts to more than half of the total number of rhythmical *clausulae* found in the *Major Declamations* (53%).

The aim of Håkanson's analysis is to suggest a fairly accurate date for each piece in that collection, on account of its particular use of rhythmical *clausulae*. The basis for this hypothesis is a rather simple assumption: Latin prose writers commonly employed rhythmical *clausulae* to give their sentences a 'musical' character, and this practice naturally evolved over time along with the taste of the individual authors and their public.[7] Through the analysis of trends in the use of rhythmical *clausulae* in texts of dubious attribution, and a comparison between them and those of well-dated texts, then, it is possible to find a guide to date even the more uncertain texts. Following this assumption, Håkanson gathers a heterogeneous sample of prose writers already well studied in terms of the use of rhythmic *clausulae*, and then compares them with the results of his own survey on the *Major Declamations*:[8]

Nachlass was left by the author in too provisional a state to be published, but will be made available at the University Library in Uppsala as well as online.

5 On this subject other studies were already available, though they eventually proved to be unreliable: Golz (1913) focused specifically on the *Major Declamations*. The main contribution in terms of method and approach, at that time, was Zieliński (1907) esp. 431–466. On the limitations of the previous investigations, see Håkanson (1986) 2293–2294; (2014d) 47–50.

6 The table, drawn from Håkanson (2014d) 97 records in percentage terms the presence of each pattern in every individual speech. The pattern of each *clausula* is reproduced in the first column; the top row lists the individual speeches, arranging them in the two groups of older (3, 6, 9, 12, 13) and later declamations (1, 2, 4, 5, 7, 8, 10, 11, 14–19) generally identified by scholars. The method followed in the collection and interpretation of those data is explained in Håkanson (2014d) 50–53.

7 See on this subject the lucid summary of Oberhelman-Hall (1984) 114–115 with bibliography at nn. 1–4. A wider assessment is provided by Oberhelman (2003) 82-194.

8 Håkanson (2014d) 98, Tab. 3B.

	Cic. Speeches	Celsus	Curtius	Suet.	Quintil.	Florus	Min. Fel.	Arnobius	Lact. *inst.* I	Symm. *ep.* I	Hier. *ep.* XXII	Ammianus
Groups 9 + 15 + 18	49.8	42.0	54.0	56.6	60.0	55.5	71.6	80.8	59.9	76.0	50.8	74.0
3	2.8	8.2	12.0	6.3	8.5	8.0	3.6	2.5	5.2	7.4	18.1	11.0
7	4.9	7.2	–	–	4.5	3.0	–	0.7	5.0	3.5	3.4	–
13	4.7	3.0	5.0	2.5	2.5	10.5	6.6	1.9	7.2	5.6	3.1	9.0
16	2.9	2.2	5.0	2.5	2.0	0.5	5.8	1.5	6.4	1.3	2.3	5.0
Tot.	65.1	62.6	76.0	67.9	77.5	77.5	87.6	87.4	83.7	93.8	77.7	99.0

The group we have already found to prevail in the *Maiores* (9, dicretic; 15, ditrochee; 18, cretic-trochee) is largely predominant in all the texts examined; it is also noteworthy that the percentage represented by this group seems to grow over time. This basic trend can provide a general guideline in dating our texts; further indications may be drawn from the analysis of a series of prosodic peculiarities individual to the style of each writer.[9] Taking into account all these factors, Håkanson suggests a dating for each of the *Major Declamations*, distributing them within a period ranging from the late first to the mid-third century CE.[10]

In an appendix to his study of the rhythmical *clausulae* in the *Major Declamations*, Håkanson applies the same statistical analysis to the excerpts of Calpurnius Flaccus, until then *terra incognita* for this kind of study. Taking into account the greater difficulties presented by the state of preservation of Calpurnius' text, Håkanson detects the presence of the same 19 patterns identified in the *Maiores*; and here as well dicretic (9), ditrochee (15) and cretic-trochee (18) turn out to be by far the most common forms:[11]

---

9 For instance, the exploitation of phenomena like hiatus, synalepha, aphaeresis, *muta cum liquida* etc.; see Håkanson (2014d) 50–52.

10 See in detail Håkanson (2014d) 95. One must not forget, however, that Håkanson regarded these assumptions, based only on prosodic analysis, as provisional, and that he was intending to verify them in the light of linguistic and stylistic factors. Håkanson's death prevented this investigation, which has been carried out independently by the authors of the monographs of the Cassino series; see for a recent overview Stramaglia (2013) 34–37.

11 Håkanson (2014d) 130, tab. 1.

		Abs. Freq.	Percent
1	⏑⏑⏑×	3	0.6
2	⏑⏑—⏑⏑×	4	0.8
3	—⏑—⏑⏑×	26	5.5
4	——⏑⏑×	6	1.3
5	⏑⏑⏑—⏑×	4	0.8
6	—⏑⏑—⏑×	9	1.9
7	—⏑—⏑×	22	4.6
8	⏑⏑——⏑×	12	2.5
9	—⏑——⏑×	90	18.9
10	⏑————⏑×	5	1.1
11	————⏑×	14	2.9
12	⏑⏑⏑⏑—×	2	0.4
13	—⏑⏑⏑—×	30	6.3
14	—⏑⏑—×	2	0.4
15	—⏑—×	75	15.8
16	⏑⏑⏑——×	32	6.7
17	—⏑⏑——×	1	0.2
18	—⏑——×	127	26.7
19	———×	11	2.3
Tot.		475	99.7

The total of these three main schemes is rather higher in Calpurnius Flaccus than in the *Major Declamations* (61.4% versus 53%), and significantly similar to the findings for Lactantius:[12]

	Lactantius	Calpurnius
Groups 9 + 15 + 18	59.9	61.4
Group 3	5.2	5.5
Group 7	5.0	4.6
Group 13	7.2	6.3
Group 16	6.4	6.7
Tot.	83.7	84.5

In order to narrow down the time span in which Calpurnius can be placed we must examine the specific features of his style: a thorough analysis of the main prosodic phenomena allows Håkanson to depict the outline of an author who is generally careful to avoid hazardous prosodies or rhythmical irregularities, who obtains proper *clausulae* without violating the most commonly used

---

12 Håkanson (2014d) 121.

forms.[13] Comparison with the sample of authors previously considered suggests a date for Calpurnius in the late second century CE.[14] Prosodic analysis, then, essentially confirms the assumptions made on other grounds by scholars who in subsequent decades have focused their research on Calpurnius Flaccus without knowing Håkanson's writings.[15]

Prosodic analysis, moreover, allows further considerations on our material. Calpurnius Flaccus' *clausulae* show a not entirely metrical character, since they do not consist exclusively of a succession of short and long syllables. Calpurnius thus seems to devote particular attention not only to traditional quantitative metrics, but also to the succession of accents of words in and before a *clausula*. We can get an accurate idea of how that is put into effect by observing the exploitation of the ditrochee (Håkanson's cl. 15: – ᵕ – ᵙ) by Calpurnius Flaccus, which is of particular prominence and importance for tracing the history of rhythmic *clausulae*.

By analysing individually all the occurrences of this pattern, Håkanson notes that in 65.4% of cases the double trochee is introduced by a trisyllabic proparoxytone, in the following combinations: [16]

1. cretic ($\acute{-}$ ᵕ – $\acute{-}$ ᵕ $\acute{-}$ ᵙ) = 22.7%;[17]
2. dactyl ($\acute{-}$ ᵕ ᵕ $\acute{-}$ ᵕ $\acute{-}$ ᵙ) = 12%;[18]
3. anapaest ($\breve{-}$ ᵕ – $\acute{-}$ ᵕ $\acute{-}$ ᵙ) = 20%;[19]

---

13 See in detail Håkanson (2014d) 127–130.

14 Håkanson (2014d) 129–130. In this case too Håkanson intended to test his hypothesis in the light of linguistic and stylistic analysis, but his sudden death prevented him from putting this into effect.

15 For a comprehensive survey see Sussman (1994) 6–10.

16 See Håkanson (2014d) 124.

17 α: *epistulae consecutae* [p. 6, 15 H.] (the excerpts of Calpurnius Flaccus are quoted according to Håkanson (1978), with reference to page and line numbers in square brackets); *exitum pernegavit* [7, 23 H.]; *filius somniavit* [10, 18 H.]; *tempus est caecitatis* [11, 4 f. H.]; *conscientiae perveniret* [12, 20 H.]; *idoneum iudicasti* [17, 18 H.]; *sanitas nasceretur* [28, 13 H.]; *viventium consenescat* [39, 14 H.]; *publice maluissem* [20, 3 H.]; *commilito laureatum* [25, 15 H.]. (β): *orbitas non habebat* [10, 10 f. H.]; *tyrannicidio non negassem* [14, 4 H.]; *arbitris non liceret* [40, 6 f. H.]. β: *potestate non est fuisse* [8, 18 H.]; *filiae vel nocenti* [22, 6 H.]; *maluit quam videri* [37, 21 H.]; *abdicatiŏ cum timetur* [27, 22 f. H.].

18 α: *tyrannide pollicetur* [6, 13 f. H.]; *ignibus adiuvantur* [7, 22 f. H.]; *credite confitenti* [9, 19 f. H.]; *paenitet indicasse* [10, 16 H.]; *iracundiă mentiendi* [12, 20 f. H.]; *agnosceret interemit* [22, 15 H.]; *altaribus educavi* [24, 19 H.]. β: *confirmaverit et tyrannus* [13, 8 H.]; *sanguine sed redemi* [40, 9 f. H.].

19 α: *Marium vindicasti* [3, 10 H.]; *redeunt orbitatis* [10, 7 H.]; *oculos perdidisset* [10, 9 H.:]; *docuit parricidae* [12, 12 f. H.]; *remedium polliceri* [13, 13 H.]; *medicum flagitabat* [13, 19 H.]; *celeriter praeparasti* [13, 19 f. H.]; *videat contumacem* [15, 21 H.]; *etiam gloriosam* [19, 1 f. H.]; *supplicio servitutis*

4. tribrach ($\smile \smile \smile \stackrel{\prime}{\smile} \smile \stackrel{\prime}{\smile} \stackrel{\smile}{\smile}$) = 4%;[20]
5. other patterns like $\stackrel{\prime}{\smile} \stackrel{\smile}{\smile} \mid - $ (2.7%)[21] and $\stackrel{\prime}{\smile} - \mid - $ (4%).[22]

In the majority of cases, therefore, Calpurnius favours a mixed *clausula*, which maintains the ditrochee ($\stackrel{\prime}{\smile} \smile \stackrel{\prime}{\smile} \stackrel{\smile}{\smile}$) as its concluding metric pattern, but introduces it with a proparoxytone ($\stackrel{\prime}{\smile} \sim \sim$); what matters in this trisyllabic base is not the quantity of the syllables but the sequence of the accents, since we find a stressed syllable followed by two unstressed, according to the pattern:

$\stackrel{\prime}{\smile} \sim \sim \quad \stackrel{\prime}{\smile} \smile \stackrel{\prime}{\smile} \stackrel{\smile}{\smile}$ (65.4% of the total).

In three other cases, however, the final ditrochee is preceded by a base of four syllables, according to the pattern:

$\stackrel{\prime}{\smile} \sim \sim \stackrel{\prime}{\smile} \stackrel{\prime}{\smile} \quad \smile \stackrel{\prime}{\smile} \stackrel{\smile}{\smile}$ (4%).[23]

To these cases we can finally add five instances in which the ditrochee is introduced by an additional oxytone:

$\stackrel{\prime}{\smile} \sim \quad \stackrel{\prime}{\smile} \smile \stackrel{\prime}{\smile} \stackrel{\smile}{\smile}$ (9.3%).[24]

While the majority of instances show a mixed structure, quantitative and accentual at the same time, a significant proportion of Calpurnius' *clausulae* feature a more pronounced accentual orientation; Håkanson's analysis reveals that 18.7% of the trochaic *clausulae* consist of a pure cadence of accented and unaccented syllables, following the pattern:

$\stackrel{\prime}{\smile} \sim \sim \stackrel{\prime}{\smile} \sim$ (18.7%).[25]

[22, 3 H.]; *alii iudicare* [29, 21 H.]; *expositum praeterire* [38, 21 H.]; *doleat caecitatem* [10, 19 f. H.]. (β): *paeniteat non novercam* [4, 13 H.]; *deseruit nec venenum* [14, 4 f. H.].
20 α: *redimat abdicatus* [15, 4 f. H.]. (β): *fuerit ad sororem* [27, 11 H.]. β: *amicitia plus nocere* [11, 13 H.].
21 *habet non sanitatem* [1, 15 H.]; *ubi non erubescas* [5, 7 H.].
22 *hostis non vindicavit* [7, 19 H.]; *mater cui mentiendum* [9, 13 H.]; *pauper non est reversus* [6, 13 H.].
23 *publica nec hos relinques* [25, 14 H.]; *divitias amare coepit* [12, 1 H.]; *argue si iure leges* [17, 20 H.].
24 *non erat cum dabatur* [32, 13 f. H.]; *rationem perdiderunt* [13, 9 H.]; *redimendo iudicastis* [39, 11 H.]; *vitam quam dedisti* [23, 12 f. H.]; *excaecare matrem* [9, 15 H.].
25 α: *illa pro te* (stressed!) *mentiatur* [9, 3 f. H.]; *quaesivit se vindicavit* [13, 14 f. H.]. β: *utriusque mortem videtis* [12, 14 H.]; *filii mei videre* [1, 9 H.]; *nobis Cimbri minantur* [3, 18 H.]; *satis fuit minari* [3, 22 H.]; *nisi captivos putarent* [7, 17 H.]; *excaecaret parentem* [9, 1 f. H.]; *de fortunā liceret* [11, 17

In summary, we can distinctly perceive in Calpurnius what scholars call *cursus*, i.e. a new way of conceiving a *clausula*. In this new approach, fully established in the Latin-speaking world only in the fifth century CE, the words in *clausulae* are interpreted no longer as a succession of long and short syllables, but as a cadence of accented and unaccented syllables. The three main patterns of the metric *clausulae* progressively evolve into the three types of *cursus* that will be preferred by the authors of Late Antiquity and the Middle Ages:

9	dicretic	$\stackrel{\prime}{-}\cup- \ \stackrel{\prime}{-}\cup\stackrel{\smile}{}$	
	⇓		
	cursus tardus	$\acute\sim\sim\ \sim\acute\sim\sim\sim$	e.g. *divína custódiet*
		paroxytone + tetrasyllabic proparoxytone	
15	(cretic)-ditrochee	$(\stackrel{\prime}{-}\cup-) \ \stackrel{\prime}{-}\cup\stackrel{\prime}{-}\stackrel{\smile}{}$	
	⇓		
	cursus velox	$(\acute\sim\sim\sim) \ \sim\sim\acute\sim\sim$	e.g. *ánimus gratulétur*
		(proparoxytone +) tetrasyllabic paroxytone	
18	cretic + trochee	$\stackrel{\prime}{-}\cup- \ \stackrel{\prime}{-}\stackrel{\smile}{}$	
	⇓		
	cursus planus	$\acute\sim\sim\ \sim\acute\sim\sim$	e.g. *fíde servántur*
		paroxytone + trisyllabic paroxytone	

If we reconsider the above-mentioned *clausulae* of Calpurnius, we will see that the most frequent pattern, the ditrochee introduced by a trisyllabic proparoxytone (cl. 15),[26] is compatible with the category of the *cursus velox*:

Trisyllabic proparoxytone + ditrochee	*cursus velox*
$\acute\sim\sim\sim \quad -\cup\stackrel{\prime}{-}\stackrel{\smile}{}$	$(\acute\sim\sim\sim)\ \sim\sim\acute\sim\sim$ (65.4%)
éxitum pērněgāvīt [7, 23 H.]	*ánimus gratulétur*

The second most frequently attested pattern, the cadence of paroxytone + trisillabic paroxytone,[27] fits exactly the scheme of the *cursus planus*:

H.]; *nihil umquam negabas* [17, 23 H.]; *abdicatorum senatus* [18, 15 H.]; *aequalem ducat volentem* [27, 2 H.]; *iudicio spectari solere* [29, 7 H.]; *appellas vocem doloris* [34, 6 H.].
26 See nn. 17-22.
27 See n. 25.

paroxytone + trisyllabic paroxytone	*cursus planus*
$\acute{\sim} \sim \ \ \sim \acute{\sim} \sim$	$\acute{\sim} \sim \ \ \sim \acute{\sim} \sim$ (18.7%)
méi vidére [1, 9 H.]	*fíde servántur*

The analysis of Calpurnius' *clausulae*, then, shows that considerable attention is paid to accentual rhythm, which, however, does not completely supplant the traditional metric system. Calpurnius seems to be located in the early stages of a long transitional process which will peak in the fifth century CE. For the purposes of our research it is crucial to examine whether Calpurnius' use of *clausulae* is compatible with his dating to the late second century proposed by previous scholars.

Two complex and debated issues are what point in time could be considered as the "date of birth" of the accentual rhythm, and what exactly happened between the first manifestation of the *cursus* and its full affirmation during the fifth century. While the characteristics of quantitative metric are largely outlined by Cicero, we do not have any theoretical treatment of the *cursus*, at least not before the works of medieval grammarians. The only reliable method of investigation is to carry out a series of statistical analyses and comparisons like those Håkanson undertook on the *Major Declamations* and Calpurnius.

A substantial contribution to these statistical studies has been provided by Steven Oberhelman, who over time has reviewed an ever-increasing sample of imperial, late antique, medieval and even modern Latin prose.[28] The conclusion he draws from these studies corresponds to the thesis hitherto predominant in this area of research: any form of accentual rhythm is considered absent in Latin prose until the early third century CE; in that period the so-called *cursus mixtus* begins to establish itself, a hybrid situation in which prose writers tend to compose *clausulae* under the old quantitative system, but at the same time take care to match the stresses of the words with the metrical *ictus*. Under the *cursus mixtus*, in other words, the *clausulae* would be metric and accentual at the same time; each author, moreover, would retain the freedom to choose whether to continue to use the old metric system or this new metric-accentual trend.

Although accurate and methodologically scrupulous, Oberhelman's analyses leave themselves open to several objections. First, the *cursus* can be given a significantly earlier date. Oberhelman identifies the oldest traces of accentual rhythm in Cyprian (210–258) and Minucius Felix (mid-third century?); prior to Oberhelman's work, however, two Swedish dissertations had already identified

---

28 See Oberhelman-Hall (1984, 1985); Oberhelman (1988a–b, 2003).

traces of accentual rhythm in the *De Platone* and *De mundo*, proved their Apuleian authorship and dated them around 170–180 CE.[29] The first appearance of accentual rhythm would then go back precisely to the time span in which, as methodologically different analyses suggest, we should date Calpurnius, namely the second half of the second century CE. The elements that point in this direction, thus, begin to show a certain consistency: a definitive demonstration will likely come from the analytic comparison of the traces of *cursus* detectable in Calpurnius and the aforementioned two Apuleian dialogues.

More substantial objections to Oberhelman's hypothesis concern the very existence of the *cursus mixtus*. As shown in a recent article by Michael Winterbottom,[30] it is of little use to conceive the opposition between quantitative and accentual rhythm as a polarisation. On the one hand, attempts to systematise the various metric-accentual types produce endless lists of schemes, which end up being almost all-encompassing, until reaching the paradox of including almost every sentence ending under some rhythmic formula. On the other hand, there are no reliable criteria to determine that a given piece of prose is completely metric or completely accentual: no Latin text can avoid some admixture of *clausulae* interpreted as metrical and *clausulae* more markedly accentual. Rather than conceiving a drastic opposition between the two systems, it is preferable to imagine an ideal scale, on which it is possible to put all Latin texts – from the orations of Cicero to the papal bulls – according to the different proportions in which the quantitative rhythm blends with the accentual one; these proportions can vary in each individual author, without necessarily following a chronological development.[31]

Despite tempering the concept of *cursus mixtus*, and adopting as our point of view the spectrum propounded by Winterbottom, there is a constant that can be observed in the data gathered by Oberhelman, and that can be a useful guide in our study of Calpurnius Flaccus. It is a matter of fact that, between the second half of the second and the early third century CE, several authors began to exploit significantly the accentual components of the prose rhythm, more so than the quantitative ones.

The earliest identified so far are:
- Apuleius (c. 125–c. 180, Madaura – Algeria);
- Cyprian (c. 200–258, Carthage – Tunisia);
- Minucius Felix (??);

---

29 Axelson (1952); Redfors (1960). See on the issue Oberhelman (1988a) 145, with previous bibliography at n. 13.

30 Winterbottom (2011).

31 Winterbottom (2011) 267–268.

- Arnobius (? – c. 330, Sicca Veneria – Tunisia);
- Lactantius (c. 250 – c. 325, Cirta[?] – Algeria).

It is striking that, throughout the period under consideration (second half of the second to the early third century), the practice of the *cursus* is connected to authors of African origin. Augustine suggests a possible explanation for this phenomenon:

> *Cur pietatis doctorem pigeat, imperitis loquentem, ossum potius quam os dicere, ne ista syllaba non ab eo quod sunt ossa, sed ab eo quod sunt ora intellegatur, ubi Afrae aures de correptione vocalium vel productione non iudicant?*

> Why should a teacher of godliness who is addressing an unlearned audience shrink from using *ossum* instead of *os*, if he fears that the latter might be taken not as the singular of *ossa*, but as the singular of *ora*, seeing that **African ears have no quick perception of the shortness or length of vowels?** (Aug. *De doctr. Christ.* 4.24 [tr. NPNF 2, 582])

Augustine explicitly states that Africans in general, and not only the *imperiti*, have a kind of innate difficulty in perceiving the Latin syllable quantity. It is clear that this evidence should be treated with great caution: Augustine is speaking about a later period and does not give us an exact measure of the possible spread of this difficulty even in the most educated strata of the African population. But we cannot exclude the hypothesis that in Africa, and more precisely in the African schools of rhetoric, a new teaching system developed, better suited to meet the needs of the local public: namely, a system able to compensate for the traditional difficulties in managing metrical *clausulae* by preferring a more marked presence of the accentual rhythm. Such a tradition of teaching may have affected also the *usus scribendi* of prominent authors like those mentioned above, determining the preponderance of the accentual rhythm in their prose.[32]

In summary, the relationship between quantitative and accentual rhythm is a balance that varies according to many factors, not only those of chronology. Among these factors, the "congenital" difficulty in perceiving and reproducing quantities that Augustine attributes to people of Africa may be of primary importance; and it could provide an explanation for the inclination of prose writers from this region to favour the accentual rather than the quantitative rhythm in their *clausulae*.

---

[32] See on this matter Oberhelman (1988b) 241–242. It should be noted, however, that this hypothesis lacks a definitive confirmation, since for this period we do not have a sample of surely non-African texts to use for comparison.

These reflections can offer two clues for research on Calpurnius Flaccus. First, the analysis of his rhythmic *clausulae* provides further argument in favour of his dating to the second half of the second century CE. Second, and more importantly, it features substantial samples of the accentual rhythm that, in the same period, seems characteristic of African prose writers. To the list of the *Afri* that, between the second and third centuries CE, reveal a progressive compliance with the system of the accentual rhythm, one is definitely inclined to add Calpurnius Flaccus, who may have been influenced in his style by some peculiarities of the teaching practices in use in the schools of rhetoric of the African provinces.

	3	6	9	12	13	1	2	4	5	7	8	10	11	14	15	16	17	18	19	Average
1	1.8	2.5	3.7	4.3	2.3	4.2	6.4	2.2	1.7	6.2	6.1	5.0	3.3	5.7	8.2	5.1	5.4	3.0	2.3	4.2
2	1.8	1.4	1.1	1.9	1.4	–	0.3	1.4	2.6	–	2.4	0.8	0.7	–	0.5	1.5	1.2	1.9	0.4	1.1
3	4.2	4.6	5.9	4.8	6.6	8.4	7.8	8.5	9.0	1.7	7.4	4.6	8.6	13.5	10.2	2.2	5.8	10.0	8.0	6.9
4	3.0	3.2	2.6	3.8	3.3	0.8	0.7	–	–	–	0.3	0.4	0.7	–	0.5	0.7	–	0.4	0.4	1.1
5	0.6	2.9	1.8	1.0	2.8	0.8	2.4	2.1	2.3	2.3	1.0	0.4	1.3	2.8	3.0	1.5	1.2	0.7	3.4	1.8
6	2.4	3.2	1.5	1.4	0.9	1.3	0.7	1.8	1.7	0.6	0.7	1.3	3.9	0.7	2.0	0.7	1.2	1.1	0.4	1.4
7	8.4	7.9	7.4	10.7	12.2	4.2	8.1	10.3	7.3	4.5	3.4	5.0	11.8	5.7	5.6	4.4	10.8	7.4	12.2	7.8
8	2.4	2.9	2.9	3.3	2.3	2.1	3.4	1.8	2.0	4.0	5.1	1.7	2.6	2.1	1.5	2.2	4.2	2.2	2.3	2.7
9	14.4	11.1	11.8	7.1	8.9	8.9	10.1	16.6	10.2	11.9	12.5	10.9	8.6	10.0	9.2	7.4	10.0	11.5	8.8	10.2
10	7.2	1.9	2.2	4.5	1.4	1.7	0.7	0.7	0.9	–	0.3	1.7	–	–	–	2.9	0.8	0.7	0.8	1.5
11	5.4	5.4	7.4	9.0	8.9	3.8	–	2.5	0.6	3.4	1.3	1.7	1.3	1.4	1.5	0.7	1.5	2.6	2.3	3.2
12	0.6	0.4	1.1	1.0	0.5	–	0.7	1.1	0.3	–	2.7	0.4	0.7	1.4	2.0	2.2	1.5	1.5	0.8	1.0
13	1.2	2.5	2.9	1.2	0.9	5.9	5.7	4.6	8.2	5.6	7.4	6.3	5.3	9.2	8.2	2.9	4.6	4.1	4.3	4.8
14	2.4	2.5	0.4	1.0	1.4	1.3	0.3	0.4	1.2	–	–	0.8	0.7	–	0.5	0.7	–	–	–	0.7
15	20.4	19.3	16.5	13.6	19.2	21.1	23.6	14.2	17.8	14.7	11.4	18.4	17.8	14.9	11.2	29.4	17.0	13.8	13.4	17.2
16	3.0	1.8	2.6	1.0	0.9	4.2	6.1	4.6	4.4	7.3	5.4	1.7	5.9	5.7	7.7	5.9	5.8	6.7	7.6	4.6
17	1.2	1.1	–	1.2	0.5	0.8	–	0.7	0.3	–	–	1.3	–	–	0.5	–	–	0.4	–	0.4
18	13.2	19.3	18.0	17.4	19.7	26.6	21.3	29.4	29.2	32.8	32.0	35.6	26.3	25.5	17.6	27.9	25.9	30.5	31.7	25.8
19	6.6	6.4	10.3	16.9	5.6	3.8	1.7	2.5	0.3	5.1	0.7	2.1	0.7	1.4	1.0	1.5	3.1	1.5	0.8	3.6
	99.9	100.2	100.1	100.1	99.7	99.9	100.0	100.0	100.0	100.1	100.1	100.1	100.2	100.0	99.9	99.8	100.0	100.0	100.2	100.2

Michael Winterbottom*

The Editors of Calpurnius Flaccus

Calpurnius' work, as we have it, does not make things easy for the reader. And I have been prompted to look at the successive editors of our author, from 1580 to the present day, and ask the question: what, if anything, did they contribute to the understanding of our author?

The first exhibit is Pierre Pithou ('Pithoeus') (1539 – 96).[1] He alone of our editors was not based in a university. He was a French grandee, procureur-général in the Parlement of Paris, who, as we shall see, moved in exalted circles. He had a remarkable track record as a purchaser of important manuscripts. All three were written in the ninth century: two in France, one in Germany. The most famous is the Montpellier Juvenal,[2] by far the best witness to the exiguous purer strain of this tradition. Pithoeus edited the author in 1585. Another P is what is recognised to be quite the most important witness to Phaedrus,[3] whom Pithoeus edited in 1596. A third of his purchases is another Montpellier manuscript,[4] which contains a considerable batch of the *Minor Declamations* ascribed to Quintilian (the only medieval witness to this text), together with the Elder Seneca, in the excerpted version, and our Calpurnius. Pithoeus edited the *Minor Declamations* in 1580. It was by no means the *editio princeps* (it had been in print since 1494), but Pithoeus' manuscript put the text on a new and far sounder basis.

Unfortunately the section of his manuscript containing Calpurnius was sadly mutilated, and Pithoeus had to fall back on a much younger book. He had ac-

---

* I am very grateful to Robin Briggs for help with the French seventeenth century, and to Antonio Stramaglia (and through him Massimo Pinto) and the late Martin West for help in tracing the career of Georg Lehnert. Professor Stramaglia was also kind enough to read a draft of this chapter and make valuable suggestions. My principal debt, however, is to Donald Russell, who discussed with me the text and translation of Calpurnius 13.

1 I do not supply references for easily accessible details of the careers of the earlier editors. See generally the still very useful survey in Sandys (1908), vol. ii; also Eckstein (1871). For other transmissions mentioned *en passant*, see Reynolds (1983).
2 Montpellier, Bibliothèque Interuniversitaire – Section Médecine, 135 (?Lorsch); see e. g. Munk Olsen (1982,1985) i. 575.
3 New York, Pierpont Morgan Library (M. A.), 906 (?Reims); Munk Olsen (1982,1985) ii. 227–8.
4 Montpellier, Bibliothèque Interuniversitaire – Section Médecine, 126 (Reims); Munk Olsen (1982,1985) ii. 298 (*Decl. Min.*); ii. 419 (Seneca rhetor, *excerpta*); i. 53 (Calpurnius Flaccus).

Michael Winterbottom, University of Oxford

https://doi.org/10.1515/9783110401554-009

quired his old manuscript '*Claudii Falceti... beneficio*'.[5] This was Claude Fauchet (1530–1601), historian and antiquary. He was premier président in the Cour des monnaies, a Paris sovereign court established in 1552. It may be added that Pithoeus dedicated his edition to Christophe de Thou (1508–1582), premier président of the Parlement of Paris: Pithoeus addresses him as '*Equiti, Regni Curiae Praesidi primario, et sacri Consistorii Senatori*'.[6] He was father of the great historian and book collector Jacques-Auguste de Thou (1553–1617), whom Pithoeus must have known. It will have been on some similar network that he got wind of a substitute for the defective old book. He does no more than refer to this as an Italian exemplar, '*non adeo vetusto*'.[7] But Håkanson showed that it was what we call N, Bern lat. 149.[8] This book was once owned by Jacques Bongars (1554–1612), diplomat, bibliophile and scholar, whose library, partly inherited from Pierre Daniel, eventually ended up in Bern.

I am going to digress on the subject of N – I hope it will be thought with good reason. Håkanson was well aware of the large number of places where readings of N coincide with corrections in B (known as B[2]), and was convinced that in such cases the corrections were taken from N (and not from N's twin in Munich, M).[9] Some of these corrections he thought might be due to conjecture; others he judged (I think rightly) to have been brought in from a source outside our tradition.[10] In his apparatus to the not very long *Decl.* 13, the piece which I shall be using throughout to illustrate this paper, Håkanson (1978) cites no fewer than seven instances where N agrees with B[2] against BC. In three cases he prints N's reading; and he says in his Preface (Håkanson (1978) XI) that two of these are not likely to be the result of conjecture. Several of the other readings are matters of dispute. In any case, it is remarkable that, despite the new witnesses that have emerged since Pithoeus, the text he printed in 1580 (see the Appendix) is basically almost identical to that printed by Håkanson (1978) four centuries later, if we ignore later conjectures made or accepted by Håkanson. There are three new readings from BC, all in the last three sentences: *nativum* for *notum* (highly dubious: Håkanson (1978) expresses no doubts *ad loc.*, but puts a question mark against it in his list on p. VIII), *moris* for *mortis* (which Pithoeus had already con-

5 See Pithoeus' dedicatory letter to Christophe de Thou and his final note on the *Minor Declamations*, reprinted in Burman (1720), 419 and 790 respectively.
6 Burman (1720) 413.
7 See the second of Pithoeus' notes referred to in n. 5 above.
8 Håkanson (1978) XIII.
9 For the manuscripts of Calpurnius see Håkanson's (1978) *Praefatio* and list of *sigla*. There is no need to go into detail here.
10 Håkanson (1978) IX-X.

jectured), and *me* for *nec* before *uenenum* right at the end (also, in fact, in N); I shall return to these passages. This does not suggest any great superiority of BC to N: rather the contrary. It looks then as though Pithoeus' luck was holding out. The manuscript to which I assume he had access through Bongars was by no means a dud, though of course the much damaged Montepessulanus would have been more valuable if it had survived intact.

However that may be, what Pithoeus printed remained the base text until the early twentieth century. It was what his successors strove to emend. He had done just a little himself to improve what he found in his manuscript. He suggested changing *consequitur* to the future *consequetur*, and he may have been right to do so. And, as we have seen, he proposed emending *mortis* to *moris*, which proved later to have manuscript support: a rather odd change, in my opinion, for *mos* can hardly have a *genus*.

Pithoeus, then, transcribed his manuscript, and made only minimal suggestions as to how its text might be improved. And he did not *explain* anything, either his conjectures or any difficulty in the Latin. This is in sharp contrast to his work on the *Minor Declamations*, where, besides exploiting his own old manuscript, he (to quote my own assessment) produced 'acute solutions to problems that Aerodius had failed to touch'.[11] This difference of approach is natural considering the different importance of the two texts, and the excitement of using an old primary manuscript for the first time. Pithoeus did not make much of Calpurnius Flaccus: '*Quis autem hic Calpurnius fuerit, alii fortasse dicturi sunt.*'[12] But others, I fear, have not been able to tell us.

Pithoeus in this way provided a text of Calpurnius, and not at all a bad one, for others to try to understand. When Calpurnius was next edited, in 1665, we have moved from the grand political and bibliophilic world of Pithoeus and his friends to the world of Dutch universities. That too was grand enough in its own way. Johann Friedrich Gronov ('Gronovius': 1611–71) was born in Hamburg, but studied at Leiden and Groningen. His predecessor in the chair at Leiden was Daniel Heinsius, and Gronovius was a friend of the brilliant Niklaas Heinsius, Daniel's son, the consummate textual critic. Gronovius was no mean critic himself, with an interest in prose (including the elder Seneca) as well as poetry. E. J. Kenney cites a fine letter of his to the young Heinsius where he talks of the art of textual criticism in terms that would be taken up by Bentley

---

11 Winterbottom (1984) XXIV.
12 See again Pithoeus' note referred to in n. 5 above.

and Housman later.[13] You need to be expert in languages, ancient customs, history, philosophy. 'When all this is brought together,' he goes on, 'and reading and diligent labour is attended by talent and judgement, the result is the ability to judge each ancient writer in his own terms'. The climax of Gronovius' list of the outcome of such wide erudition is 'to restore corrupt passages'. This he himself did with panache. In the *Minor Declamations* I speak of 'a galaxy of fine emendations' on his part.[14] His ideas shine in the *Major Declamations* too, and in the Elder Seneca. No one could have been better qualified to understand and where need be correct Calpurnius Flaccus.

Explanation, as with Pitheous, is in short supply. In *Decl.* 13 he reports Pithoeus' two conjectures, but does not print either in his text. *moris*, indeed, he improves to *timoris*, superficially a good deal more convincing, and to be accepted by Håkanson: the context does after all concern fear. But I am not very happy with the resulting phrase. I have wondered about keeping Pithoeus' text, including *mortis*. The city doctor has been given an objection: 'I had a better opportunity' (that is, than you, the citadel doctor) 'to administer poison: the tyrant himself had provided it' (that is, by summoning him to his bedside). To this the citadel doctor ripostes: '[But poisoning] is a common cause of death, so that previous experience results in a cautious attitude to everything.' Accordingly, the argument goes, the city doctor did *not* have a better opportunity. But, as we shall see, there is even more to say about this crux.

I have spoken as though Gronovius *edited* our work. In fact, the 1665 edition of the declamations '*ex officina Hackiana*' (Leiden and Rotterdam) is a *Variorum* text: '*cum variorum notis*', as it proclaims. The companion volume, also of 1665, which was devoted to Quintilian's *Institutio oratoria*, mentioned the notes of Turnebus, Camerarius, Gronovius 'and others'; but only Gronovius had, it seemed, worked on Calpurnius. Nor was the whole operation coordinated by him. Perhaps it was just a question of notes from his own private margin being taken over into the common stock.

Further on in the 1665 *Hackiana* we find a letter, dated in the same year, from another scholar who made his mark on declamatory texts, Johann Schultingh.[15] It is addressed 'Henrico Bentingio', that is, Hendrik Bentinck, scion of an important

---

13 Kenney (1974) 58 (Latin in n. 1): '*Haec cum conjuncta sunt, et lectio diligensque labor ingenio & judicio non destituitur, existit inde praeclarum illud egregium, posse de unoquoque Scriptorum veterum... judicium ferre, genium uniuscujusque penetrare, ... locos corruptos restituere.*'
14 As above, n. 11.
15 At pp. 759–60. The notes to Calpurnius follow on pp. 761–84.

family.[16] The Bentincks came from the Netherlands, where their family estate has for centuries been Schoonheten House in Overijssel; but they were to make a wider fortune when Hans Willem accompanied the Prince of Orange to England in the Glorious Revolution of 1688. In my own country they are still represented by the 12th Earl of Portland, who plays David Archer in the BBC Radio 4 programme *The Archers* (fame at last!). It appears that Hendrik and Johann had both been pupils '*summi Gronovii*'. Schultingh expresses the very proper conviction that he regarded it as part of his job to remove any injury inflicted on ancient texts by the ignorance or audacity of scribes or others, and to restore corrupted passages. He has begun this task by turning his attention to 'the Quintilians', but time has been short, and he can only offer his friend, in memory of their *condiscipulatus*, a specimen of his work. There follow around fifteen pages of '*emendationes et notae*' on Calpurnius' declamations. The letter is dated from Nijmegen, where Schultingh held a chair, and the year is given as 1665. Poignancy is added by the fact that Johann died in the following year, only seven years after the birth of his son Anton, who was to become professor in Leiden in the middle age of a life that was presumably a good deal longer than his father's.

We learn more specifically from Burman (of whom more later) that Johann had hoped to write a commentary on the *Major Declamations* and on Calpurnius, but had not got far into the task when he died, leaving somewhat chaotic notes behind.[17] These Burman was able to draw on with the permission of Anton Schultingh. We therefore have news of Schultingh's work both directly from the *Hackiana* and indirectly via Burman: though I must say that I have not found anything in Burman's reports of his ideas on Calpurnius that goes much beyond what had been published in the *Hackiana*.

Before saying something of Schultingh's work on *Decl.* 13, I must stress that, whatever its quality, it marks a distinct advance on Pithoeus and Gronovius in a significant sense. The idea of producing notes as well as emendations was new for Calpurnius, and it reflects Schultingh's realisation that this is a difficult text that requires explication as well as correction. The idea of writing a commentary was a sound one, even if it was not completed. Burman took the idea further, and at last in our own day we have a full commentary by Lewis A. Sussman (1994). Sussman also provides a translation, and that too was a happy thought. The more recent French version published under the name of Paul Aizpurua (2005) is not to be ignored, as we shall see. Declamation, apart from the elder

---

16 He is addressed as 'nobilissime'. Bentinck is styled 'Domino in Werckeren.' Werckere was a manor house in the hamlet of Mastenbroek in the 'north west' of the municipality of Zwolle. Thanks are due to Jasper de Mooij for his help with Dutch geography.
17 Burman (1720) *Praefatio*, p. **** 3.

Seneca, has little attracted translators until quite recently. I name *honoris causa* the quaint and acute English translation of the *Major Declamations* by (as the title page splendidly puts it) 'a learned and ingenious hand', that of John Warr, which came out in 1686. I know of hardly any successors until the remarkable Cassino series began in 1999.

What then of Schultingh, as we see him grappling with *Decl.* 13? Before discussing his emendations, I should stress his ability to provide declamatory parallels for particular usages, as here of *perdere*, and to explain (rather than emend) difficult phrases. Thus, on *Poenas meas hinc cogitate, in quibus nec ira nec natura cessavit*, he comments that *ira* refers to the torturers and the cruel tyrant, while *natura* 'seems' to refer to the flames employed by them. He compares *Decl.* 7, where the general is *iratus* and *ignes* are deployed. I doubt if this is correct, but seeing problems is one step towards solving them and may spark off ideas in others. Burman, after citing Schultingh's note, said he preferred to refer *natura* to the innate cruelty of the tyrant, *ira* to the temporary access of rage caused in him by the situation. I myself wonder if we should not, while taking *ira* of the tyrant, refer *natura* to the *patientia* of the doctor under torture. In any case, one would like some help with the word *hinc*: is it in effect explained by the relative clause that follows? The harshness of the torture can be judged both from the cruelty of the tyrant and the ability of the doctor to withstand the pain.

If one now turns to some of Schultingh's emendations, one is struck by his desire to give point where point seems to be lacking. In adding *huic* before *virus serpebat* and *non* before *longa*, he comments on the *languida oratio* of the received text. But in this instance, where the previous sentence is so doubtful and we are not sure if a new *sententia* starts at *virus*, the addition seems over-bold. Again, in emending the last sentence of the piece to *In arce enecavi: non deseruit me venenum*, he comments that this would be *declamatorium* as well as restoring the sense. We now know what Calpurnius really wrote here; but this feeling for declamatory Latin is one of Schultingh's great strengths in conjecture.

Finally, we come to his treatment of the major crux, or series of cruces, in this piece. He felt, as Håkanson did after him, that *Ultio... vindicavit* should be transposed to follow *emergit*. For, as Håkanson put it, 'these words belong to the description of the torture, whereas *praemium... polliceri* is probably [!] logically connected with *o quam facile* etc.'.[18] Håkanson later dropped this idea, no doubt rightly: one cannot be sure about connections of this sort when all we have is a series of *sententiae*. As in Seneca the Elder, a great difficulty for the critic is not being sure where the breaks between quotations should be set. As to

---

18 Håkanson (1974) 57.

what follows here in Calpurnius, Schultingh saw what for me is the key point: that *illecebra* refers to the temptation of the prize for tyrannicide, which replaces in the mind of the city doctor his previous desire to win a reward by saving the tyrant's life. He accordingly wrote '*inlecebraque* in contrarium *transferuntur*' (the passive was later found in BC). This seems to me to be on the right lines, though what should be made of the preceding *gerunt* is very doubtful. Schultingh thought of *cedunt*, where *persuasiones* is nominative, and *vertunt*, where it is accusative. I prefer it to be accusative, and suggest something like *suggerunt*, 'supply'. The subject of both this and *transferuntur* is the city doctor together with his advocate, as in *confingunt* earlier.

It should always be borne in mind that Schultingh's notes on Calpurnius are only a kind of draft; he did not live to perfect them. But he consistently displays an acute mind at work, concerned to help the reader to understand a difficult text, and to encourage him to think further for himself. What he did not do, any more than Gronovius, was to look for new manuscript evidence. He did a little in this direction for the *Institutio oratoria*, but not for the declamations.

When Ulrich Obrecht came to edit Calpurnius in Strasbourg in 1698, he added little, and indeed nothing at all in *Decl.* 13, where he in effect reproduces Gronovius' text. But that his flair was unabated is clear from a passage in *Decl.* 12, where from *o noverca! est alta crudelitas* he produced *o novercae stulta crudelitas!* Lehnert rejected this palmary emendation, Håkanson accepted it: no further comment on the comparative judgement of these two editors is necessary. Similar strokes aroused my admiration when I was editing the *Minor Declamations*. This was a clever man, who did not perhaps give his full attention to Calpurnius. He lived from 1646 to 1701 (he died not long indeed after the publication of his work on Quintilian and Calpurnius). He was a Strasbourg man, and presumably related to another Obrecht from that city (Elias, born in 1653 and professor in Uppsala). Ulrich's teacher, and his father-in-law, was Johann Heinrich Boekler (d. 1672), who also taught at Uppsala; there was a link between the two universities, fostered by Queen Christina of Sweden. Boekler worked on prose texts too, though historical ones. Ulrich followed him to the extent of editing the pseudo-historical *Scriptores Historiae Augustae* and *Dictys Cretensis*, as well as Quintilian. His career merits further investigation.

With Pieter Burman the Elder (1668–1741) we return to the Netherlands and to *Variorum* editions. Indeed he is the natural heir of Gronovius, whose son Jakob had taught him at Leiden. He himself ended up as professor at that university after a spell at Utrecht. No one contributed more freely to the genre of *Variorum* quarto editions, which so flourished in his time. In forty years he produced editions of around eleven major Latin authors. His declamation collection is more elaborately annotated than Gronovius' *Variorum*. For Calpurnius, as we have seen, he adduces Schultingh's notes, as well as those of Pithoeus and Gronovius. And he adds a good deal of his own from a well-stocked mind: rather surprisingly, considering that he did not value the declamations very highly. He only adds this second volume, he admitted, 'so that nothing should be found to be missing in this edition rather than because I think they deserve the expenditure of much time and trouble'.[19] He did adduce some new manuscript readings for the *Major Declamations*, but none for the *Minor*, let alone for Calpurnius.

Burman, no doubt, worked too fast and spread himself too widely. But he was nobody's fool. In commenting on *Decl.* 13, he reacts to the notes of the scholars whose work he draws upon rather than branching out on his own. But he has helpful things to say in the process. We have seen him countering Schultingh's view of *ira* and *natura*. Further on, though, he approves of Schultingh's *<non> longa poenarum dilatione*, comparing the haste seen in *instantem* and *festinans* nearby. I myself feel that the addition is not necessary. The punishment of the citadel doctor went on a long time, during which the condition of the tyrant got worse, giving him the opportunity to identify the poison (or, as I once suggested, the poisoner). What is perhaps more important is to explain *dilatione*, which does not mean 'continuation'.

When Burman does suggest changes of his own, he does not much convince, at least in *Decl.* 13. Near the end, he suggests '*notum hoc genus morbi*'; perhaps not very persuasively, but he knows parallels for the confusion of this word with *mortis* (though he does not cite more than one). That sort of argument is not often found in the material I have examined, and has a modern ring. He would also like *clamabant* in the last sentence but one, and Lehnert accepted this. But there is perhaps no real problem in *tota arce:* the tyrant started to range all over the citadel, shouting 'Doctor!'. Burman thought he was asking for the citadel doctor; but the city doctor must be meant, as in the phrase *medicum flagitabat* above, which defends both the singular *clamabat* and its tense. What is the point, though, of *quasi ego de tyrannicidio non negassem?* Aizpurua, whose translation I mentioned earlier, noted: 'Le tyran savait donc parfaitement, malgré les dénégations du médecin de la citadelle, que celui-ci l'avait empoisonné, et il en réclamait un autre, ne voulant plus des "soins" du premier.' This gives point: the citadel doctor is using the tyrant's call for a second opinion to prove that he had administered poison and so merited the prize. We may compare for this *quam et medicus confirmauerit et tyrannus* earlier. The tyrant (it is argued) acted as

---

19 Burman (1720) *Praefatio* *** 3: '...*Declamationibus, quas magis ne quid desiderari in hac editione posset, quam ut eas admodum dignas censeam, in quas multum temporis et laboris impendatur, subjiciendas putavi...*'.

though he did not believe the citadel doctor's denials. Here as elsewhere the speaker is reacting to the difficulty that the citadel doctor had, despite torture, claimed that he had *not* administered poison.

I do not understand why in an earlier sentence Burman proposed to read '*unde venenum tam celeriter parasti*' rather than *praeparasti*. But here I hope to contribute something of use to critics of our author, while at the same time keeping to my principle of never writing a paper without mentioning prose rhythm. When Calpurnius ends a sentence with a word forming a dichoreus or double trochee, his normal practice is to precede it with a proparoxytone word. Thus in a passage recently mentioned, the (paroxytone) dichoreus *flagitá-bat* is preceded by the proparoxytone *médicum*. The rule is observed even when the dichoreus is divided into monosyllable + trisyllable: thus at the end of the piece *non venénum* is preceded by the proparoxytone *deséruit*. I call it a rule. It holds good in about 36 cases out of the 45 (80%) which I count in the whole of Calpurnius.[20]

I shall not enlarge on the fact that this *clausula* is what is in the *cursus* system called the *velox*. I have written in one of my more impenetrable articles about the way in which dichorei over the centuries turn from elements in the metrical system of rhythm into elements of the *cursus*.[21] But Calpurnius is very relevant to this story, and it may be relevant to the question of his date (later rather than earlier, I should personally judge).

In view of this rhythmical practice, it would perhaps be unwise to abandon *praeparasti* in favour of *parasti* in the passage from which we started. We may also look at an early sentence in the piece, printed by Håkanson as *Confingunt nocendi voluntatem, postquam sanandi rationem perdiderunt. rationem* is a conjecture introduced by Håkanson,, the manuscripts being divided between *rem* (BC) and *remedium* (B²MN). The latter had never been questioned until B and C were discovered, for Pithoeus bequeathed N's *remedium* to his successors. *rem*, and *rationem* too, break my rule, so far as it is a rule.[22] But *remedium* conforms to it. I do not say that this decides the matter (for the locution is strange), but rhythm is a factor to be weighed, here and in other places in Calpurnius.

To return to my story: I should not omit mention of Peter de Fransz, Latinised as Francius, whose ideas are occasionally reported in Burman's *Variorum*. He has not had a good press, but he was certainly not without gifts. He was part of the Dutch network. Younger than Schultingh but older than Burman, he lived from 1645 to

---

20 Details in Håkanson (2014d) 124; Håkanson, counting on a different system, reckoned about 65%. He did not apply these findings to the cruces I discuss. See also Santorelli in this volume.
21 Winterbottom (2011).
22 *Rationem* is classified by Håkanson ((2014d) 125) under a much less common type of rhythm.

1704, serving first as professor of History and Eloquence at Amsterdam, then of Greek in the same university. He was not an editor. Rather, his métier of eloquence led him to compose poetry and many orations, two on the *Ratio Declamandi*.[23] In his Preface Burman speaks of having access to a codex which had once belonged to Francius.[24] It contained the *Institutio oratoria* and the declamations (what could it have been? – it would be nice to track it down). Burman got it from 'Johannes Bouersius' (*sic*), professor at Deventer, whom I cannot trace. It is apparently from this manuscript that Burman cites some conjectures by Francius. For instance, he thought to read *tyrannicidio* in the first sentence of *Decl.* 13, and the dative is certainly normal after the markedly Quintilianic locution *detrahere fidem*.[25] But Schultingh (Burman attests) had made this emendation before him.

Ever since Pithoeus first published Calpurnius, progress had been made only in conjectural emendation. No search was made for new manuscripts; editors merely felt it their task to improve and sometimes explain the text as they found it in printed editions. The nineteenth century saw new conditions that made tracking down manuscripts easier than before. Books passed from monasteries or private collections into city libraries. Catalogues began to be made. Lachmann, theorist as well as practitioner, laid the foundations for a scientific approach to textual criticism. Such developments brought distinguished results in some authors. Karl Halm in the 1860s recognised for Quintilian's *Institutio oratoria* three primary manuscripts, an Ambrosianus that had been known but little exploited before him, and books from Bern and Bamberg that had not been known at all. These three remain the basis for any modern text. But, equally important, Halm brought to his task an admirable acuteness in conjecture. His new witnesses were the foundation of his masterly text, but they did not dictate it. So too with the Elder Seneca. H. J. Müller in 1887 combined identification of the primary witnesses with excellent critical acumen. The *Minor Declamations* did not need such basic work on the manuscripts, for, as we have seen, Pithoeus had edited this text from the only old witness. And the *editio princeps* of 1494, for all its faults, did give access to a different, though much less good, branch of the tradition. It was left to Constantin Ritter to build on these foundations. But the value of his Teubner of 1884 lies especially in his own excellence in conjecture, and that of his mentor Erwin Rohde.

---

23 I have looked at these; they are hardly relevant to what we think of as declamation.
24 Burman (1720) *Praefatio* page following **** 2. For more on Francius' library see Winterbottom (1962) and Winterbottom (1964).
25 *Institutio* 2.17.15 (and nine other instances); also *Decl. Mai.* 10.13.

The fate of the *Major Declamations* and of Calpurnius Flaccus during this period was less happy. Both were edited by Georg Lehnert, the declamations in 1905, Calpurnius, a little earlier, in 1903. For the declamations, Hugo Dessauer had recently produced a thorough analysis of the manuscripts, which Håkanson later did little to modify.[26] Lehnert himself worked out the relationships of the far fewer witnesses to Calpurnius. On this basis he might have been able to produce satisfactory texts for both Calpurnius and the *Major Declamations*. That he did not was the result of his own deficiencies. He did not lack intelligence or diligence, but he was in the grip of a textual conservatism that might have been appropriate to some classical texts, but made no sense at all in the books he chose to edit. Few ancient books in Latin are more difficult to understand than these; and, to make matters worse, they are not well transmitted. It is just not good enough for an editor to print what he judges to be the archetype of his authors with insufficient citation (let alone acceptance) of earlier conjectures, and with little attempt to explain any difficulties.[27] Lehnert's texts have minimal value apart from their apparatuses, and even these Håkanson found could not be trusted in detail. The texts themselves represent an abnegation of the task of an editor. That task, I take it, is at a minimum to print a text founded on the manuscripts and to emend it where the editor judges it necessary. If the printed text is hard to understand, the apparatus should suggest possible remedies or refer us to printed discussions by earlier scholars. An *obelus* should be used in moments of despair. These principles were unknown to Lehnert, or rejected by him.

In Lehnert's defence I can only cite his own words in the preface to the *Major Declamations*. After remarking on the proliferation of emendations on display in Burman's edition, of which he promises to cite a selection in his apparatus, he goes on: 'I myself have purposely made few innovations. The wording of the declamations is better transmitted than you might think at first sight. If one more *carefully* examines the connection of sentences, and takes account not only of the (so to say) corrupt eloquence of the declamations but also of the manner of expression, which needs to be observed as *carefully* as possible and to be illuminated from texts that indulge in the vulgar language, it will become evident that many of the emendations that looked easy [*lenes*] in fact lack weight [*leves*]. Accordingly, my only aim in this edition was to put on display the readings of the manuscripts as *carefully* as possible, and with their help, so far as possible, to try

---

26 Dessauer (1898).
27 This is not true of the *Major Declamations*, on which he published some *adversaria* in Lehnert (1903b) (not listed in Håkanson (1982) XXVII-XXIX).

to recover the pristine form of the text after the removal of blots and errors.'[28] 'Care' is appealed to three times in this apologia, but that is not the only virtue required of an editor. And it is not clear how blots and errors in such a text are to be removed if not by conjectural criticism. Lehnert's next sentence (with a further appeal to carefulness) looks forward to a *felix eventus* of work by others on these declamations. He certainly did not achieve such a happy result himself.

I know nothing in Lehnert's philological background that accounts for his editorial practice. He seems to have trained at Leipzig when Otto Ribbeck (1827–1898) was still in post; but Ribbeck was by no means a conservative critic. The slightly younger Alfred Klotz (1874–1956), whom he mentions as a friend in both volumes, was not (I think) conservative either. Another friend was the excellent Dessauer, mentioned earlier for his work on the manuscripts of the *Major Declamations* (Dessauer 1898). He died very young, and did not live to be an editor. His friend's edition is dedicated to his *manes*.

Lehnert himself was born in 1871. It is presumably he who wrote a Leipzig dissertation *De scholiis ad Homerum rhetoricis* (1896). In 1901 he signed himself as being at Munich when he briefly introduced an article by the now deceased Dessauer.[29] But in January 1903 he was back in Leipzig, where he dated the Preface of his Calpurnius (dedicated PATRI OPTIMO). There is no similar indication in the *Major Declamations* edition of 1905. But he worked in the Giessen University Library from 1903 to 1913, and was later occupied in library and archival activities in and around Giessen.[30] Two brief pieces on declamatory topics came out in the early 1930s (Lehnert 1930 and 1932) and, for the Hepding Festschrift in 1938, a piece on 'Zauber und Astrologie in den erhaltenen römischen Deklamationen' (Lehnert 1938). Lehnert also contributed to Bursians Jahresbericht, the final item being a report on Greek and Roman Rhetoric in the years 1915 to 1925.[31] This was published (for some reason) only in the volume dated 1944–1955; its author died in 1944.

---

28 Lehnert (1905) *Praefatio* XXVII: '*ipse pauca novavi neque id sine consilio. melius enim quam primo aspectu credideris, declamationum verba tradita sunt. accuratius enim sententiarum nexu perspecto et ratione habita non modo corruptae, ut ita dicam, declamationum eloquentiae sed etiam loquendi usus qui quam accuratissime observandus atque ex scriptis quae indulgent sermoni vulgari, illustrandus est, apparebit multas earum emendationum quae videbantur esse lenes re vera leves esse. quam ob rem meum tantum erat hac in editione codicum lectiones quam accuratissime proferre atque earum auxilio quantum fieri potuit, maculis detersis mendisque deletis conari pristinam textus formam recuperare.*'
29 Dessauer (1901) 416.
30 Cf. Gundel (1957) 206.
31 Among his many reviews Lehnert (1934) and (1944/1955) are of particular relevance.

We can see Lehnert's principles, and his judgement, at work in miniature in Calpurnius 13. He cites several conjectures, but accepts only two, one of them Burman's perhaps unnecessary *clamabant*. He accepts from BC the new reading *nativum*, without mentioning that B², like Pithoeus, has the more plausible *notum*. He does register that all the manuscripts give not *deseruit me* but *deseruit nec* in the final sentence. Håkanson was able to base on this a brilliant and elegant conjecture, but Lehnert does not seem aware that his own new version of the sentence is as meaningless as the earlier. In sum: Lehnert gives us materials for a text, but not a text, or at least not one superior to that of Pithoeus.

I am aware of having spoken harshly of this scholar, and shall make some amends by quoting from a letter written me by the humane Antonio Stramaglia while we were jointly investigating Lehnert's hitherto obscure life: 'E' bello avere un'immagine un po' più concreta di uno studioso che non è certo stato in prima linea fra i "più bravi", ma che comunque si è dato da fare, pur dovendosi contentare di un lavoro di secondo piano.'

I come now, and finally, to Lennart Håkanson, about whom such reservations do not need to be expressed. Lennart, whom I was privileged to know as a friend, died at the age of 47. He had done a great deal that had won him the highest admiration of textual scholars working on Latin prose and Latin verse. But he was cut off in his prime. He should be alive today, and should have contributed to this volume.

I shall, however, try to avoid hagiography, tempting though that is.[32] First, as a background to the dry details of the career, some words from Alf Önnerfors' obituary on the man:[33] 'the thoughts he exchanged with his friends over the chessboard or during fishing expeditions on Lake Bosarp' (where the family owned a summer house) 'were about other (*sc.* than academic) matters, the essential ones. Lennart was an exceptionally well-integrated and harmonious human being. Those of us who knew him cannot forget his open, unspoiled boyish spirit, his genuine modesty, and the spontaneous pleasure he took in the good things of life; but most of all his warm friendship.' But he did, as people often said, live for his work. When I went to stay with him in Lund, he retired to work in the evening. Meanwhile, his wife Monica (with whom I am still in touch) turned over the pages of family photograph albums with me in the sitting room. His colleagues in the university told

---

32 In what follows, I draw (with the permission of the editors) on my account of Håkanson's career, which has appeared, in German translation, in the second volume of his *Unveröffentlichte Schriften* (Håkanson (2016), ix–xiii); this book contains a complete list of his writings (ibid., xiv–xvi).

33 Önnerfors (1988); kindly supplied to me (with other material) by Gerd Haverling, and kindly translated for me by Francis Lamport.

me that he was well known for forgetting to turn off the lights of his Volvo, and had regularly to summon assistance when his battery failed.

I also met him on academic occasions, first when he lectured in Oxford on the text of Lucan. I think we felt in advance that this young man could not improve on A. E. Housman. By the time the lecture was over, we were all aware that a new star had swum into our view: at least as acute as Housman, and quite without Housman's absurdly polemical tone. Later, I heard him give a paper at Cambridge for an occasion in honour of C. O. Brink; his topic, the historical fragments in the *Suasoriae* of the Elder Seneca, was a precursor of his posthumously published work, the Teubner of that difficult author. But for me the climax of our acquaintance was our correspondence while I was editing the *Minor Declamations*. It was typical of him that, when he heard of the progress I had made on my edition, he not only abandoned his own project of editing this text with the German scholar J. Dingel, but sent, over a long period, more and more emendations and interpretations for me to make free use of. When I say that I was also at the same time receiving similar help from D. R. Shackleton Bailey and W. S. Watt, you will be able to judge how exciting that period was for me.

Håkanson was born in Karlsborg in 1939, and at the University of Lund was taught by another Latinist of the highest distinction in Latin textual criticism, Bertil Axelson, himself the pupil of Einar Löfstedt: an apostolic succession indeed. Axelson found fault with his thesis on Statius' *Silvae:* he wrote of 'numerous faulty judgements', of an 'irritating lack of rigour and pregnancy in presentation'. Later, when Håkanson was a lecturer at Lund, the tone changed: 'H. has matured remarkably quickly: latterly he has tackled the major pseudo-Quintilian declamations and in our seminars has produced a surprisingly long series of really excellent emendations.'

Axelson noted correctly, though in apparent depreciation of Håkanson's efforts, that the *Major Declamations* had been seriously neglected by scholars. That observation cuts both ways. Håkanson was breaking new ground, and it needed an original talent to do justice to a whole genre that (in both Greek and Latin) called for more sympathetic and scholarly treatment than it had ever received before. That of course was true also of the edition of Calpurnius (1978), which came out four years before that of the *Major Declamations* (1982). It had been preceded by three articles in *Eranos* discussing individual passages (published in 1972, 1974 and 1976). In a letter to me dated 1975 enclosing offprints of two of these, he says: 'I must admit, that I have changed my mind on more than one or two of the problems discussed, partly because I have now collated all MSS existant to this author and prepared an edition, which will be published as soon as I can find anyone willing to print it (for the moment I am trying to tempt the venerable Teubner Verlag).' Teubner was indeed tempted, and the book came out in 1978.

Let us look, for almost the last time, at *Decl.* 13, and at the concluding sentence: *In arce enecavimus: deseruit nec venenum.* This is what Lehnert printed, noting that BC read *arcem*. Håkanson had already seen in 1972 that in this unintelligible string of words we must read: *In arce me nec animus deseruit nec venenum*. Clarity and point result from the change of a U/V to an N. This is the sort of emendation that looks obvious once someone else has made it; it was not obvious to Lehnert, and it might not have been obvious to any of us either.

For all Håkanson's work on manuscripts, it was of course textual criticism that was his real forte, as can be seen from the long list of his works. He published, beside the editions I have mentioned, major collections of conjectures and interpretations on Statius and Silius Italicus, and articles on the text of many other authors, some of them late. It may well be that, had he lived, he would have done yet more for late and medieval Latin, in the great tradition of Swedish scholarship. But the authors he most favoured were those which raised the problems in which he excelled, by their often tortured cleverness not only of expression but of argument that constantly keeps readers on their toes. It is by no means always a matter of emending the wording. A solution may often lie in the elucidation of a bizarre train of thought, or the re-positioning of a comma misplaced in previous editions. In this kind of writing Håkanson moved as easily as if he had himself sat at the feet of a Roman rhetor. In working on the texts he did, he showed a sure sense of what he did best.

Håkanson buttressed his critical work by some publications on wider topics: on homeoteleuton and adverbs in Latin dactylic poetry, and on prose rhythm. He also published a translation into Swedish of Apuleius' *Metamorphoses*, judged by an obituarist to be 'surely one of the most successful in any modern language'.[34] What he did *not* pronounce upon, at least in public, was what we distinguish as 'literary' criticism. In an age of theory he may well have felt that silence was the best course of action, and that the authors of antiquity are best served by trying to understand exactly what they were saying. At any rate, he told Alf Önnerfors that for the moment he was much too occupied with projects in textual criticism to turn in that other direction.

By 1980 Håkanson had been elected to the chair of Latin at Uppsala, only to die in the sea off Crete on 19 June 1987. He left behind, as eventually transpired, a corpus of unpublished work. Two volumes drawn from it have recently been published.[35]

---

34 Staffan Fogelmark (*Sydsvenska Dagbladet Snallposten*, 27 June 1987).
35 Håkanson (2014) and Håkanson (2016).

If, then, we look back over the story I have been telling, we can discern a pattern familiar (*mutatis mutandis*) from the story of many, though by no means all, classical texts. In the early period, down to 1800 or so, scholars, free-lance (Pithoeus) or, later, holding academic appointments (Obrecht, Burman), worked to correct texts without taking much interest in tracking down further manuscripts. In the nineteenth century, it became possible, and normal, to search for better manuscripts than those used hitherto. Lehnert did this service for Calpurnius Flaccus. In the twentieth century, it became easier and easier, and it was seen more and more to be desirable, to try to look at as many witnesses as possible. But at the same time the law of diminishing returns was asserting itself. R. A. B. Mynors, for all the thoroughness of his work on the manuscripts, produced a text of Pliny's Letters that hardly differed from H. Keil's. The same is true of L. D. Reynolds' work on the younger Seneca, and my own on Cicero's *De Officiis*.

If modern texts do improve on their predecessors, it is normally because they draw on the work of exceptional textual critics. Håkanson's Calpurnius, and his editions of the *Major Declamations* and Seneca Rhetor also, fall into this category. He by no means neglected the manuscripts. But the basic work on them had been done before him. What he brought to them was something only he could bring: a sure judgement and a conjectural flair that marks him off from the other editors I have discussed, good as some of them were. D. R. Shackleton Bailey did not praise lightly; but of Lennart Håkanson's critical powers he judged that they 'would have been remarkable at any period in the history of philology'.[36]

* * *

I should like to finish with a word or two about someone who has done a great deal for declamation without ever editing a declamatory text. Lennart Håkanson was cut off in his prime. His elder, Donald Russell, is still very much alive at the age of 97. I had the pleasure of discussing Calpurnius 13 with him some weeks before the Paris conference, and very much benefited from our talk; he was as sharp and engaged as he had been when he first introduced me to the Elder Seneca in 1954. We disputed over some of the cruces I have been talking about. On one, near the end of the piece, he suggested that we should accept *moris*, Pithoeus' conjecture confirmed by BC, but disjoin it from *genus:* 'it is customary that ...'. If that is right, we may perhaps take the short phrase *notum hoc genus* to mean 'This sort of thing is well known'. It was sad that we could not proceed to email Lennart and ask him what *he* thought.

---

36 Shackleton Bailey (1976) 73.

Appendix

XIII Medicus tyrannicida

TYRANNICIDAE PRAEMIVM. Tyrannus suspicatus sibi venenum datum ab eo medico quem in arce habebat, torsit eum. ille pernegauit. Misit ad medicum ciuitatis. dixit datum illi ab illo venenum, sed se remedium daturum, dedit poculum, quo exhausto statim perijt tyrannus, contendunt de praemio.

Pro medico arcis

Absit, sanctissimi iudices, vt hanc vos fidem tyrannicidij detrahatis, quam & medicus confirmauerit & tyrannus. Confingunt nocendi voluntatem, postquam sanandi remedium perdiderunt. Poenas meas hinc cogitate, in quibus nec ira, nec natura cessauit. Tolerabilis vis est vbi ad consuetudinem mali, caussa necessitatis emergit. Præmium consequitur qui ausus est & confirmare meum venenum, & suum remedium polliceri. Vltio quidem illa non quæstio. Tyrannus venenum quæsiuit? sed vindicauit. O quam facile gerunt persuasiones, inlecebramque in contrarium transferunt. Vt virus serpebat interius, & artus omnes longa pœnarum dilatione languebant, veneficium iam tyrannus agnouerat, quia instantem interitum sentiebat. festinans medicum flagitabat. vnde venenum tam celeriter præparasti? dicis forte, Maior mihi dandi veneni fiebat occasio, quæ ex ipsius voluntate veniebat. Notum hoc genus mortis est, vt ex sensu priore, ad cuncta cautior sollicitudo procedat. nonne iam apud tyrannum cuncta suspecta præsens formido faciebat? Medicum tota arce clamabat. quasi ego de tyrannicidio non negassem. In arce enecauimus. deseruit me venenum.

Proposed text[1]

Tyrannicidae praemium. Tyrannus, suspicatus sibi venenum datum ab eo medico quem in arce habebat, torsit eum. Ille pernegavit. Misit ad medicum civitatis.

---

1 The apparatus given here is not what I should print in an edition of Calpurnius. It includes all the emendations mentioned in the course of this paper, and excludes manuscript variants except those mentioned there.

Dixit datum illi ab illo venenum, sed se remedium daturum. Dedit poculum; quo exhausto statim periit tyrannus. Contendunt de praemio.

1. Absit, sanctissimi iudices, ut hanc vos fidem tyrannicidii detrahatis, quam et medicus confirmaverit et tyrannus. 2. Confingunt nocendi voluntatem, postquam sanandi remedium perdiderunt. 3. Poenas meas hinc cogitate, in quibus nec ira nec natura cessavit. 4. Tolerabilis vis est ubi ad consuetudinem mali causa necessitatis emergit. 5. Praemium consequitur qui ausus est et confirmare meum venenum et suum remedium polliceri? 6. Ultio quidem illa, non quaestio. 7. Tyrannus venenum quaesivit? Se vindicavit. 8. O quam facile suggerunt persuasiones, illecebraque in contrarium transferuntur! 9. Virus serpebat interius, et artus omnes longa poenarum dilatione languebant: veneficium iam tyrannus agnoverat. 10. Quia instantem interitum sentiebat, festinans medicum flagitabat. Vnde venenum tam celeriter praeparasti? 11. Dicis forte: 'Maior mihi dandi veneni fiebat occasio, quae ex ipsius voluntate veniebat.' Notum hoc genus: moris est ut ex sensu priore ad cuncta cautior sollicitudo procedat. Nonne iam apud tyrannum cuncta suspecta praesens formido faciebat? 12. Medicum tota arce clamabat, quasi ego de tyrannicidio non negassem. 13. In arce me nec animus deseruit nec venenum.

Thema	venenum datum B2N: verecundatus BC
1	tyrannicidio *Schultingh, Francius*
2	remedium B²N: rem BC: rationem *Schaub ap. Håkanson*
5	consequetur *Pithoeus*
6	ultio … vindicavit *post* emergit (4) *transpos. Schultingh*
8	suggerunt *tempt. Winterbottom:* gerunt *codd.:* cedunt *uel* vertunt *Schultingh*
	inlecebraque *Schultingh:* inlecebramque *codd.*
	transferuntur BC: transferunt ut B²N
9	<huic> serpebat … <non> longa *Schultingh*
	serpebat B²N: scribebat BC
	veneficum *Winterbottom* (1995) 42
10	parasti *Burman*
11	veneni B²N: bene BC
	notum B²N: nativum BC
	post genus *distinxit Russell*
	moris BC, *Pithoeus* (*e coniectura*): mortis B²N: timoris *Gronovius:* morbi *Burman*
12	clamabant *Burman*
13	in arce me nec animus *Håkanson:* in arce (arcem BC) enecavimus *codd.:* in arce enecavi: non *Schultingh*
	nec *codd.:* me *Pithoeus, errore legendi, et sic edd. usque ad Lehnert*

Translation

The doctor who killed the tyrant

A tyrant-killer is to receive a prize. A tyrant, suspecting he had been given poison by the doctor he kept in the citadel, tortured him. He absolutely denied it. The tyrant sent word to the city doctor,[2] who said that he [the tyrant] had been given poison by him [the castle doctor], but that he would supply a cure. He gave him a draught, on draining which the tyrant fell dead on the spot. They dispute the prize.

1. Far be it from you, most reverend judges, to refuse to believe in a tyrannicide that has been confirmed both by a doctor and a tyrant.[3]
2. They [the doctor and his advocate] are fabricating an intention to harm <the tyrant>, after failing to cure him.
3. Picture my punishment from this: neither anger [the tyrant's] nor nature [the doctor's endurance] failed.
4. Force can be borne when necessity results in[4] habituation to evil.
5. Is the prize going to one who had the face both to confirm my poison and to promise a remedy of his own?[5]
6. That was revenge, not an investigation.[6]
7. The tyrant did not inquire into poison, but revenged it.
8. How easily they supply convictions,[7] and are put into reverse by the lure [of the prize]!
9. The poison crept further in, and all the limbs grew languid as the punishment was prolonged: by now the tyrant had recognised he had been poisoned/who had poisoned him.
10. Because he felt death was upon him, he asked for a doctor in a hurry. How <then> did you manage to prepare a poison so quickly?
11. Perhaps you say: 'I had a better opportunity to administer poison because it arose from his own wish.' This is a familiar situation: it is customary that as

---

2 Rather than 'sent for'?

3 The (city) doctor by saying the citadel doctor gave poison to the tyrant (cf. §5), the tyrant by suspecting he had.

4 Though *emergit* is odd.

5 Perhaps not a question.

6 I.e. the tyrant had decided in advance what the answer was.

7 *Persuasio* in the plural is found in Quintilian, e.g. 3. 1. 6 with *mutare*.

a result of previous experience one is more cautious towards everything. Did not his present terror now make everything suspect?[8]

12. He called for a doctor all over the citadel, as though I had not denied I had tried to kill him.

13. In the citadel I was failed neither by my spirit nor by my poison.

---

8 *Moris est* is common in Quintilian. The city doctor claims that he had intended to give poison, and that he had had a better opportunity to give it than the citadel doctor because the tyrant had sent for him. The reply is: no, you didn't, because the tyrant would have been more cautious this time round.

Bibliography

Achard, G. (1994) *Cicéron. De l'invention.* Paris.

Adams, J. N. (1982) *The Latin Sexual Vocabulary.* London.

Aizpurua, P. (2005) *Calpurnius Flaccus. Les plaidoyers imaginaires.* Paris.

Alston, R. (1998) 'Arms and the man: soldiers, masculinity and power in Republican and Imperial Rome', in: L. Foxhall and J. Almon (eds.) *When Men Were Men: Masculinity, Power, and Identity in Classical Antiquity.* New York: 205–23.

Appleton, C. (1924) 'Trois épisodes de l'histoire ancienne de Rome: les Sabines, Lucrèce, Virginie', *Revue Historique de Droit Français et Étranger* s. IV 3: 193–271; 592–670.

Axelson, B. (1952) *Akzentuierender Klauselrhythmus bei Apuleius. Bemerkungen zu den Schriften* De Platone *und* De Mundo. Lund.

Badius Ascensius, I. (1528) *Commentarii familiares ... in M. Fabii Quintiliani declamationes, nuper editi.* Paris.

Balbo, A. (2011) 'Tra *sententia* e proverbio. Problemi di paremiografia in Seneca il Vecchio', *Philologia Antiqua* 4: 11–34.

Balbo, A. (2014) *Ricognizioni sul tema della fortuna in Seneca,* in: E. Guglielminetti (ed.) *Fortuna, Spazio filosofico* 12: 555–65 (http://www.spaziofilosofico.it/).

Balbo, A. (2015) *Declamazione e paremiografia,* in: M. Lentano (ed.) *La declamazione latina. Prospettive a confronto sulla retorica di scuola a Roma antica.* Naples: 1–17.

Balbo, A. (2016) *Ri-leggere un retore: riflessioni lessicali su Calpurnio Flacco,* in: R. Poignault and C. Schneider (eds.) *Fabrique de la déclamation antique (suasoires et controverses grecques et latines).* Lyon: 49–65.

Baraz, Y., and van den Berg, C. S. (eds.) (2013) 'Introduction', *American Journal of Philology* 134.1 (Special Issue: *Intertextuality and its discontents*): 1–8.

Beall, S. (1997) 'Translation in Aulus Gellius', *Classical Quarterly* 47: 215–26.

Beard, M. (2007) *The Roman Triumph.* Cambridge, MA.

Beard, M. (1993), 'Looking (Harder) for Roman Myth: Dumézil, Declamation and the Problem of Definition', in: F. Graf (ed.), *Mythos in mythenloser Gesellschaft. Das Paradigma Roms,* Stuttgart, 44–64.

Becker, A. (1904) *Pseudo-Quintiliana.* Ludwigshafen a. Rh.

Bernay-Vilbert, J. (1974) 'La répression de l'homosexualité dans la Rome antique', *Arcadie* 21 [n° 250]: 443–56.

Bernstein, N. W. (2009) 'Adoptees and exposed children in Roman declamation. Commodification, luxury, and the threat of violence', *Classical Philology* 104: 331–53.

Bernstein, N. W. (2012) '"Torture her until she lies": torture, testimony, and social status in Roman rhetorical education', *Greece and Rome* 59: 165–77.

Bernstein, N. W. (2013) *Ethics, Identity and Community in Later Roman Declamation.* Oxford.

Berti, E. (2007) Scholasticorum Studia. *Seneca il Vecchio e la cultura retorica e letteraria della prima età imperiale.* Pisa.

Bianco, M. M. (2010) '*Urbana militia.* L'oratore e il generale', *Res publica litterarum* 31: 3–27.

Biville, F. (ed.) (1999) *Proverbes et sentences dans le monde romain.* Paris.

Biville, F. (1999a) 'Les proverbes: nature et enjeux', in: F. Biville (ed.) *Proverbes et sentences dans le monde romain.* Paris: 11–25.

https://doi.org/10.1515/9783110401554-010

Bloomer, M. (1997a) *Latinity and Literary Society at Rome*. Philadelphia, PA.

Bloomer, M. (1997b) 'Schooling in persona: imagination and subordination in Roman education', *Classical Antiquity* 16: 57–78.

Bloomer, W. H. (2007) 'Roman Declamation: the Elder Seneca and Quintilian', in: W. Dominik and J. Hall (eds.) *A Companion to Roman Rhetoric*. Malden, MA – Oxford – Carlton: 83–97.

Bonner, S. F. (1949) *Roman Declamation in the Late Republic and Early Empire*. Liverpool.

Bornecque, H. (1902) *Les déclamations et les déclamateurs d'après Sénèque le père*. Lille (= Hildesheim 1967).

Bornecque, H. (1992³) *Sénèque le Père, Sentences, divisions et couleurs des orateurs et des rhéteurs (Controverses et Suasoires)*. Paris (corrected reprint of 1932²).

Boulanger, A. (1949) *Cicéron, Discours, Tome XVII, Pour C. Rabirius Postumus; Pour T. Annius Milon*. Paris.

Braun, M. (2005) 'Prolepsis', in: G. Üding (ed.) *Historisches Wörterbuch der Rhetorik 7*. Tübingen: 197–201.

Breij, B. (2006) '*Vitae necisque potestas* in Roman declamation', *Advances in the History of Rhetoric* 9: 55–81.

Breij, B. (2006a) '"Post exitum unici revertor in patrem". *Sententiae* in Roman declamation', in: A. Lardinois, M. van der Poel and V. Hunink (eds.) *Land of dreams*. Leiden: 311–27.

Breij, B. (2009) 'Pseudo-Quintilian's *Major Declamations:* Beyond School and Literature', *Rhetorica* 27: 354–69.

Brescia, G. (2004) *Il* Miles *alla sbarra. [Quintiliano]:* Declamazioni maggiori *III*. Bari.

Brescia, G. (2006) *La sfida impossibile: Ps. Quint.* Declamazioni minori *317*. Bari.

Brescia, G., and Lentano, M. (2009) *Le ragioni del sangue. Storie di incesto e fratricidio nella declamazione Latina*. Naples.

Brescia, G. (2012) *La donna violata. Casi di* stuprum *e* raptus *nella declamazione latina*. Lecce.

Brescia, G. (2015) 'Ambiguous Silence: *stuprum* and *pudicitia* in Latin Declamation,' in: E. Amato, F. Citti and B. Huelsenbeck (eds.) *Law and Ethics in Greek and Roman Declamation*. Berlin – Munich – Boston: 75–93.

Brzoska, J. (1897) 'Calpurnius Flaccus [40]', in *Pauly-Wissowa Realencyclopädie der classischen Altertumswissenschaft* III.1. Stuttgart: 1371–72.

Burman, P. (1720) *M. Fabii Quinctiliani, ut ferunt, Declamationes XIX majores, et quae ex CCCLXXXVIII supersunt CXLV minores et Calpurnii Flacci Declamationes, cum notis doctorum virorum*. Leiden.

Calboli, G. (1999) 'Sentences et proverbes dans la littérature et la rhétorique', in: F. Biville (ed.) *Proverbes et sentences dans le monde romain*. Paris: 42–54.

Calboli Montefusco, L. (1979) *Consulti Fortunatiani* Ars rhetorica. Bologna.

Calboli Montefusco, L. (1986) *La dottrina degli* status *nella retorica greca e romana*. Hildesheim – Zurich – New York.

Calboli Montefusco, L. (1999) 'La *gnome* et l'argumentation', in: F. Biville (ed.) *Proverbes et sentences dans le monde romain*. Paris: 27–39.

Calboli Montefusco, L. (2007) 'La funzione strategica dei *colores* nella pratica declamatoria', in: L. Calboli Montefusco (ed.) *Papers on Rhetoric* VII. Rome: 157–77.

Callies, H. (1971) 'Zur Vorstellung der Römer von den Cimbern und Teutonen seit dem Ausgang der Republik', *Chiron* 1: 341–50.

Cameron, A. (2011) *The Last Pagans of Rome*. Oxford.

Cantarella, E. (1987) 'Etica sessuale e diritto. L'omosessualità maschile a Roma',
Rechtshistorisches Journal 6: 263–92.

Cantarella, E. (1991) *Selon la nature, l'usage et la loi: la bisexualité dans le monde antique.*
Paris (French translation of: *Secondo natura. La bisessualità nel mondo antico.* Rome
1988).

Casaceli, F. (1986) 'Sulla composizione di alcuni *argumenta* nelle *Controversiae* di Seneca
Padre', in: G. Resta and S. Calderone (eds.) *Hestíasis. Studi di tarda antichità offerti a
Salvatore Calderone*. Messina: 397–406.

Casamento, A. (2002) Finitimus oratori poeta: *Declamazioni retoriche e tragedie senecane.*
Palermo.

Casamento, A. (2004) 'Le mani dell'eroe: in nota a Sen. *Contr.* 1.4', Pan 22: 243–53.

Casamento, A. (2016) 'Come un figlio: variazioni tematiche e modalità narrative. A proposito
di Sen. *contr.* 10.2 e decl. 258', in: A. Casamento, D. van Mal-Maeder and L. Pasetti
(eds.) *Le* Declamazioni minori *dello Pseudo-Quintiliano. Discorsi immaginari tra
letteratura e diritto.* Berlin – Boston: 191–212.

Citti, F. (2007) 'La declamazione greca in Seneca il Vecchio', in: L. Calboli Montefusco (ed.)
Papers on Rhetoric VIII. Rome: 57–102.

Citti, F. (2015) 'Nature and Natural Law in Roman Declamation', in: E. Amato, F. Citti and B.
Huelsenbeck (eds.) *Law and Ethics in Greek and Roman Declamation.* Berlin – Boston:
95–131.

Citti, F., and Pasetti, L. (2015) 'Declamazione e stilistica', in: M. Lentano (ed.) *La
declamazione latina. Prospettive a confronto sulla retorica di scuola a Roma antica.*
Naples: 19–57.

Coffee, N. (2009) *The Commerce of War. Exchange and Social Order in Latin Epic.* Chicago.

Connell, S. (2016) *Aristotle on Female Animals: A Study of the* Generation of Animals.
Cambridge.

Connolly, J. (2007) *The State of Speech.* Princeton, NJ.

Conte, G. B. (1986) *The Rhetoric of Imitation: Genre and Poetic Memory in Virgil and Other
Latin Poets.* (ed. and trans. C. Segal). Ithaca, NY.

Corbeill, A. (2007) '*Rhetorical Education* and Social Reproduction in the Republic and Early
Empire', in: W. Dominik and J. Hall (eds.) *A Companion to Roman Rhetoric.* Malden,
MA – Oxford – Carlton: 69–82.

Coroï, J. (1915) *La violence en droit criminel romain.* Paris.

Courtney, E. (1995) Musa lapidaria. *A Selection of Latin Verse Inscriptions.* Atlanta, GA.

Cousin, J. (1975–1980) *Quintilien, Institution oratoire. Tomes I-VII, Livres I-XII.* Paris.

Dalla, D. (1987) Ubi Venus mutatur. *Omosessualità e diritto nel mondo romano.* Milan.

Danesi Marioni, G. (2011–12) 'Lo spettacolo della crudeltà. Mutilazioni e torture in due
Controversiae (1,4 e 5) di Seneca Retore (e nel cinema d'oggi)', *Quaderni di Anazetesis*
9: 17–45.

Dangel, J. (1999) 'Proverbes et sentences. Rhétorique, poétique et métatexte', in: F. Biville
(ed.) *Proverbes et sentences dans le monde romain.* Paris: 55–74.

Dauge, Y.-A. (1981) *Le Barbare. Recherches sur la conception romaine de la barbarie et de la
civilisation.* Brussels.

Delarue, F. (1979) 'La *sententia* chez Quintilien', in: *Formes brèves. De la* γνώμη *à la pointe,
métamorphoses de la sententia. La Licorne.* Poitiers: 97–124.

Desanti, L. (1990) *'Interpellare de stupro* e *iniuriae in corpus:* P. S. 5,4,4', *Annali dell'Università di Ferrara. Sezione Vᵃ: Scienze Giuridiche* 4: 129–42.

Dessauer, H. (1898) *Die handschriftliche Grundlage der neunzehn grösseren pseudo-quintilianischen Declamationen.* Leipzig.

Dessauer, H. (1901) 'De codice rescripto Parisino 7900 A', *Rheinisches Museum für Philologie* 56: 416–22.

Di Capua, F. (1946) *Sentenze e proverbi nella tecnica oratoria e la loro influenza sull'arte del periodare.* Naples (= F. Di Capua (1959) *Scritti minori* I. Rome: 41–188).

Dingel, J. (1988) Scholastica Materia. *Untersuchungen zu den* Declamationes Minores *und der* Institutio Oratoria *Quintilians.* Berlin – New York.

Dinter, M. T. (2016) *'Fama* in Ps-Quintilian's Declamations', in: M. T. Dinter, C. Guérin and M. Martinho (eds.) *Reading Roman Declamation: The Declamations Ascribed to Quintilian.* Berlin – Boston: 127–46.

Doblhofer, G. (1994) *Vergewaltigung in der Antike.* Stuttgart – Leipzig.

Dobrov, G. (2001) *Figures of Play. Greek Drama and Metafictional Poetics.* Oxford.

Dumont, J. C. (2003) 'Les données économiques', in: F. Hinard and J. C. Dumont (eds.) Libitina. *Pompes funèbres et supplices en Campanie à l'époque d'Auguste. Édition, traduction et commentaire de la* Lex Libitinae Puteolana. Paris: 69–74.

Dunkle, R. (1971) 'The rhetorical tyrant in Roman historiography. Sallust, Livy and Tacitus', *Classical World* 65: 12–20.

Dupont, F., and Éloi, T. (2001) *L'érotisme masculin dans la Rome antique.* Paris.

Echavarren, A. (2007) *Nombres y personas en Séneca el Viejo.* Pamplona.

Eckstein, F. A. (1871) *Nomenclator philologorum.* Leipzig.

Edmunds, L. (2001) *Intertextuality and the reading of Latin poetry.* Baltimore, MD – London.

Edwards, C. (1997) 'Unspeakable professions. Public performance and prostitution in ancient Rome', in: J. P. Hallett and M. B. Skinner (eds.) *Roman Sexualities.* Princeton, NJ: 66–95.

Fairweather, J. (1981) *Seneca the Elder.* Cambridge.

Fairweather, J. (1984) 'The Elder Seneca and declamation', in: *Aufstieg und Niedergang der römischen Welt* II.32.1: 514–56.

Fantham, E. (1978) 'Imitation and decline: rhetorical theory and practice in the first century after Christ', *Classical Philology* 73: 102–16.

Fantham, E. (1991) *'Stuprum.* Public attitudes and penalties for sexual offences in Republican Rome', *Echos du monde classique* 10: 267–91.

Fantham, E. (2004) 'Disowning and dysfunction in the declamatory family', *Materiali e discussioni* 53: 65–82 (= E. Fantham (2011) *Roman Readings. Roman Response to Greek Literature from Plautus to Statius and Quintilian.* Berlin – New York: 302–19).

Favreau Linder, A.-M. (2006) 'Le sophiste et son public dans les déclamations de Lucien', in: G. Abbamonte, L. Miletti and L. Spina (eds.) *Discorsi alla prova.* Naples: 421–47.

Feddern, S. (2013) *Die Suasorien des älteren Seneca.* Berlin.

Flacelière, R., and Chambry, E. (1971) *Plutarque, Vies Tome VI.* Paris.

Forbes, R. J. (1971) *Studies in ancient technology* VIII. Leiden.

Franceschi, T. (2004) 'La formula proverbiale', in: V. Boggione and L. Massobrio (eds.) *Dizionario dei proverbi.* Turin: ix–xxii.

Franchet D'Espèrey, S. (2006) 'Rhétorique et poétique chez Quintilien: à propos de l'apostrophe', *Rhetorica* 24: 163–185.

Frazel, T. D. (2009) *The Rhetoric of Cicero's* In Verrem. Göttingen.

Garbarino, G., and Tabacco, R. (2008) *M. Tullio Cicerone*, Ad familiares. Turin.

Gardner, J. F. (1998) *Family and* Familia *in Roman Law and Life*. Oxford.

Gleason, M. (1995) *Making Men. Sophists and Self-Presentation in Ancient Rome*. Princeton, NJ.

Golz, G. (1913) *Der rhythmische Satzschluss in den grösseren pseudoquintilianischen Declamationen*, Diss. Kiel. Breslau.

Grimal, P. (1979) *L'amour à Rome*. Paris.

Gronov, J. F. (1665) *M. Fab. Quintiliani Declamationes undeviginti. M. Fabii Avi et Calpurnii Flacci Declamationes. Auctoris Incerti Dialogus* De causis corruptae Eloquentiae. Leiden – Rotterdam.

Guérin, C. (2010) 'Référence aux orateurs et usages de la citation chez Cicéron et Sénèque le rhéteur', in: L. Calboli Montefusco (ed.) *Papers on Rhetoric* X: 141–56.

Gundel, H. G. (1957) 'Die klassische Philologie an der Universität Giessen im 20. Jahrhundert', in: *Ludwigs-Universität, Justus-Liebig-Hochschule 1607–1957. Festschrift zur 350-Jahrfeier*. Giessen: 192–221.

Gunderson, E. (2003) *Declamation, Paternity, and Roman Identity*. Cambridge.

Hagendahl, H. (1936) 'Rhetorica', in: *Apophoreta Gotoburgensi Vilelmo Lundström oblata*. Göteborg: 282–338.

Hagendahl, H. (1937) *La prose métrique d'Arnobe. Contributions à la connaissance de la prose littéraire de l'Empire*. Göteborg.

Håkanson, L. (1972) 'Some critical remarks on Calpurnius Flaccus', *Eranos* 70: 59–71.

Håkanson, L. (1974) 'Some more critical remarks on Calpurnius Flaccus', *Eranos* 72: 53–64.

Håkanson, L. (1976) 'On two passages in Calpurnius Flaccus', *Eranos* 74: 67–68.

Håkanson, L. (1978) *Calpurni Flacci Declamationum Excerpta*. Stuttgart.

Håkanson, L. (1982) *Declamationes XIX maiores Quintiliano falso ascriptae*. Stuttgart.

Håkanson, L. (1986) 'Die quintilianischen Deklamationen in der neueren Forschung', in: *Aufstieg und Niedergang der römischen Welt* II.32.4: 2272–306.

Håkanson, L. (1989) *L. Annaeus Seneca Maior. Oratorum et rhetorum sententiae, divisiones, colores*. Leipzig.

Håkanson, L. (2014) *Unveröffentlichte Schriften* I: *Studien zu den grösseren pseudoquintilianischen Deklamationen* (ed. B. Santorelli). Berlin – Boston.

Håkanson, L. (2014a) 'Zu den Themata der *Größeren Deklamationen*', in: L. Håkanson, *Unveröffentlichte Schriften* I (ed. B. Santorelli). Berlin – Boston: 5–14.

Håkanson, L. (2014b) 'Zu den literarischen Vorbildern der *Declamationes maiores*: Cicero, Seneca, *Declamationes minores*', in: L. Håkanson, *Unveröffentlichte Schriften* I (ed. B. Santorelli). Berlin – Boston: 15–38.

Håkanson, L. (2014c) 'The Murder of a Manuscript', in: L. Håkanson, *Unveröffentlichte Schriften* I (ed. B. Santorelli). Berlin – Boston: 39–46.

Håkanson, L. (2014d) 'Der Satzrhythmus der 19 *Größeren Deklamationen* und des Calpurnius Flaccus', in: L. Håkanson, *Unveröffentlichte Schriften* I (ed. B. Santorelli). Berlin – Boston: 47–130.

Håkanson, L. (2016) *Unveröffentlichte Schriften* II: *Kritischer Kommentar zu Seneca Maior, Controversiae, Buch* (eds. F. Citti, B. Santorelli and A. Stramaglia). Berlin – Boston.

Håkanson, L., and Winterbottom, M. (2015) '*Tribunus Marianus*', in: L. Del Corso, F. De Vivo and A. Stramaglia (eds.) *Nel segno del testo. Edizioni, materiali e studi per Oronzo Pecere*. Florence: 61–90.

Hallik, S. (2007) Sententia *und* Proverbium. *Begriffsgeschichte und Texttheorie in Antike und Mittelalter.* Cologne.

Häussler, R. (1968) *Nachträge zu A. Ottos 'Sprichwörter und sprichwörtlichen Redensarten der Römer', eingeleitet und mit einem Register.* Hildesheim.

Haye, T. (1999) Oratio. *Mittelalterliche Redekunst in lateinischer Sprache.* Leiden – Boston.

Henry, D. (2006) 'Understanding Aristotle's Reproductive Hylomorphism', *Apeiron* 39: 257–87.

Hermans, L. (1995) *Bewust van andere lusten. Homoseksualiteit in het Romeinse keizerrijk.* Amsterdam.

Hill, T. (2004) Ambitiosa Mors. *Suicide and Self in Roman Thought and Literature.* New York – London.

Hinds, S. (1998) *Allusion and Intertext: Dynamics of* Appropriatio *in Roman Poetry.* Cambridge.

Hölkeskamp, K. J. (2004) Senatus Populusque Romanus. *Die politische Kultur der Republik – Dimension und Deutungen.* Stuttgart.

Hölscher, T. (2006) 'The transformation of victory into power. From event to structure', in: S. Dillon and K. Welch (eds.) *Representations of War in Ancient Rome.* Cambridge: 27–48.

Hömke, N. (2002) *Gesetz den Fall, ein Geist erscheint. Komposition und Motivik der ps-quintilianischen* Declamationes maiores *X, XIV und XV.* Heidelberg.

Hömke, N. (2007) '"Not to win, but to please". Roman declamation beyond education', in: L. Calboli Montefusco (ed.) *Papers on Rhetoric* VIII. Rome: 103–27.

Hömke, N. (2009) 'The declaimer's one-man show. Playing with roles and rules in the pseudo-Quintilian *Declamationes maiores*', *Rhetorica* 27: 240–55.

Huelsenbeck, B. (2009) *Figures in the Shadows: Identities in Literary History from the Anthology of the Elder Seneca.* Diss. Duke University.

Huelsenbeck, B. (2011a) 'Seneca *contr.* 2.2.8 and 2.2.1: The rhetor Arellius Fuscus and Latin literary history', *Materiali e discussioni* 66: 175–94.

Huerta Cabrera, Y. V. (2015). *La retórica de los* colores. *Tipología en las Controversias de Séneca el Viejo.* Diss. UNAM, Mexico.

Imber, M. (2001) 'Practiced speech: oral and written conventions in Roman declamation', in: J. Watson (ed.) *Speaking Volumes: Orality & Literacy in the Greek & Roman World.* Leiden: 201–16.

Innes, D., and Winterbottom, M. (1988) *Sopatros the Rhetor. Studies in the text of the* Διαίρεσις Ζητημάτων. London.

Janson, T. (1964) *Latin Prose Prefaces.* Stockholm.

Johansson, M. (2015) 'Nature over Law: Themes of Disowning in Libanius' Declamations,' in: E. Amato, F. Citti and B. Huelsenbeck (eds.) *Law and Ethics in Greek and Roman Declamation.* Berlin – Munich – Boston: 269–86.

Jonkers, E. J. (1949) '*Macte virtute esto*', *Mnemosyne* 4: 63–7.

Joshel, S. (1992) 'The Body Female and the Body Politic: Livy's Lucretia and Verginia,' in: A. Richlin (ed.) *Pornography and Representation in Greece and Rome.* New York: 112–30.

Kaser, M. (1956) '*Infamia* und *ignominia* in den römischen Rechtsquellen', *Stimmen der Zeit* 73: 220–78.

Kenney, E. J. (1974) *The Classical Text.* Berkeley – Los Angeles – London.

Knapp, R. (2011) *Invisible Romans.* Cambridge, MA.

Knobel, M., and Lankshear, C. (2007) 'Online memes, affinities, and cultural production', in: M. Knobel and C. Lankshear (eds.) *A New Literacies Sampler.* New York: 199 – 227.

Kohl, R. (1915) *De scholasticorum declamationum argumentis ex historia petitis.* Paderborn.

Kolendo, J. (1981) 'L'esclavage et la vie sexuelle des hommes libres à Rome', *Index* 10: 288 – 97.

Korenjak, M. (2000) *Publikum und Redner. Ihre Interaktion in der sophistischen Rhetorik der Kaiserzeit.* Munich.

Korneeva, T. (2011) Alter et ipse. *Identità e duplicità nel sistema dei personaggi della* Tebaide *di Stazio.* Pisa.

Krüger, P. (1877) *Corpus Iuris Civilis* II *(Codex Iustinianus).* Berlin (= Hildesheim 1967[14]).

Krüger, P., and Mommsen, T. (1872) *Corpus Iuris Civilis* I *(Digesta. Institutiones).* Berlin (= Hildesheim 1988[24]).

Kunst, C. (2005) *Römische Adoption. Zur Strategie einer Familienorganisation.* Hennef.

Ladmiral, J.-R. (2009) '*Epilegomena*', in B. Bortolussi *et al.* (eds.) *Traduire, transposer, transmettre dans l'Antiquité gréco-romaine.* Paris: 215 – 23.

Lamacchia, R. (1968) *M. Tulli Ciceronis* Epistula ad Octavianum. Florence.

Lanfranchi, F. (1938) *Il diritto nei retori romani.* Milan.

Langer, V. I. (2007) Declamatio Romanorum. *Dokument juristischer Argumentationstechnik, Fenster in die Gesellschaft ihrer Zeit und Quelle des Rechts?* Frankfurt a. M.

Langlands, R. (2006) *Sexual Morality in Ancient Rome.* Cambridge.

Lanzarone, N. (2008) *L. Annaei Senecae Dialogorum Liber I.* De Providentia. Florence.

Lausberg, H. (1990[3]-1998) *Handbuch der literarischen Rhetorik.* Stuttgart. (München 1960[1]; Engl. tr.: *Handbook of Literary Rhetoric.* Leiden.)

Leach, E. W. (1999) 'Ciceronian "Bi-Marcus". Correspondence with M. Terentius Varro and L. Papirius Paetus in 46 B.C.E.', *Transactions of the American Philological Association* 129: 139 – 79.

Lehnert, G. (1903) 'Zum Texte der Pseudo-Quintilianischen *declamationes maiores*', *Philologus* 62: 419 – 44.

Lehnert, G. (1908) 'Das *Corpus decem rhetorum minorum*', *Philologus* 67: 479 – 80.

Lehnert, G. (1920) 'Bericht über die Literatur zu den lateinischen Deklamationen bis 1914', *Jahresbericht über die Fortschritte der Altertumswissenschaft* 183: 204 – 67.

Lehnert, G. (1930) 'Zu Seneca, *Suas.* 3,3 (S. 548, 10 Müller)', *Philologische Wochenschrift* 50: 766.

Lehnert, G. (1932) 'Der Rehdigeranus der sogenannten grösseren quintilianischen Deklamationen', *Philologische Wochenschrift* 52: 1051 – 54.

Lehnert, G. (1934) 'Bericht über die Deklamationen aus den Jahren 1907 – 1914', *Jahresbericht über die Fortschritte der Altertumswissenschaft* 248: 106 – 10.

Lehnert, G. (1938) 'Zauber und Astrologie in den erhaltenen römischen Deklamationen', in: *Volkskundliche Ernte H. Hepding dargebracht.* Giessen: 131 – 39.

Lehnert, G. (1944/1955) 'Griechisch-römische Rhetorik. Bericht über das Schrifttum der Jahre 1915 – 1925', *Jahresbericht über die Fortschritte der Altertumswissenschaft* 285: 5 – 198.

Lelli, E. (2006) *I proverbi greci. Le raccolte di Zenobio e Diogeniano.* Soveria Mannelli.

Lentano, M. (1998) *L'eroe va a scuola. La figura del* vir fortis *nella declamazione latina.* Naples.

Lentano, M. (1999) 'La declamazione latina. Rassegna di studi e stato delle questioni (1980 – 1998)', *Bollettino di studi latini* 29: 571 – 621.

Lentano, M. (2007) *La prova del sangue. Storie di identità e storie di legittimità nella cultura Latina.* Bologna.

Lentano, M. (2009) *Signa culturae. Saggi di antropologia e letteratura latina.* Bologna.

Lentano, M. (2014) *Retorica e diritto. Per una lettura giuridica della declamazione latina.* Lecce.

Lentano, M. (2015) '*Parricidii sit actio:* Killing the Father in Roman Declamation', in: E. Amato, F. Citti and B. Huelsenbeck (eds.) *Law and Ethics in Greek and Roman Declamation.* Berlin – Munich – Boston: 133–53.

Lentano, M. (2016) '*Auribus vestris non novum crimen.* Il tema dell'adulterio nelle *declamationes minores'*, in: A. Casamento, D. van Mal-Maeder and L. Pasetti (eds.) *Le declamazioni minori dello Pseudo-Quintiliano. Discorsi immaginari tra letteratura e diritto.* Berlin – Boston: 63–80.

Lentano, M. (2017) *La declamazione a Roma: breve profilo di un genere minore.* Palermo.

LeVen, P. (2013) 'Reading the Octopus: Authorship, Intertexts, and a Hellenistic Anecdote (Machon Fr. 9 Gow)', *American Journal of Philology* 134: 23–35.

Levy, E. (1932–1963) 'Zur *Infamie* im römischen Strafrecht', in: S. Perozzi (ed.) *Studi in onore di S. Riccobono nel XL anno del suo insegnamento* II. Palermo: 79–100. (= E. Levy (1963) *Gesammelte Schriften* II. Cologne: 509–26.)

Lilja, S. (1983) *Homosexuality in Republican and Augustan Rome.* Helsinki.

Lindsay, H. (2009) *Adoption in the Roman World.* Cambridge.

Lyotard, J.-F. (1979). *La condition postmoderne: rapport sur le savoir.* Paris. Trans. (1984) by Bennington, G. and Massumi, M. as *The Postmodern Condition: A Report on Knowledge.* Minneapolis.

Mal-Maeder, D. van (2007) *La fiction des déclamations.* Leiden.

Malpas, S. (2003) *Jean-Francois Lyotard.* London.

Massaro, M. (1997) 'L'epigramma per Scipione Ispano (CIL, I^2, 15)', *Epigraphica* 59: 97–124.

McAuley, M. (2016) *Reproducing Rome: Motherhood in Virgil, Ovid, Seneca, and Statius.* Oxford.

McDonnell, M. (2006) *Roman Manliness: Virtus and the Roman Republic.* Cambridge.

McGill, S. (2013) *Plagiarism in Latin Literature.* Cambridge.

Mencacci, F. (2007) 'L'equivoco felice. Lettura gemellare dei *Menaechmi'*, in: R. Raffaelli and A. Tontini (eds.) *Lecturae Plautinae Sarsinates* X: Menaechmi. Urbino.

Meyer, E. A. (1990) 'Explaining the Epigraphic Habit in the Roman Empire. The Evidence of Epitaphs', *Journal of Roman Studies* 80: 74–96.

Meyer-Zwiffelhoffer, E. (1995) *Im Zeichen des Phallus. Die Ordnung des Geschlechtslebens im antiken Rom.* Frankfurt – New York.

Migliario, E. (2007). *Retorica e storia. Una lettura delle* Suasoriae *di Seneca Padre.* Bari.

Monier, R. (1948⁴) *Vocabulaire de droit romain.* Paris.

Munk Olsen, B. (1982, 1985) *L'Étude des auteurs classiques latins aux XIe et XIIe siècles.* 2 vols. Paris.

Naschert, G. (1994) 'Ethopoeia', in: G. Üding (ed.) *Historisches Wörterbuch der Rhetorik* 2. Tübingen: 1512–16.

Nicholson, N. (2013) 'Cultural Studies, Oral Tradition, and the Promise of Intertextuality', *American Journal of Philology* 134: 9–21.

Nosarti, L. (2010) *Forme brevi della letteratura latina.* Bologna.

O'Gorman, E. C. (2005) 'Beyond Recognition. Twin Narratives in Statius' *Thebaid*', in: M. Paschalis (ed.) *Roman and Greek Imperial Epic*. Rethymno: 29 – 46.

Oberhelman, S. M. (1988a) 'The *cursus* in late Imperial Latin prose: a reconsideration of methodology', *Classical Philology* 83: 136 – 49.

Oberhelman, S. M. (1988b) 'The history and development of the *cursus mixtus* in Latin literature', *Classical Quarterly* n. s. 38: 228 – 42.

Oberhelman, S. M. (2003) *Prose Rhythm in Latin Literature of the Roman Empire*. Lewiston, NY.

Oberhelman, S. M., and Hall, R. G. (1984) 'A new statistical analysis of accentual prose rhythms in Imperial Latin authors', *Classical Philology* 79: 114 – 30.

Oberhelman, S. M., and Hall, R. G. (1985) 'Meter in accentual *clausulae* of late Imperial Latin prose', *Classical Philology* 80: 214 – 27.

Olsen, S. (2012) 'Maculate conception. Sexual ideology and creative authority in Heliodorus' *Aethiopica*', *American Journal of Philology* 133: 301 – 22.

Önnerfors, A. (1988) 'Lennart Håkanson', in: *Vetenskapssocietetens i Lund årsbok*. Lund: 159 – 62.

Otto, A. (1890²) *Die Sprichwörter und sprichwörtlichen Redensarten der Römer*. Leipzig (= Hildesheim – Zurich – New York 1962).

Papadopoulou, T. (2004) 'Herakles and Hercules. The hero's ambivalence in Euripides and Seneca', *Mnemosyne* 57: 257 – 83.

Pasetti. L. (2009) '*Mori me non vult*. Seneca and Pseudo-Quintilian's IVth Major Declamation', *Rhetorica* 27: 274 – 93.

Pasetti, L. (2011) *[Quintiliano]. Il veleno versato* (Declamazioni maggiori, *17*). Cassino.

Pasetti, L. (2013) 'Spudorati eufemismi, false definizioni', *Griselda online* 13.

Patarol, L. (1743) '*In tertiam M. Fabii Quintiliani declamationem antilogia. Miles Marianus*', in: L. Patarol (ed.) *Opera Omnia quorum pleraque Nunc primum in lucem prodeunt* II. Venice: 137 – 53.

Peirano, I. (2013) '*Non subripiendi causa sed palam mutuandi:* Intertextuality and literary deviancy between law, rhetoric, and literature in Roman Imperial culture', *American Journal of Philology* 134: 83 – 100.

Penella, R. J. (2009) *Rhetorical Exercises from Late Antiquity. A Translation of Choricius of Gaza's Preliminary Talks and Declamations*. Cambridge.

Phang, S. E. (2008) *Roman Military Service. Ideologies of Discipline in the Late Republic and Early Principate*. Cambridge.

Pianezzola, E. (1981) 'Spunti per l'analisi del racconto nel thema delle *Controversiae* di Seneca il Vecchio', *Materiali e contributi per la storia della narrativa greco-latina* 3: 253 – 67 (= E. Pianezzola (2007) *Percorsi di studio: dalla filologia alla storia*. Amsterdam: 251 – 63).

Pingoud, J., and Rolle, A. (2016) '*Noverca* et *mater crudelis:* la perversion féminine dans les *Grandes Déclamations* à travers l'intertextualité', in: M. T. Dinter, C. Guérin and M. Martinho (eds.) *Reading Roman Declamation: The Declamations Ascribed to Quintilian*. Berlin – Boston: 147 – 66.

Poel, M. van der (2009) 'The Use of *Exempla* in Roman Declamation', *Rhetorica* 27: 332 – 53.

Polla-Mattiot, N. (1990) 'Il silenzio nella τέχνη ῥητορική. Analisi della *Contr.* 2,7 di Seneca il Vecchio', in: A. Pennacini et al. (eds.) *Retorica della comunicazione nelle letterature classiche*. Bologna: 233 – 74.

Quignard, P. (1990) *Albucius*. Paris.

Redfors, J. (1960) *Echtheitskritische Untersuchung der apuleischen Schriften* De Platone *und* De mundo. Diss. Lund.

Reeve, M. (1989) 'Conceptions', *Proceedings of the Cambridge Philological Society* 215: 81–112.

Reynolds, L. D. (ed.) (1983) *Texts and Transmission. A Survey of the Latin Classics*. Oxford.

Richlin, A. (1992²) *The Garden of Priapus. Sexuality and Aggression in Roman Humor*. New York – Oxford (1983¹).

Richlin, A. (1997) 'Gender and rhetoric: producing manhood in the schools', in: W. J. Dominik (ed.) *Roman Eloquence. Rhetoric in Society and Literature*. London: 90–110.

Rizzelli, G. (1997) Lex Iulia de adulteriis. *Studi sulla disciplina di* adulterium, lenocinium, stuprum. Lecce.

Rousselle, A. (1998) *La contamination spirituelle. Science, droit et religion dans l'Antiquité*. Paris.

Rupprecht, K. (1949) 'Paroimia', in: *Pauly-Wissowa Realencyclopädie der classischen Altertumswissenschaft* XVIII.2: 1707–35.

Russell, D. A. (1979) '*De Imitatione*', in: D. West and A. J. Woodman (eds.) *Creative Imitation and Latin Literature*. London: 1–16.

Russell, D. A. (1983) *Greek Declamation*. Cambridge.

Saller, R. P. (1994) *Patriarchy, Property and Death in the Roman Family*. Cambridge.

Saller, R. P., and Shaw, B. D. (1984) 'Tombstones and Roman Family Relations in the Principate. Civilians, Soldiers and Slaves', *Journal of Roman Studies* 74: 124–56.

Sallmann, K. (1997) 'Calpurnius Flaccus', in: K. Sallmann (ed.) *Handbuch der lateinischen Literatur der Antike* IV. Munich: 321.

Samuelsson, G. (2013²) *Crucifixion in Antiquity*. Tübingen.

Sandys, J. E. (1908) *A History of Classical Scholarship*. 2 vols. Cambridge.

Santorelli, B. and Stramaglia. A. (2017). *[Quintiliano]. Il muro con le impronte di una mano* (Declamazioni maggiori 1). Cassino.

Santorelli, B., Stramaglia, A. and Winterbottom, M. (forthcoming). *[Quintilian]: The Major Declamations*. Cambridge, MA.

Schanz, M., and Hosius, C. (1922) 'Der Deklamator Calpurnius Flaccus', in: C. Hosius and G. Krüger (eds.) *Geschichte der römischen Literatur bis zum Gesetzgebungswerk des Kaisers Justinian* 3. Munich: 153–54.

Schneider, C. (2000a) 'Quelques réflexions sur la date de publication des *Grandes déclamations* pseudo-quintiliennes', *Latomus* 59: 614–32.

Schneider, C. (2000b) 'Littérature et propagande au IVᵉ siècle de notre ère dans le recueil des *Grandes déclamations* pseudo-quintiliennes: l'exemple du *Miles Marianus* (ps.-Quint., *Decl. Mai.* III)', in: F. E. Consolino (ed.) *Letteratura e propaganda nell'occidente latino da Augusto ai regni romanobarbarici*. Rome: 45–66.

Schneider, C. (2004) *[Quintilien]. Le soldat de Marius* (Grandes déclamations, 3). Cassino.

Schneider, C. (2005) 'L'histoire dans la rhétorique: les enjeux politiques du *Miles Marianus* dans le recueil des *Grandes déclamations* pseudo-quintiliennes', *Cahiers des Études Anciennes* 42: 99–122.

Schneider, C. (2016) 'Le *Tribunus Marianus* par Lorenzo Patarol (1674–1727). Un essai de traduction', in: G. Herbert de la Portbarré-Viard and A. Stoehr-Monjou (eds.) Studium in libris. *Mélanges en l'honneur de Jean-Louis Charlet*. Paris: 371–87.

Schröder B.-J. and Schröder, J.-P. (eds.) (2003) Studium declamatorium. *Untersuchungen zu Schulübungen und Prunkreden von Antike bis Neuzeit.* Munich – Leipzig.

Shackleton Bailey, D. R. (1976) 'Review of Lennart Håkanson, *Textkritische Studien zu den grösseren pseudoquintilianischen Deklamationen,* Lund 1974', *American Journal of Philology* 97: 73–79.

Shackleton Bailey, D. R. (1977) *Cicero,* Epistulae ad familiares. Cambridge.

Sinclair, P. (1995) *Tacitus the Sententious Historian: A Sociology of Rhetoric in* Annales *1–6.* College Park, PA.

Simmonds, T. S. (1899) *The Themes Treated by the Elder Seneca.* Baltimore, MD.

Stramaglia, A. (2002) *[Quintiliano].* La città che si cibò dei suoi cadaveri *(Declamazioni maggiori, 12).* Cassino.

Stramaglia, A. (2006) 'Le *Declamationes maiores* pseudo-quintilianee: genesi di una raccolta declamatoria e fisionomia della sua trasmissione testuale', in: E. Amato (ed.) *Approches de la Troisième Sophistique.* Brussels: 555–84. (Appendix: F. Ronconi, *Il codice palinsesto* Paris. Lat. *7900 A: una nuova ispezione della* scriptio inferior, 585–88.)

Stramaglia, A. (2009) 'An international project on the pseudo-Quintilianic *Declamationes Maiores*', *Rhetorica* 27: 237–39.

Stramaglia, A. (2010) 'Come si insegnava a declamare?', in: L. Del Corso and O. Pecere (eds.) *Libri di scuola e pratiche didattiche: Dall'Antichità al Rinascimento.* Vol. 1. Cassino: 111–51.

Stramaglia, A. (2013) *[Quintiliano].* L'astrologo *(Declamazioni maggiori, 4).* Cassino.

Stramaglia, A. (2016) 'The Hidden Teacher. "Metarhetoric" in Ps.-Quintilian's *Major Declamations*', in: M. T. Dinter, C. Guérin and M. Martinho (eds.) *Reading Roman Declamation. The Declamations Ascribed to Quintilian.* Berlin – Boston: 25–48.

Sussman, L. (1972) 'The Elder Seneca's Discussion of the Decline of Roman Eloquence', *California Studies in Classical Antiquity* 5: 195–210.

Sussman, L. (1978) *The Elder Seneca.* Leiden.

Sussman, L. (1984) 'The Elder Seneca and Declamation Since 1900: A Bibliography', *Aufstieg und Niedergang der römischen Welt* II.32.4: 557–77.

Sussman, L. (1994) *The Declamations of Calpurnius Flaccus. Text, Translation, and Commentary.* Leiden.

Sussman, L. (1995) 'Sons and fathers in the *Major Declamations* ascribed to Quintilian', *Rhetorica* 13: 179–92.

Sussman, L. (1999) 'Interpreting racism in Calpurnius Flaccus *Declamatio* 2. The evidence of Ovid *Amores* 2, 7–8 and Juvenal *Satires* 6', in: W. Schubert (ed.) *Ovid. Werk und Wirkung* II. Bern – Frankfurt am Main: 841–60.

Syme, R. (1968) 'People in Pliny', *Journal of Roman Studies* 58: 135–51.

Szelinski, V. (1892) *Nachträge und Ergänzungen zu Otto, Die Sprichwörter und sprichwörtlichen Redensarten der Römer.* Jena (= Häussler 1968: 15–50).

Szelinski, V. (1903–4) 'Zu den Sprichwörtern der Römer', in: *Rheinisches Museum für Philologie* 58: 471–475; 59: 149–57; 316–17; 477–78; 635–38 (= Häussler 1968: 231–49).

Tabacco, R. (1985) 'Il tiranno nelle declamazioni di scuola in lingua latina', *Memorie dell'Accademia delle Scienze di Torino* 9: 1–141.

Tabacco, R. (1994) 'Calpurnio Flacco: un retore da leggere [Review of Sussman (1994)]', *Bollettino di studi latini* 24: 187–91.

Tarwacka, S. (2012) 'Searching for the Roots. *Vis vi depulsa* in the Concept of Cicero', *Miscellanea Historico-Iuridica* 11: 77–88.

Thomas, J.-F. (2005) '*Pudicitia, impudicitia, impudentia* dans leurs relations avec *pudor*: étude sémantique', *Revista de Estudios Latinos* 5: 53–73.

Thomas, J.-F. (2006) '*Pudor* et *verecundia*: deux formes de la conscience morale?', *Euphrosyne* 34: 355–68.

Thomas, J.-F. (2007) *Déshonneur et honte en latin. Étude sémantique.* Paris – Louvain.

Till, R. (1970) 'Die Scipionenelogien', in: D. von Ableitinger and H. Gugel (eds.) *Festschrift Karl Vretska zum 70. Geburtstag überreicht von seinen Freunden und Schülern.* Heidelberg: 276–89.

Tosi, R. (1991) *Dizionario delle sentenze latine e greche.* Milan.

Tosi, R. (1995) 'La tradizione proverbiale', in: U. Mattioli (ed.) Senectus. *La vecchiaia nel mondo classico.* Bologna: 365–78.

Tosi, R. (2009) 'Introduzione a E. Lelli (ed.) Paroimiakos. *Il proverbio in Grecia e a Roma*', *Philologia Antiqua* 2: 13–29.

Traina, A. (2000) *Seneca. La provvidenza.* Milan.

Varvaro, M. (2013) 'Legittima difesa, tirannicidio e strategia difensiva nell'orazione di Cicerone a favore di Milone', *Annali del Seminario Giuridico dell'Università degli Studi di Palermo* 56: 215–55.

Vesley, M. E. (2003) 'Father-son relations in Roman declamation', *Ancient History Bulletin* 17: 158–80.

Walters, J. (1993) *Ancient Roman Concepts of Manhood and their Relation with other Markers of Social Status.* Diss. Cambridge.

Walters, J. (1997a) 'Invading the Roman Body: Manliness and Impenetrability in Roman Thought', in: J. P. Hallett and M. B. Skinner (eds.) *Roman Sexualities.* Princeton: 29–43.

Walters, J. (1997b) 'Soldiers and Whores in a pseudo-Quintilian Declamation', in: T. Cornell and K. Lomas (eds.) *Gender and Ethnicity in Ancient Italy.* London: 109–14.

Walz, C. (1832–36) *Rhetores Graeci vol. VII/1.* Stuttgart – Tübingen (= Osnabrück 1968).

Watson, P. A. (1995) *Ancient Stepmothers. Myth, Misogyny and Reality.* Leiden.

Weber, H. (1898) *Quaestiones Calpurnianae.* Donauwörth.

Weil, R., and Nicolet, C. (1977) *Polybe, Histoires. Tome VI, Livre VI.* Paris.

Welch, T. (2013) 'Was Valerius Maximus a hack?', *American Journal of Philology* 134.1: 67–82.

Weyman, C. (1893) 'Zu den Sprichwörtern und sprichwörtlichen Redensarten der Römer', *Archiv für lateinische Lexikographie* 8: 23–38; 397–411 (= Häussler 1968).

Weyman, C. (1904) 'Zu den Sprichwörtern und sprichwörtlichen Redensarten der Römer', *Archiv für lateinische Lexikographie* 13: 253–70 (= Häussler 1968).

Williams, C. (1999, 2010[2]) *Roman Homosexuality. Ideologies of Masculinity in Classical Antiquity.* Oxford.

Winterbottom, M. (1962) 'Almeloveen's manuscript of Quintilian', *Classical Review* 12: 121–22.

Winterbottom, M. (1964) 'More about Almeloveen', *Classical Review* 14: 243.

Winterbottom, M. (1974) *The Elder Seneca.* 2 vols. Cambridge, MA.

Winterbottom, M. (1974a) 'Problems in the Elder Seneca', *Bulletin of the Institute of Classical Studies* 21: 20–42.

Winterbottom, M. (1982) 'Schoolroom and Courtroom', in: B. Vickers (ed.) *Rhetoric Revalued.* Binghamton, NY: 59–70.

Winterbottom, M. (1983) 'Declamation, Greek and Latin', in: A. Ceresa-Gastaldo (ed.) Ars Rhetorica *antica e nuova.* Genoa: 57–76.

Winterbottom, M. (1983) 'Quintilian (?)', in: L. D. Reynolds (ed.) *Texts and Transmission. A Survey of the Latin Classics.* Oxford: 337.

Winterbottom, M. (1984) *The Minor Declamations Ascribed to Quintilian.* Berlin – New York.

Winterbottom, M. (1995) 'Review of Lewis A. Sussman, *The Declamations of Calpurnius Flaccus*', *Classical Review* 45: 40–42.

Winterbottom, M. (2011) 'On ancient prose rhythm', in: D. Obbink and R. Rutherford (eds.) *Culture in Pieces. Essays on Ancient Texts in Honour of Peter Parsons*, Oxford: 262–76.

Zieliński, T. (1907) *Das Ausleben des Clauselgesetzes in der römischen Kunstprosa.* Leipzig.

Zinsmaier, T. (2009) 'Zwischen Erzählung und Argumentation: *colores* in den pseudoquintilianischen *Declamationes maiores*', *Rhetorica* 27: 256–73.

Subject Index

Compiled by Astrid Khoo

https://doi.org/10.1515/9783110401554-011

Index locorum

Compiled by Astrid Khoo

N.b. Håkanson's page and line numbers have been given in brackets only where they are needed to locate specific passages in Calpurnius' *Declamations*. Similar references have been provided for the *Major Declamations* ascribed to Quintilian.

For passages that are cited in footnotes the page number only is given.

https://doi.org/10.1515/9783110401554-012

CPSIA information can be obtained
at www.ICGtesting.com
Printed in the USA
LVHW091930061219
639727LV00002B/15/P

9 783110 685138